MEDIA ETHICS

MEDIA ETHICS
A Philosophical Approach

Matthew Kieran

Westport, Connecticut
London

Library of Congress Cataloging-in-Publication Data

Kieran, Matthew, 1968–
    Media ethics : a philosophical approach / Matthew Kieran.
       p.   cm.
    Includes bibliographical references and index.
    ISBN 0–275–95634–2 (alk. paper)—ISBN 0–275–96694–1 (pbk.)
    1.   Mass media—Moral and ethical aspects.   I. Title.
  P94.K54   1997
  174—dc21   97–1916

British Library Cataloguing in Publication Data is available.

Library of Congress Catalog Card Number: 97–1916
ISBN: 0–275–96694–1 (pbk.)

First published in 1997

Praeger Publishers, 88 Post Road West, Westport, CT 06881
An imprint of Greenwood Publishing Group, Inc.
www.praeger.com

Printed in the United States of America

The paper used in this book complies with the
Permanent Paper Standard issued by the National
Information Standards Organization (Z39.48–1984).

10 9 8 7 6 5 4 3 2 1

Contents

Preface

One of the difficulties in taking a philosophical approach to media ethics is that many people often fail to grasp the difference between a philosophical and a sociological, political, or critical–cultural studies position on the issues discussed. This is exacerbated by the fact that there is no clear body of empirical findings or theory that constitutes a philosophical approach and is waiting to be learned. Of course, there is a sociological reason for this. Although historically concerned with central moral and social issues, philosophers have yet to consider many of these issues in relation to the distinctive problems arising from our contemporary media and journalistic practices. But there is a deeper reason too. For philosophy is not so much a subject where we learn information, but one in which we learn how to think about various issues. This is not to deny that many philosophers have made distinctive contributions to the stock of human knowledge. But, rather, there are certain kinds of questions and issues—those concerned with right and wrong, what constitutes a good life, and the nature of evil—that can only really be thought of and argued about in a philosophical manner, and only philosophical thinking can deepen our understanding of them.

The topic of this book, media ethics, is an extension of such philosophical concerns. For the question is, in essence, what constitutes ethical media practice and why? Just what is it that journalists, morally speaking, should do? Is it really news to print a story about the sex life of a public celebrity? Are they justified in lying and cheating to get a story? Are intrusions into privacy always justifiable in the name of the public interest? Is showing sexually explicit films on television morally dubious? Should we worry about gratuitously violent films? And, lastly, do we have good rational grounds for justifying censorship, or is our right to freedom of expression absolute? It is important to recognize that although sociological and psychological concerns, together with contributions from other areas, may be important, they cannot get us to a deeper understanding of the possible answers to these questions. For example, merely knowing that many people would prefer to watch violent films or ban sexually explicit ones does not, as yet, lead us any way toward answering whether or not such films are morally dubious. For the relevance of such information depends on an understanding of how and why people's preferences are, morally speaking, important. And that is a philosophical question.

The method of philosophical argument employed in this book is primarily dialectical. For thousands of years, since the time of Socrates, dialectical argument has been an essential philosophical method. Essentially it consists in examining our intuitions and trying to articulate the conclusion to which they lead us. Once we have marshaled our intuitions in this manner, we need to examine more closely what the position articulated involves. How should we understand the basic terms in the argument? For example, what exactly do we mean by "harm"? Are the premises used in the argument plausible? Even if they are plausible, do they entail the conclusion? Or could we agree with the premises and draw an entirely different conclusion? Can this be shown by counterexample? The point is to test, critically, the claims made at each stage of the argument, draw out their implications, and test them. Thus the conclusions reached are not merely a matter of assertion or opinion but, rather, the result of a reasoned cumulative process that leads us toward what we have most reason to believe and thus to a deeper understanding of why certain other positions, rationally speaking, may be flawed.

Given the nature and emphasis of the book, I have tried to keep notes to a minimum and avoid the kind of scholasticism and jargon we might sometimes expect from an academic book. For the important thing is not so much to glean information about what particular thinkers have said about the issues being discussed but to present the critical development of certain kinds of arguments. You should be concerned not so much to learn arguments or conclusions but to examine critically, for yourself, the kinds of arguments presented. In essence the book is an attempt to show what philosophical reasoning can achieve in relation to issues in media ethics, through actually engaging in philosophical argument. You may not agree with the conclusions, but you should grasp what the underlying argument is and, hopefully, be in a better position to articulate just why you find the various arguments satisfactory or flawed. The aim of the book is not just to put forward substantive positions regarding particular questions, but to enable you to argue philosophically about these issues for yourself.

Conversations with many colleagues and students on my media ethics course have certainly helped to give the book its present shape, and I am grateful to them all. I would especially like to thank David Morrison, Piers Benn, Darren Brierton,

Chris Megone, Rebecca Roache, and Louisa Dale. Finally, my thinking on these matters has certainly been improved by Sarah's journalistic experience and her ability to put up with me working away at all hours; I owe a debt to her in many ways, and it is to her that I dedicate this book.

MEDIA ETHICS

1 *Media Ethics?*

INTRODUCTION

Despite an increasing concern with media ethics there are many who remain skeptical about the very idea. Most normative research presumes that the media ought to be ethical in their professional conduct, thus concentrating on journalistic codes, guidelines, and ideals of media responsibility.[1] But before we pursue such an avenue of enquiry we must at least entertain and critically assess arguments that suggest that the entire aim of media ethics is fundamentally mistaken. It is important to see how and why these arguments are flawed if we are to convince those who presume that journalism and the media remain outside the demands of commonsense morality that they are wrong.

The point is that the very notion of media ethics appears paradoxical: the very phrase itself seems to constitute an oxymoron. Many professional journalists in Britain, for example, often greet the suggestion that they ought to be ethically sensitive with sneers of disdain.[2] After all, how could journalists possibly hope to get at stories that matter, or ones the public want to know about, if they have to be wholly honest in their investigations or straightforwardly respect the feelings, wishes, and privacy of the subjects of their reports? Moreover, the public at large tends to take for granted the commonsense presumption that journalists are ultimately concerned with only one thing: what sells.[3]

Given such attitudes, it is hardly surprising that the news media are perceived to be predominately interested only in crisis stories, sordid events, sleazy allegations, and the secular iconography of the rich and famous in order to boost readership or ratings.[4] Indeed, this picture is reinforced when journalists cite the right to freedom of speech, or the First Amendment, in defence of apparently dubious actions involving bribery, deceit, sensationalism, fabrication, or the giving of gratuitous offense.[5] For such appeals are often perceived to be no more than mere camouflage for activities and behavior which, ordinarily, would not be considered either legal or ethical. Of course, such a picture of the media profession may well be a partial caricature. Nonetheless, I hope to show that even if such a caricature of journalism were sound, the sense of a paradox here is misplaced.

PHILOSOPHICAL ETHICS AND THE MEDIA

The news press and media have a variety of functions to fulfill: from investigating domestic, corporate, and political scandals to relaying news about significant events elsewhere in the world. Of course, many journalists and media institutions may presume that ethics can bear no significant relation to the realization of these goals. But it does not follow that the demand that journalists and the news media should be ethical is misplaced. Indeed, on face value at least, we have good reason to believe that such a self-understanding must be mistaken.

What is the point of news and investigative journalism? Presumably it is to investigate and report on significant events in the world, including the exposure of corrupt, deceitful, illegal goings on by corporations, politicians, organized crime, or the rich and famous. It is by virtue of this function that we tend to talk of the news media in terms of the fourth estate: as constituting a public check and balance on those in positions of power and influence in our society.[6] Given that the news media's function, at least in part, is to seek out and expose wrongdoing as such, it had better not be guilty of the very same sins it exposes in others if it is to avoid the charge of hypocrisy.[7] That is, journalists have a moral duty to report faithfully and expose wrongdoing. Hence journalists and the news media must themselves consistently aim to respect the very same ethical standards of behavior that they demand others should adhere to or strive for.

It is important to point out that though communications studies, psychology, sociology, and cultural theory have an admirable recent history in terms of critically investigating journalistic practice and the public's understanding of the media, such forms of enquiry cannot help us in answering questions as to what journalists (morally) may, should, or should not do. To enquire into what the demands of ethics are in relation to journalism is, necessarily, to engage in a distinctively philosophical enquiry.

Of course, many people would quite properly conceive of philosophical enquiry as a highly formal, abstract mode of theorizing. Indeed, in certain domains—for example, logic—that is all it is. But philosophy also properly involves, in the light of theoretical considerations, the critical examination of our practical experience and actions. After all, the significance of abstract ethical questions arises from their bearing on our ordinary, everyday deliberations and actions. That is, the very purpose of ethical reflection is to point us toward what might be required in order to live a good life.

In recent times, we have witnessed a dramatic proliferation in the number of journalism courses, communications studies, and public initiatives concerned with journalism and the news media.[8] However, the attention paid to ethical issues tends toward the pragmatic and is typically framed in response to particular press scandals, worries raised by certain pressure groups, or perceived government interference.[9] The problem is that such responses necessarily involve certain normative commitments that often remain unexamined. Hence philosophical reflection, at least potentially, has a significant role to play in the field of media ethics. Philosophers, minimally, may hope to explicate and critically assess the commitments involved. Furthermore, in the light of various scandals, there is an increasing wish on the part of the media to examine and reevaluate their ethical, social, and political values. Hence a philosophical approach to media ethics is broadly concerned with what good media practice amounts to and whether it is as it should be. As a matter of principle, a philosophical approach to media ethics can hope, at the very least, to deepen our understanding in this way.

Yet the skeptical challenge, for which there are distinct motivations, should not be underestimated. There are some interesting and often highly persuasive considerations that tend to suggest that any such enquiry is doomed to failure. Although they come in a variety of guises, there are two basic ideas that motivate the skeptical challenge. On the one hand, there is the notion that ethical sensitivity may be incompatible, in certain cases at least, with carrying out a journalist's job professionally. For journalism, or good journalism at least, perhaps requires a certain clinical detachment from and disregard for some of the ethical niceties and sensitivities of everyday ethical life. On the other hand, there is the thought that ethical theory or ideals are necessarily inapplicable in relation to journalistic practice. That is, the kind of news interest taken by journalists in current events or tragedies, and the means they must use to get at and relay the stories, may themselves be intrinsically immoral. Thus, as a matter of principle, journalistic professionalism and ethical responsibility may be incompatible.

Nonetheless, despite the arguments considered, I suggest here that philosophical reflection may help us to grasp why certain media practices may be ethically admirable, permissible, or even immoral and thus, hopefully, show us what ought to be done. Furthermore, such reflection will enable us to see that good media practice is far from being incompatible with the demand to be ethical. Hence I hope to show that, as a matter of principle, the skeptical challenge regarding media ethics is flawed.

MORAL SKEPTICISM

A crude source of skepticism about media ethics may arise from a presumed fact–value distinction. Basically the presumption is that propositions that can be assessed as true or false, facts being true propositions, cannot concern values. We can definitively state that the earth is, in fact, round and, at least as a matter of principle, verify the assertion with reference to evidence that supports the hypothesis. But, the thought is, where is the evidence for a news report being just or a journalist being generous or kind? These are merely expressions that voice our own subjective approval of certain states of affairs or people. Hence the last thing we ought to seek to do is to impose our opinions on others, whereas we can meaningfully dispute and be right or wrong about facts concerning whether an event actually happened and who was involved.

One way we might bring out this thought more clearly is if we contrast scientific discourse with moral discourse. Science involves the theoretical investigation and explanation of the world; hence terms are carefully explicated, hypotheses carefully postulated and tested, and theoretical presumptions critically examined. By contrast, the nature of moral discourse appears radically distinct and hardly appears to constitute critical argument at all. Think, for example, of the way objections to news reports or pornographic material are often expressed: couched in emotional language suggesting offense, outrage, and hurt feelings. It would seem that the normal currency of moral discourse is constituted by rhetoric rather than philosophical rigor.

Indeed, on the basis of particular sentiments, prejudices, and emotions many people generalize from their own reactions to what can only be partial conclusions. For example, someone may uncritically leap from the intuition that a morbid interest in the dead and dying is morally wrong to the conclusion that therefore most war journalism, crime reporting, and coverage of tragedies is ethically suspect. The thought is that normal ethical discourse is polemical, a matter of declaring which value someone chooses to promote against another through over-generalizing on the basis of particular intuitions and feelings. Taking such a view we ought to be very suspicious of those who claim to provide a framework for what constitutes ethical journalism and media practice, for such a framework can only be the schematic formalization of their own particular prejudices and preferences.

Of course, as a mode of conceptual analysis, philosophical reflection may explicate and clarify the nature of the concepts involved. Nonetheless, given the difference in kind between scientific discourse, directed toward finding out truths about the world, and moral discourse, directed toward expressing what we feel about everyday life and the way our responsibilities and dilemmas have evolved, perhaps philosophy cannot hope to engage in a meaningful way with the practicalities involved at a pragmatic professional level of activity.[10] If true, reflection cannot hope to be normative or action-guiding in the way any philosophical approach to media ethics must presume.

It is unfortunate that the presumed fact–value distinction is so deeply ingrained within liberal culture for, in certain cases, laudable but misconceived motives. Arguing about what ought to be done is reduced to the mere grunting of approval or disapprobation. But such a view rules out the very possibility of moral disagreement. Yet when we argue about whether a journalist's actions were justified or scandalous we are not merely asking what someone else feels. We want to know, and are disputing, what was the case and how we should describe it. The whole point of moral discourse and reflection is to iron out apparently meaningful disagreements and guide our action toward good rather than bad examples.

To see just how misconceived the fact–value separation is, consider the apparently value-neutral method of scientific enquiry. Science aims to increase our knowledge of the natural world. Yet science, like ethics, aims at some good: a true description of the natural world through mathematical description. Hence, relative to this evaluative aim, we classify science as good or bad. That is, science itself depends on the pursuit of at least one value, truth, and good science does so via truth-promoting methods. In science, truth-promoting methods include the recording and testing of evidence against hypotheses to see which theory retains the greatest functional simplicity, coherence, and explanatory value. Conversely, bad science is indifferent to truth and may disregard evidence, involve faking results, be only partially explanatory, or build in huge redundancies. So too with journalism. If a journalist's methods are poor, then truth-promoting methods are abandoned, and if stories are faked, then truth is obviously not sought. Hence we would condemn such cases.

The point is that we do not merely respect certain values in order to get at the truth. Rather, what is warranted or rationally acceptable is determined by the cognitive virtues the relevant theory has. Similarly, we appropriately form moral judgments, make character appraisals, and evaluate particular actions as morally good, bad, or permissible in terms of their appropriateness. Hence value judgments are not merely subjective because they correspond to aspects of the person or action being judged. Thus when we judge a war-reporter's actions to be courageous we are putting forward the term as the most appropriate description and explanation for his action. If we describe a reporter who stood his ground in the face of danger as courageous, when in fact he was merely paralyzed with fear and would have run if he could, then our description would be wrong. Of course, as with science, we may not be able to know what the most appropriate descriptions are in a particular case. But it does not follow from this that some descriptions are not more or less appropriate than others.

Moreover, the recognition that our moral judgments are about the way things really are, in a significant sense, captures something the subjectivist or moral skeptic cannot—namely, that moral disagreements do in fact have a certain force and that how they are to be resolved does matter. After all, if the skeptic were right there would be no such thing as moral argument. But in saying "genocide is always evil" or "checkbook journalism is wrong" we are categorically denying what someone else asserts if they say "genocide is good" or "checkbook journalism is ethically permissible": we are not merely talking past one another.

Indeed, far from avoiding harm, which is often the misplaced motivation for denying the status of value judgments, the idea that there are no justifiable value judgments plays into the very hands of those who perpetrate evil. For the appropriate condemnation of certain motivations, actions, or exploitation as immoral can then, falsely, be dismissed by fiat as mere opinion. The fact that our moral judgments do matter in this way is brought out by the need to judge and evaluate in order to know what kinds of actions or practices we ought to be avoiding or aiming to emulate.[11] Of course, to a large extent, the point of critical reflection here depends on the point and value of journalism and media communications. But, at the very least, conceptual clarification enables us to attain a deeper understanding of the commitments involved in journalism and the media (to truth, say) and may modify our understanding of how we ought to act.

JOURNALISM AND MORAL INNOCENTS

Given that, on face value, ethical reflection on media behavior and practices seems straightforwardly relevant, why is it that so many people both within the media world and external to it may remain skeptical of such enquiry? The basic thought appears to be that ethical reflection per se is wholly irrelevant to the messy, everyday realities of a practical and professional life. Indeed, some might go so far as to claim that even journalistic codes of practice, to the extent that they are taken seriously, can only confuse decisionmakers. For, except as a matter of rhetoric, the demand that the media could or should be ethical may be considered misplaced. Hence, on this view, ethical reflection could only be, at best, an irrelevance and, at worst, play a distortive role in relation to established journalistic practices and media interests.

The underlying intuition here seems to concern an implicit opposition between the world of experience and the utopian ideals we might aspire to. After all, if nothing else, the world of the press and media is one of intense practical activity. Thus, it might be thought, ideals concerning how we ought to act cannot apply. For, in order to report about the way the world is, one has to be capable of dealing in the ways of the world. The moral innocent, unfamiliar with the more pragmatic ways of the world, is likely to reject the necessary compromises of professional life and ethical integrity which may be required to get the job done. The morally innocent journalist may well retain his integrity, but it may be at the expense of fulfilling his function as a reporter.

Take, for example, the world-wide reporting in April 1994 of the huge size and scale of genocide in Rwanda. It was a newsworthy item precisely because of the nature and scale of the killings. Hence it was important to get across the magnitude of what was happening, rather than seek to convey a particular individual human experience and fate. On 23 April the press photographer Luc Delahaye

(Rex Features), among others, was taken to the site of a massacre. Hutu troops had thrown a grenade into a crowd in the middle of the road just above Kigali, the capital of Rwanda, and then proceeded to shoot dead those who had not died in the explosion.

Now, it may well be true that one who was a moral innocent, and naive about some of the more humanly depraved ways of the world, could not have taken a newsworthy photograph. In the face of such a horrific mass of dead men and mutilated women and children a moral innocent might have been unable to do anything but walk away. Indeed, even if such a person could stomach the sight, it does not follow that the photographs he might tremblingly take would be professional, appropriate, or newsworthy. In good photojournalism, as with good news-reporting generally, a certain capacity for critical detachment and appraisal is absolutely essential. Apart from anything else, taking a good journalistic picture depends on bearing in mind and addressing the kinds of news interests involved, a matter that may be quite distinct from the ethically sensitive human response to a particular individual's plight.

In the case of the massacre above Kigali, the picture had to convey the horror and brutality of the massacre appropriately but not in a way that is so graphic as to cause people not to look at all or to seem wholly offensive. Hence it was important for Delahaye deliberately to step away from the pile of bodies and take the photograph at a distance, which he did while also including a dead child offset from the mass of bodies. Thus the details of the wounds, mutilations, and individual faces in his photograph are lost in a way that serves to foreground the immense scale and callousness of the massacres while simultaneously avoiding the graphic portrayal of horrific wounds in all their detail.

But we might have good reason to think that someone lacking experience of the world and prone to moral sensitivity would be unable to achieve the kind of critical detachment required. After all, if someone is in a state of shock or is overwhelmed by sympathy for and outrage on behalf of the massacre victims, then, even assuming that they can cope psychologically with the task of taking pictures of the mass of dead bodies, they may be far less likely to bear in mind the news requirements involved. Hence an outraged witness may be naturally in-clined to take many photographs that detail in all their particularity the grotesque wounds and fatalities caused. But such photographs would probably not be usable, given their graphic nature, in any news medium and, moreover, would probably fail to convey the scale and nature of the massacre as the focus would naturally be ____ as individuals. In ethical terms, we should be sensitive to the horrifi____ ____ heinous and inhuman crime, but, the thought may be, ____ ____ne they should push such reactions aside.

How ____ ____derlies the intuition that ethics and journal____ ____ is misconceived. For, as a journalist, if anyth____ ____ a case surely it is to channel one's sensitivities into taking the best photograph possible in order to bear witness to the terrible events occurring. As Luc Delahaye himself said, "I don't think there is a lot to say about it. I just took this picture because I thought it would have been immoral not to do it."[12]

Sometimes our moral sensitivities can and do trouble us when performing the right or a good action; in this case, surely it would be right for us to feel uneasy at photographing so many people lying dead, mutilated, and undignified as one large mass of carcasses. That our ordinary, human affective reaction may be one of repulsion does not entail that we ought to retreat from action. Indeed, if such a reaction is appropriate then it suggests that, if anything, as journalists we ought to make damn sure that we take a newsworthy photograph. After all, we are quite rightly repulsed by many of the effects of and acts in war, but our repulsion in no way entails that war can never be justified. This is not to say that our feelings of repulsion are themselves unjustified or inappropriate. We would worry about soldiers and journalists who, having become so used to atrocities, warfare, and inhumanity, remain unmoved in the face of great human suffering. Rather it is to point out that we think that in certain kinds of cases, despite our feelings of repulsion, we may have a moral duty to act—whether it be to fight in the case of war, or witness and report on a horrific event in the case of journalism.

Furthermore, in the case of Delahaye's photograph, we are troubled precisely because we are appropriately shocked at the nature of the massacre, and should be so troubled by the resultant photograph. What the example in fact brings out is not an opposition between the sphere of practical activity and morality or ethical reflection but, rather, the fact that morality, making ethical judgments, and guiding our action, is itself primarily a practical matter.[13] Thus the experience, judgment, and capacities required—in this case, from the technical skills required of a good cameraman to the appropriate judgment about the nature of and news interest in such a tragedy—ought to be cultivated by any ethically responsible journalist. If someone in Delahaye's position felt squeamish at the prospect of taking the photographs they still had a duty to overcome their sensitivities in order to capture the nature of the event on film. Thus the demand that journalists should be ethical, and reflect on their actions in this light, is in no way akin to, and indeed precludes, the unrealistic and utopian notion that journalists should be or behave as moral innocents.

UNDERSTANDING THE MEDIA FROM THE INSIDE

However, the idea that fulfilling a journalistic function may be incompatible with ethical reflection and integrity is not just reducible to the idea that certain, possibly appropriate, moral feelings may cloud a moral innocent's judgment. It might still be thought that recognizing the nature of value judgments and the clarificatory role that critical thinking may play entails a very weak conclusion. For media professionals may retain a deep skepticism based on the idea that only those involved in a given practice or profession can properly understand or critically reflect upon it. Presumably it is something like this thought that underlies the indignation of journalists subjected to criticism by lobby groups, academics, or sections of the public.[14] It is often presumed by journalists, program producers, and media institutions that nonpractitioners, typically clueless regarding the very basic methods and goals in journalism and the media, are the very last people who should have the gall to criticize something that they can only view externally.

Thus the underlying presumption might be that in order to understand something aright, we must ourselves have first-hand experience of it. Just as we cannot know how to play tennis or ride a bike unless we have already attempted to do so, philosophers cannot expect to contribute anything to our understanding of what good media practice amounts to (given that they have little or no experience of working in the media).[15] To understand a particular practice, and grasp the various problems appropriately in all their particularity, we must already be engaged in that very practice ourselves. So unless we have moved within the media world already, whether working in a newsroom or producing community programming, there can be no epistemological justification for the beliefs and ethical demands we are inclined to make of the media. Only those with first-hand experience of the sphere concerned or internal to a practice may properly deliberate about and reflect upon it.

In order to flesh the point out more fully, consider how problematic it is to apply philosophical principles or codes of practice appropriately without some kind of experience. For instance, take the familiar journalistic practice of making "collect calls." These are calls made by journalists to the friends and families of murder or accident victims to get a photograph for the news story. Obviously the more poignant the photograph the better for the story, hence photographs of children, the elderly, policemen, and nurses involved in tragedies tend to be particularly popular. Typically, a reporter will approach friends or neighbors of the bereaved to ask what kind of state they are in. Then they will approach the family directly, or through an intermediary, to ask if the family would mind supplying a photograph to accompany the news report.

Now those outside the practice of journalism might ordinarily consider such a routine ghoulish, intrusive, and offensive. For what seems to be involved is a kind of parasitic preying upon the victims of misfortune which effectively exploits the grief and distress of those most affected for the benefit of media sensationalism. Thus for someone who presumes that privacy should be respected, especially in instances of bereavement, illness, or misfortune, such a routine may well appear to be highly unethical. But if one actually has experience of making such calls or listens to those who have, it is far from clear that things are how an outsider might presume. Of course, just as policemen do not enjoy similar kinds of calls, most journalists positively dislike making collect calls. They are approaching people in the midst of great suffering and asking for something that is highly personal and deeply emotionally charged: what they do not want to be is an intruder. Hence sensitive journalists will make use of various strategies, from the possible use of intermediaries to expressing sorrow and regret at the unfortunate events, to show an appropriate concern for and sensitivity for the family concerned.

Yet given such sensitivity, there in fact seems to be nothing inherently wrong with requesting a photograph of an accident or murder victim to illustrate a paper's story. The point of using the photograph to accompany such a story is not merely as a means of increasing circulation. Rather, any increase in circulation is dependent on the inherent reason for using such photographs: namely that they convey more vividly the nature of what has happened, as a good newspaper should. Hence when journalists from the Pacemaker news agency in Northern Ireland made their collect calls after the IRA bombing of the Remembrance Day service in Enniskillen, they explained that the photographs would vividly show, in a way mere words cannot, the evil nature of the bombing; namely, that innocent men, women, and children who had played no part in the conflict had been cruelly and calculatedly murdered.

As human beings, we quite naturally respond more deeply and in more complex, profound, and intricate ways to particular individuals. Through representing particular individuals, photographs can bring home to us, indeed show us, the persons whose lives have been taken from them. Thus the tragedy can be conveyed to us much more vividly by the judicious use of a photograph than by a longer story without one. When presented with the picture of young boys who have been abducted, abused, and murdered—the way they smile, the freckles that one has, the toothy grin, the way the tie on the school uniform is proudly done up or only half tied—it is harder to dismiss the news story as yet just another murder statistic. Photographs bring home the particular, individual, human nature of the tragedy. Hence, despite the uncomfortable nature of the task, when journalists explain to the families of victims why they want a photograph, many if not most will commonly consent and produce a cherished photograph of their loved one for the media to use.

Of course, such photographs may be obtained in unethical ways. A journalist lacking in sensitivity may attempt to hound or bully the family into producing a photograph. Indeed, where consent is not forthcoming a journalist may even stoop to deceptive means of acquiring a photograph for his editor. For example, one way of getting a photograph from an uncooperative family is to ask for a cup of tea and, while alone in the living room, snatch a treasured photograph from the living-room mantelpiece. When the photograph is returned after use a week later, the editor might even include a note thanking the family for their cooperation. No doubt in their grief the family would probably not have much recollection of the fact that they had not consented. Hence a journalist might prey upon the vulnerable in a deceitful, manipulative, and immoral way. But what is wrong here is not the routine of collect calls per se, but rather the way in which the end was achieved. Where the reporter is suitably sensitive, the family's consent is asked for and received, and the photograph is used appropriately, there would in fact appear to be nothing morally dubious about the practice.

What such an example might be thought to illustrate is the idea that routines or practices of which we have no experience or are external to may appear highly dubious. Yet when one examines such practices more closely it may turn out that what is actually involved, in terms of the experience of those involved, shows the practices not to be intrinsically unethical and, moreover, as constitutive of good practice when carried out with proper sensitivity. A good journalist, through his experience, will know that collect calls can be made without resorting to bullying, manipulation, or deceit. Without direct experience or knowledge informed by the experience of those within the practice, outsiders might wrongly presume that respect for privacy precludes the possibility of making collect calls. Hence, the thought is, we must have experience of journalism in order to deliberate fully and properly about the ethics of what is, should, or may be involved.

However, we should recognize that first-hand experience is not sufficient for sound critical reflection about a particular practice. Many ordinary journalists may unquestioningly follow the precedents set for them without being able to articulate clearly the rationale for what they do. Indeed, given the time constraints and institutional pressures, journalists may be less likely than outsiders to examine questions of probity, deceit, privacy, and malpractice. No one aspires to alienate friends, disparage colleagues, or offend his or her employer. More importantly, why should merely being external to a practice disqualify someone from understanding or critically reflecting on it? Some of the best arts commentators are not artists, nor political scientists politicians, which is probably a good thing. Many commentators on journalism and the media are not themselves practicing journalists, but it is far from clear that this precludes their ideas or criticism from having any value.

True, there is good reason to hold that knowledge depends on experience. I might appreciate the underlying principles of tennis, but unless I actually try to play myself I am not going to be able to do so. Similarly, I may understand the rationale for making collect calls on recently bereaved families for the photographs of victims of tragic misfortunes, accidents, or murders. Yet unless I actually follow those who make such calls, as an apprentice might, or attempt to make such calls myself and learn the intricacies actually involved, I may be unable to perceive the kinds of difficulties involved. This is, after all, precisely why we learn from experience. But it is quite compatible with holding that true understanding depends on experience to recognize that critical reflection can deepen our understanding of what is involved, possibly leading to changes in our practices. Indeed if critical reflection could not play such a role then our understanding would be unable to transcend our actual experience.

Furthermore, critical reflection enables us to consider more clearly the rationale for something independently of the way those imbued into the practice may feel about it. In trying to understand those involved in a given practice, whether journalism or politics, we should try to see how they themselves understand it. Yet their self-understanding is no guarantor of truth. For example, in trying to understand those involved in the practice of slavery it may be necessary to see them as they understood themselves: as trading in subhuman species or tribes who were not worthy of moral consideration. Yet from a critical viewpoint we can see that those treated as slaves were human and, moreover, that ethnic, religious, or cultural differences are insufficient to exclude people from the sphere of moral concern. The point is that practices that we now accept, just as slavery once was, may in the light of critical examination turn out to be problematic. Hence it may be that journalistic deceit, invasion of privacy, sensationalism, and voyeurism, though perhaps a common part of contemporary media practice, are morally problematic. Whether or not they are and why can only be discovered in the light of critical philosophical enquiry.

Unless we try to examine the possible grounds for our practices, we cannot know whether what we do is in fact justifiable or not. That we can and do recognize the possibility of being mistaken at both the individual and communal level precludes a crude moral relativism, a relativism that aligns itself with an uncritical arrogance about the way things are. It is important to realize that this does not rule out relativism as such. There may be, as I am inclined to think, a blameless, ineliminable divergence in what we value in the moral sphere distinct from categorical morality. But even if this is so regarding the moral principles we hold as good, it cannot follow from the false assumption that our values and principles are not subject to external examination and critical assessment. Thus it is that theoretical reflection can and does allow us to modify more effectively existent practices or institute new ones.

I am not denying that probably many philosophers, interest groups, and assorted critics of media practices may possess only a superficial grasp of the realities of journalistic and media practices. Hence media criticism and ethical debate tends to belie the messy, complex cases and dilemmas that actually arise. The ethical codes and prescriptions suggested in relation to journalistic practice or media censorship are often highly simplistic and inapplicable: from the plainly useless to the highly damaging. But this is not to deny the point and purpose of critical reflection. Indeed, media professionals themselves show the need to reflect critically on what they do from merely technical matters to more obviously ethical ones.[16] But, at best, what this shows is that the experience of those within the practice should inform our ethical reflections about it. Hence in order to critically examine substantive ethical issues we must at least be familiar with the experiences of those involved in journalism and the media.

After all, our judgments of the practices and conventions involved are necessarily comparative. Hence we require the ability to make previous comparisons which relies on a sense of the history and evolution of journalism and the media. Such an awareness will also lessen the chances that one is shackled by contemporary media fashion or the hidden prejudices of a particular party or institutional agenda. Moreover, such a basis for comparison enables us to clarify more clearly the reason for one's judgment in a particular case. If we are to trust external critics we must assume that they are sympathetic, sufficiently discriminating, and capable of recognizing the point of the practices and conventions even though they may disagree with them. For example, we would not listen overmuch to someone who dismissed all advertisements on the grounds that they lie. Such a critic misunderstands the point and purpose of advertising. This does not exclude external criticism but only criticism that is ill-informed: after all, a practice may itself be corrupt in a manner that only external critics may be able to see.

Critical enquiry and media practice are not hermetically sealed off from each other. Indeed, without philosophical input, those who report, produce, and film cannot themselves be expected to be clear about various issues, such as the point of news in the first place, the nature of individual and institutional responsibility, conflicts of loyalty and public interest, the force of censorship considerations, and so on. We are not engaged merely in the abstract analysis of principles or in showing the arguments involved. Rather, we are concerned with why certain descriptions are more appropriate than others and why journalism and the media are to be valued. Hence, in part, argument should proceed by trying to show how it is that someone may simply be missing the point. It is this interplay between intuition, appropriate description, and the analysis of principles with which we try to grapple in this book to deepen our understanding of the values, concepts, and principles that good journalists and those in the media should live by.[17]

IMMORALISM AND THE MEDIA

Nonetheless, there is one last and significant challenge to the motivation behind media ethics. The idea, in essence, is that the news media and journalists must themselves be quite prepared to be immoral in order to carry out their professional functions properly.[18] After all, many people think politicians cannot be expected to be moral saints and tell the truth all the time, especially not to our enemies. Similarly, in order to uncover scandals and to serve the public's wants, journalists may find themselves engaged in sensationalism, deceit, and bribery. Alternatively expressed, the idea might be that those in the media, as journalists at least, are not bound by ordinary, commonsense morality.[19] In the Delahaye example, I suggested that the journalist's moral duty actually coincided with the news interest involved in the massacre. The relevant news interest and the journalist's moral duty both entailed that Delahaye should take a photograph that captured the nature and scale of the massacre, without focusing too graphically on any one particular individual or atrocity. But there are, of course, many cases where a journalist's moral duty and professional interest seem to come apart almost completely. That is, it might be thought that acting as a professional journalist in fact requires one to be immoral in certain kinds of cases.

Consider, for example, how journalists responded when, on 21 December 1988, Pan American Flight 103 from London to New York exploded over Lockerbie, Scotland. As a result of the bomb planted on board, 270 people were killed in mid-flight. Within a few hours of finding out that their nearest and dearest had been cruelly killed, friends, family, and acquaintances were rung up by journalists and networks to find details out about those who had died, just after they had actually learned of the tragedy for themselves. Of the people killed, 35 were students from Syracuse University, where a memorial service for the students was held. But at the memorial service, at Hendricks Chapel, students were badgered prior to, during, and after the service by photographers and reporters. The aisles were overflowing with journalists, television equipment, camera mechanisms, and triggered strobe lights all distracted away from and interrupted the memorial service itself, while studied camera shots tracked people in their most private moments of grief, intruding vicariously upon the cruel effects that such tragic events may have on those left behind.[20] Such journalistic behavior, though professionally required in order to cover the story, itself seems to run counter to what we might consider to be an ethically appropriate response. Asking someone whose friends or parents have just been killed in a plane crash "how they feel" seems entirely inappropriate at best and, at worst, entirely lacking in sensitivity to the nature of the tragedy for those concerned. The journalistic response may be that, professionally speaking, they still have to cover such things, no matter how distasteful. The story has to be covered, photographs have to be taken, and questions have to be asked to report on or convey the information, grief, and nature of the tragedy. After all, if the plane had not been blown up there would be no story, no grief, no tragedy, and thus the journalists would not have to be there.[21]

In the particular case of one woman's hysterical grief, we can see how this kind of view crystallizes into an opposition between professional journalism and ethical responsibility. The television camera crews and reporters were at New York airport before many of the friends and relatives waiting for passengers on Flight 103 had arrived or even heard about their possible deaths. Understandably those waiting for the passengers became worried and were made ever more frantic by the increasing presence of television cameras and journalists. Eventually the information concerning the plane crash was given to those waiting for the passengers. One couple had only just arrived at the airport after most of the reporters, photographers, and television cameras had camped down near to the First-Class Lounge which had been sectioned off. The woman approached a Pan Am official standing near the journalists and cameramen and asked why there was all this fuss. She was told that Flight 103 had gone down—her daughter's flight. She then collapsed into a hysterical fit, screaming and howling for her baby, crawling on the floor, her skirt up, in what can only be described as the most painful exhibition of grief and rage for the death of her daughter.

The cameras immediately zoomed in on her for the duration of the fit: people were fighting to get shots of her howling on the floor, and some of the shots were almost instantly relayed onto television. As one freelance reporter directing his camera crew for the BBC put it: "I didn't really know what was going on. I didn't realize that this was someone who'd come to the airport, had her daughter on the flight and just discovered it. . . . I'd never heard anything like it. I just had an immediate reaction. . . . Look, just get it."[22]

The footage went out almost immediately on CNN. In such a case the obviously telegenic image, electrifying in its horror, of this woman bestially writhing on the floor is what drew the cameramen and journalists to her. Yet many would, I think rightly, be outraged at the way her essentially private grief, rage, impotence, and despair was put on display for all viewers, without her consent and regardless of any sympathy for or understanding of her position. In the very act of deploring the tragedy before them, journalists and the news media seem to encourage an appalling curiosity and morbid delight in the tragedies of others.[23] Although most journalists would consider it to be their professional duty to catch such events on tape, it seems to constitute a paradigmatic case of unethical journalism.

What the journalistic coverage of the Pan Am disaster might be thought to show is that, generally, journalism is inherently ghoulish and parasitic: primarily it involves preying upon the tragedies and misfortunes of others. When Jacqueline Kennedy Onassis was dying in her apartment in New York there were rumours going around that she had died already or that she was, at the very least, on her last legs. So hundreds of reporters, cameramen, and television crews gathered outside her apartment on Fifth Avenue. The following excerpt from a conversation between two reporters from *The New York Daily News*, as to whether Jackie Kennedy's body will come out the front or the back of the apartment block, seems to bear this analysis out:

Rob Speyer, *Daily News* Reporter: "I think if they bring the body out, they bring it out on the other side, they ain't gonna bring it out the front door . . . can you imagine what a zoo it would be if they brought the body right out of the awning?"

Daily News Reporter 2: "I know, but it's like a little respect—there's like trash bags out back and . . . "

Rob Speyer: "I don't know . . . I can't imagine anything less respectful than 5,000 cameramen stomping on her body."[24]

In a similar vein the political correspondent of the *Daily News,* Paul Schwartzman, in discussing the fact that he spends most of his time following Mayor Giuliani around New York, implied that news journalism is an inherently morbid business: "You never know what's going to happen. A lot of times we do things just because there's a chance that he'll be shot in the head."[25]

So it would seem that the very kind of interest taken in events by news journalists might itself be intrinsically dubious. Moreover, the professional journalistic activities involved in acquiring the information that fuels the public's interest in newsworthy events may themselves be unethical. Strategies ranging from offering payment for information to subterfuge, deceit, and bribery all have a long history in journalistic practice and are often involved in the acquisition of various journalistic scoops and exclusives. Reporters on to stories about tragedy victims used to take snatchmen with them to the relatives' house. It was the job of the snatchman to steal a picture of the dead to accompany the story in the paper, without the relatives realizing that it had gone: sometimes the picture was returned with an editor's note thanking the relatives for their cooperation.[26] Thus the conclusion drawn from such cases might be that in order to fulfill their function—in the Lockerbie case, by relaying information about a plane crash and the effects on the nearest and dearest of those killed—journalists must pay scant regard to the ethical niceties that we observe in normal, day-to-day life. Professional journalists, at least to the extent that they are truly professional, cannot respect commonsense morality.

MEDIA ETHICS VINDICATED

However, such considerations suggest quite the reverse. The very fact that the general public was itself outraged by aspects of the coverage of the Lockerbie disaster, as well as many media professionals, ought to suggest at least one significant role for media ethics. For what critical reflection may enable us to do is to clarify the intuitions, concepts, and beliefs that we actually have in relation to journalistic and media practices. Thus philosophical thought can usefully aspire to formalizing, critically explicating, and thus assessing the principles that we think ought to govern our behavior. Hence we can seek to iron out possible inconsistencies in our journalistic commitments and media practices.

Such a role is significant because once we have formulated principles that we can reasonably assent to they can be referred to in governing our future actions, especially where our judgment fails us. Thus, in the Lockerbie case, it seems clear that the nature of the plane crash, the grief felt by those waiting for the passengers' arrival, and the resultant memorial services could have been conveyed without the kind of intrusion and insensitivity that occurred. The hysteria of the woman need not have been shown; people need not have been asked how they felt, when the very picture itself conveys their grief well enough.

Moreover, the same kind of reasoning will clarify what might well be appropriate in similar but distinct cases. The identical considerations that mitigated against showing the woman's hysteria may prohibit showing the burned remains of charred bodies in Bosnia because the images are so horrific and yet, conversely, permit certain photographs of the massacre in Rwanda, given that the particular bodies and injuries themselves are backgrounded.

Of course, many journalists do quite rightly follow public figures in case misfortune, or even good luck, should strike. But, of itself, this stems from the necessity to do so in order to inform the public about significant events in the world within which they live. There is nothing, of itself, intrinsically immoral about that. The reporters and cameramen outside Jackie Kennedy's apartment had to be there to get the photographs and reports that enabled them to convey to an interested public that she was dying and to anchor the more general reflections on her death. Thus the *Daily News*, among other papers like the *Post*, could run with a 16-page pull-out special on Jackie Kennedy, selling an extra 16,000 copies.

The fact that reporters gathered while Jackie Kennedy was dying and, later on, at her funeral service may be distasteful to some, but it seems no more or less immoral than the distasteful job of being an undertaker. The undertaker must perform certain tasks in order for the appropriate burial and form of public grief to be expressed, just as the journalist must report and photograph events, whether tragic, unfortunate, or admirable, as they happen. What is important is that reporters, journalists, and the media perform this function with courtesy and respect for those involved. Indeed, to carry out their function well, the media must respect certain ethical values to maintain public trust and respect for what they are told.[27] The incompatibility alluded to then is not one of principle, media ethics is not an oxymoron, but it does relate to certain ways in which the functions involved may be, more or less reputably, carried out. Professionalism need not come apart from ethical responsibility.[28]

The objection to ethical journalism is a strange and highly implausible line to take. After all, philosophical ethics typically involves not just understanding ethical theories but critically modifying ethical principles and their application, principles that, since they are both normative and practical, have a direct bearing on the deliberations and decisions of everyday life. Indeed, the objection to media ethics is bizarre, given that we recognize that the demand to be ethical applies over every aspect of our practical lives, including that most pragmatic of all practical activities, politics. Part of the value of philosophical ethics lies in its very application to our ordinary lives. There is no distinctive feature that ought to exempt media institutions and journalistic practices from ethical obligations and requirements. Thus we should demand of those in journalism and the media that they act in an ethically respectable manner while pursuing the end of informing us about significant events in the world.

NOTES

1. Excellent examples of this include Philip Meyer's *Ethical Journalism* (New York: Longman, 1987), Edmund B. Lambeth's *Committed Journalism*, 2nd edition (Bloomington, IN: Indiana University Press, 1992), and Clifford Christians, John Ferré, and Mark Fackler, *Good News: A Social Ethics of the Press* (New York: Oxford University Press, 1993).

2. In contrast to attitudes in the United States where training journalists take courses in media ethics and journals such as the *Columbia Journalism Review* and *Quill* regularly focus on such matters, in Britain the cardinal rule seems to be only that one should always try to avoid admitting any mistakes. Hence Peregrine Worsthorne, of *The Sunday Telegraph*, has complained that "journalism does less harm when it disgusts by its genuine vulgarity than when it deludes by its spurious sanctity," and the journalist Christopher Fildes, of *The Daily Telegraph* and *The Spectator*, has claimed that ethics is a growth industry we can do without.

3. For example, a detailed MORI public-opinion poll carried out in 1990 found that less than half of the public questioned agreed with the claim that "the press behaves responsibly in Britain" and 73 percent believed that the press intruded far too much into the lives of public figures. See Raymond Snoddy, *The Good, The Bad and The Unacceptable* (London: Faber, 1993), pp. 16–17.

4. See, for example, Paul Weaver's *News and the Culture of Lying* (New York: Macmillan, 1994).

5. The automatic incantation of the right to freedom of speech by the press seems especially cynical in cases where news reporting has had a prejudicial effect on the course of justice. The role of the media in the 1995 nearly year-long trial of O. J. Simpson, for example, certainly may have had a prejudicial effect on the way witnesses took the stand, lawyers pursued their task, and the public perceived the case, never mind possible influences on jurors, just by virtue of the mere presence of television cameras and the resultant media frenzy. In the United Kingdom the Taylor sisters had their convictions for murder quashed in 1993 because the Appeal Court judged that news reports had been prejudicial. Justice requires a certain distance from the public sphere rather than complete exposure to and manipulation by public prurience, prejudices, and media agendas.

6. See Lucas A. Powe, Jr., *The Fourth Estate and Constitution: Freedom of the Press in America* (Berkley and Los Angeles, CA: University of California Press, 1991).

7. An obvious case involving downright lying to the public is Janet Cooke's "Jimmy's World," which was an entirely fabricated story about the drug abuse of an eight-year-old boy. The Pulitzer prize it won in 1980 was withdrawn a year later, and *The Washington Post* ran its own investigatory article about the story. A more complex case in the United Kingdom was the July 1995 *Sunday Times* investigation into allegations about M.P.s in the British parliament asking questions in return for financial payment; the investigation itself involved lying and various forms of subterfuge. The point here is that it is much harder for reporters or papers lacking integrity and willing to engage in such deception then to denounce public figures who themselves are involved in deceiving the public at large.

8. The increasing proliferation and variety of media programs, the increasing numbers of texts concerned with the activities and practices of the news media, many public campaigns, such as gay campaigns to out public figures, and the increasing numbers of initiatives, such as the Voices Against Violence Cable Television Initiative, touch upon, in many different ways, aspects of press and media ethics.

9. For example, the incorporation of journalistic codes of practice, programming guidelines, and advertising regulations may be seen as useful instruments for allaying public worries. In the United States, papers such as the *Los Angeles Times* have a written code of ethics for their journalists, and in the United Kingdom, after the 1990 Report of the Calcutt Committee on Privacy and Related Matters, the Press Council's function became the supervision of a code created by the newspaper industry.

10. Michael Oakeshott, *Experience and Its Modes* (Cambridge: Cambridge University Press, 1933), pp. 69–81 and pp. 331–346, claims that philosophical theorizing, by its very nature, is inapplicable to particular practices and professions.

11. Mary Midgley, "Trying Out One's New Sword," in *Heart and Mind* (London: Routledge, 1981), also in *Vice and Virtue in Everyday Life*, ed. Christina Sommers and Fred Sommers, 5th ed. (Fort Worth, TX: Harcourt Brace, 1993), pp. 174–180.

12. Luc Delahaye in *Decisive Moments: Photographs That Changed the World*, BBC TV 1994.

13. As Aristotle recognized, the role of reason and reflection is to enable us to recognize which dispositions ought to be cultivated, which appetites suppressed and thus what the most appropriate and moderate course of action is in any given case. See Aristotle on moral responsibility in his *Nichomachean Ethics*, trans. J. A. K. Thomson (Harmondsworth: Penguin, 1953), Book III, 1109b30–1110a16, pp. 111–141.

14. For example, most American editors decried the suggestions put forward by the Hutchins Commission in 1947, which critically examined press performance and responsibilities, on the grounds that they would involve imposing the useless ideas of intellectuals who "don't know anything about newspapers." See Gene Gilmore and Robert Root, "Ethics for Newsmen," in *Ethics and the Press*, ed. John C. Merrill and Ralph D. Barney (New York: Hastings House, 1975), p. 33. This kind of complaint is not unique to journalism and the media. Lawyers, businessmen, health care workers, and social workers all make complaints against philosophers interested in the rationale for certain practices on the grounds that, as a matter of principle, they cannot understand what is involved. See Anne Maclean, *The Elimination of Morality* (Routledge: London, 1993), for an articulation of something like this claim in relation to medical ethics.

15. See Stephen R. L. Clark's "Abstract Morality, Concrete Cases," in *Moral Philosophy and Contemporary Problems*, ed. J. D. G. Evans (Cambridge: Cambridge University Press, 1987).

16. See Meyer, *Ethical Journalism*, pp. 189–200.

17. In Plato's *Protagoras and Meno*, trans. W. K. C. Guthrie (Harmondsworth: Penguin, 1956), Socrates argues that the definitional question, as to what constitutes virtue, must take epistemological priority before any meaningful enquiry concerning whether we should be virtuous, or whether virtue is teachable, can proceed. But by the time Plato came to write *The Republic*, trans. H. D. P. Lee (Harmondsworth: Penguin, 1974), Socrates' enquiry into the nature of justice and the just state is conducted in a symbiotic interplay between the formal and substantive considerations.

18. This thought is clearly articulated in Robert Aibel, "Ethics and Professionalism in Documentary Film-making," in *Image Ethics*, ed. Larry Gross, John Stuart Katz, and Jay Ruby (New York: Oxford University Press, 1988), pp. 108–118. The classic genesis of this kind of thought is obviously Niccolò Machiavelli's *The Prince,* where he states, in relation to a Prince's state governance: "It is essential, therefore, for a Prince who desires to maintain his position, to have learned how to be other than good, and to use or not to use his goodness as necessity requires." See Niccolò Machiavelli, trans. N. H. Thomson, *The Prince* (New York: Dover, 1992), p. 40.

19. This claim is made by Stephen H. Daniel, "Some Conflicting Assumptions of Journalistic Ethics," in *Philosophical Issues in Journalism*, ed. Elliot D. Cohen (New York: Oxford University Press, 1992), pp. 50–58.

20. See Joan Deppa, *The Media and Disasters: Pan Am 103* (London: David Fulton, 1993), and Saul E. Wisnia, "Private Grief, Public Exposure," in *Impact of Mass Media*, ed. Ray Eldon Hiebert, 3rd edition (New York: Longman, 1995), pp. 113–118.

21. See Jody Powell, "No Consequences," in *Impact of Mass Media,* ed. Ray Eldon Hiebert, 3rd edition (New York: Longman, 1995), pp. 119–122, for a discussion of the way that the suicide of the Clinton White House lawyer, Vincent Foster Jr., was covered by the news media and the cynical forms of justification given by journalists for their conduct.

22. Deppa, *The Media and Disasters: Pan Am 103*, p. 29.

23. Alistair Cooke's "The Obscenity Business," in his *The Americans: Fifty Talks on Our Life and Times* (New York: Alfred A. Knopf, 1979), identifies quite succinctly the kind of hypocritical interest often taken in such horrific events by the news media.

24. *Naked News: The Tabloid*, Channel 4 TV, 1995.

25. Paul Schwartzman, *Daily News* Political Correspondent, in *Naked News: The Tabloid*, Channel 4 TV, 1995.

26. See Snoddy, *The Good, The Bad and The Unacceptable*, p. 35. Unfortunately, even in contemporary journalism the practice has not disappeared altogether.

27. See Andrew Belsey and Ruth Chadwick, "Ethics as a Vehicle for Media Quality," *European Journal of Communication, 10* (1995): 461–473.

28. However, the force of certain ethical demands may depend on special norms by virtue of features particular to journalism and the functions of the media.

2 *News and the Fourth Estate*

INTRODUCTION

Naturally enough, we tend to presume that we know what news is. As the very term suggests it is surely constituted by new information, the reporting of fresh events, or the casting of new light upon old ones. Hence, presumably, the function of journalism is to report accurately and in a complete manner the truth concerning new events or insights. However, what makes the news is far from simple. If all new events were appropriately considered news and reported as such, then there would not be enough air time on television and radio for anything else, newspapers would be the size of the *Encyclopaedia Britannica*, and anything of interest to us would be lost in a welter of information that we could not possibly process.

An apt analogy might be made to the cartographer's map in Lewis Carroll's *Sylvie and Bruno Concluded*: the cartographer's aim is to make the most faithful map of England possible.[1] But, in order to achieve his goal, the cartographer presumes he must represent every geographical detail, every highway, byway, and blade of grass. Consequently he ends up with a map that would literally cover the entire country and, no doubt, under which many people would suffocate. Obviously the map is useless: one can hardly fold it up and put it in one's pocket or tell, without actually going to the place, what the landscape ahead is like. In being so literal-minded the cartographer undercuts the very point and purpose of making a map in the first place. News, like maps, must necessarily be selective.

So not all new events can usefully be considered news; hence we need some idea as to what guides the process of selection. What enables us to distinguish newsworthy events from merely new events? The point is not just that newspapers cannot store all the information in a user-friendly way. Imagine a Gibsonian "news" society of the future where we could access a news service listing every event in the world. Such a service would inform us less about the world than the papers we presently read. Infinite storage capacity with bulletins of standard-length summaries would hardly attain the minimum threshold required to be a news service of informative value and interest. The point of the news is to select, highlight, and treat appropriately what we ought to know about what is happening in our world.

A SOCIOLOGICAL ACCOUNT

A popular sociological account of whether something constitutes news presumes that the issue is a purely classificatory matter, which depends on the conventions of presentation, narrative style, and whether the news institutions, programs, or editors consider a story news. Whether the story covered as news is any good or of much interest is a further distinct and unrelated question. The thought is that accounts that assess news in terms of the performance of a particular function conflate, falsely, the classificatory and evaluative senses of the term "news."[2] The virtues of such a distinction mean that we need not be overly narrow about what is considered to be news. According to this sociological account, Bill Clinton's commitment to affirmative action, a Zenith take-over bid, Heather Locklear's steamy sex secrets, Hollywood gossip, and Michael Jordan's foray into baseball are all thus considered news because the papers, radio, and television stations cover them as such, even though we might evaluate them negatively.

However, despite its virtues, such a sociological account can only prove deeply inadequate because it nimbly sidesteps the difficult questions concerning judgement and value that we must get clear about. In the first instance, who exactly counts in conferring the status of news upon a particular story? Organizations? Proprietors? Editors? Journalists? Proprietors need not have any intrinsic connection to or understanding of news and journalism. They may just be interested in owning a given paper or news network for profit maximization, power, or influence. Journalists may write up stories as news, and yet the story may still fail to qualify because editors refuse to take it or see the public interest involved. Perhaps editors are the key figures in the news-making process? Typically editors started out as journalists and thus have a fairly thorough grounding in the skills and understanding of a reporter's job. Moreover, and this is increasingly true in the world of corporate journalism, they have the power to reject, rewrite, and tailor the report's content and style. Yet even so, news editors or institutions cannot adequately be taken to be conferrers of news status. This is not merely because journalists often discover stories by themselves, independently of editorial direction, and will bring a story to the editor expecting them to recognize it as news. More importantly it is because—as all journalists, editors, and the public at large recognize—big news stories can be and sometimes are missed by the press.

For example in the 1980s the activities of the Department of Housing and Urban Development (HUD) were hardly considered newsworthy.[3] Yet even in the early years of the Reagan administration it was becoming clear that something was seriously wrong. Sam Pierce, a New York lawyer appointed to head the agency, was flown all over the United States by various builders and bankers. Industry bodies facilitated trips abroad by various administration officials, including to Italy, and expenses bills were rocketing through the roof for trips to Europe. Unfortunately, contracts were awarded to those with the right political allegiances, bribery proliferated, and federal mortgage applications falsified. Despite evidence of a wide-scale problem, and the effect such corruption had on the weakest and most vulnerable in society, the HUD scandal was not deemed to be news. It was only in April 1989 that the story was considered newsworthy, because of the angle of human hypocrisy involved. James Watt had become well known for his denunciations of federal poverty programs and resultant subsidy handouts, influence-seeking punditry that inflated the cost and inefficiency of the programs. But he was among a group of consultants identified as seeking to cash in on various grants from one of the HUD's housing programs. Suddenly the HUD became big news overnight. But the real story, as it had been happening, had been and gone. For many years the federal programs had been manipulated by those in authority and subsumed for personal interest or advantage, and most of the key information had been released in audits five years previously.

Conversely, hard-news "exclusives" may turn out not to be worth the paper on which they are printed. For example, a recent *Sunday Times* exclusive reported that the one-time leader of the British Labour Party, Michael Foot, had in fact worked for the Russian KGB. But it rapidly turned out that the source's account was, at best, misdirected and that *The Sunday Times* had apparently misrepresented their own source's claims. The mere fact that Michael Foot had met various Russian emissaries was hardly news, given that most left-wing politicians had, during their political careers, been approached in this way. Subsequently *The Sunday Times* was obliged to retract and pay damages.[4]

The sociological account effectively defines news in terms of what is covered by the media as news. Yet papers or television sometimes miss big stories and, conversely, actually cover stories that turn out not to be news at all. This is not merely the trivial point that in the bulky sections of Sunday papers there are cookery, travel, and car sections that, marketing considerations aside, would normally not be considered news at all. Nor is it merely to point to the recent phenomenon of papers like *The Sunday Sport,* which "report" such stories as "Elvis Found on Mars." For these stories are not intended, nor taken by their readership, to constitute real news at all: they are a parody in news form of outlandish freak stories and tall tales. Rather, if we limit news to these stories actually covered by the media and recognized as such by those within it, our understanding of news would be both too wide and too narrow. It falsely includes joke stories treated in news form and falsely excludes stories that it was a mistake not to cover. Unfortunately the latter kind of case is not as rare as many journalists would like to believe.

All these problems point to the fundamental misconception endemic to the sociological approach. For the account presupposes the institutional existence of journalists, media institutions, and the process of making news. But this is the very thing any account of the news ought to seek to explain: just why do we have the news media, and what exactly is their function? The sociological account puts the cart before the horse. How did the institutions of the media, newspapers, and journalists get going if not by building on a recognition of certain things as news in the first place? This is not to deny that evolving institutions and modes of communication shape and influence the nature of the news. After all, the demands of advertisers or the need for pictures to go with a story covered by television may have a strong determining influence on the shape and nature of news programming. But, without the primary recognition of something as news, the media institutions could not have got going and there would be nothing for the evolving institutions and modes of communication to have a modificatory influence on.

Our natural and fitting presumption is that what matters is what journalists discover. We talk of recognizing a news story rather then merely creating one. A journalist convinced that something is a news story will not try to convince others by saying that it has been written up as one or that the editor said it was. Rather, a good journalist will try to explain why it is newsworthy by attempting to show the news editor or doubter that something of crucial public or human interest is involved. He or she will try to show us how we should see the essential aspect of the story rather than appeal to institutional considerations. What is relevant is not the appearance of a story in newsprint or production by CNN and the BBC. This is precisely why it is only when we fail to recognize whether or why we are supposed to be interested in a news story that we tend to seek institutional-type explanations. Thus only when we think a news item is not really newsworthy do we start thinking about distorting institutional influences such as the possible demands made by advertisers. After all, we may watch the news and complain "that's not news," a complaint that makes no sense on the sociological account. Conversely, a story or event not covered by the media may be big news. We judge news stories, not confer news status on them. The value of news, and the implicit ethical commitments involved, cannot be explained by the sociological account: it leaves us unclear about the very thing it sets out to explain.

THE FOURTH ESTATE AND THE IMPLICIT CONTRACT

We still require an understanding of the values that enable us to pick out what the salient news stories are. The traditional presumption is that the primary principle concerns what affects our lives as citizens: the media have a duty to inform us about events in the world that significantly affect our lives.

This traditional conception of the role of the news media generally underwrites the presumption that the press constitutes the fourth estate.[5] The three estates of the legislature, executive, and judiciary are all semiautonomous and official spheres of government. In a democratic state, we elect the legislature to legislate on the people's behalf. The law is enforced impartially by the executive, and the judiciary rule on how the law is to be applied and, moreover, whether the legislation is within the bounds of a constitutional liberal state. Democratic accountability is the primary means of ensuring that those in power cannot manipulate their position for their own self-interest at the expense of the public interest. As Winston Churchill once intimated, democratic government may be bad, but the alternatives are worse.[6]

Although the political arrangements of checks and balances aim to prevent the domination of one sphere of government on another, it remains possible for devious, powerful individuals and institutions within government to conspire in their own private interest. This is a perversion of the transparent functioning of government, the aim being to avoid accountability, in order to achieve private ends independently of legality and the public interest. But due to the complexity, size, and levels of government, the mechanisms, bodies, personnel, and interrelations involved in the democratic process are often far from transparent. As with any political state, the question arises, who keeps guard over the guardians? The question is particularly acute for liberal democratic societies because the fundamental presumption of a liberal state is that the arms of government are accountable to the people.[7] But there is no absolute guarantee, and the trappings of power and influence can often corrupt those in positions of authority. It is often possible for those in the political sphere to club together and to attempt to pervert the democratic process to further their own aims and goals.

This is where the notion of the press as an unofficial fourth estate comes in. Obviously we cannot all hope to get to grips with the opaque workings of government or hope to grasp the nuances of political maneuverings. But those who study the process itself on a day-to-day basis, comment on it, and relay reports to us through the news media are not only there to report to us the public workings of government but can hope to explain to us what the significance of certain events might be. Thus journalists reporting on the day's proceedings in Congress, parliament, the courts, or the behavior of the police are, in effect, watchdogs for the people over those who occupy positions of power and rule in our name for our benefit.

The fundamental point is not merely an empirical one about the kinds of corruption to which those who control the levers of power are open. After all, the watchdog role of the press brings with it its own form of power to shape and influence events. Rather, it is to point up the implied contract between the citizens in a liberal state and the news media. The point of the press is to keep a watch on those in positions of power over us, in order to report what is actually happening and being done in our name. We need this information both to know what is happening and so that we can judge whether our representatives are doing their job, whether the right policies are being pursued, whether we should make representations to government against some policy, and whether true justice is being carried out.

It is important to realize that the implicit contract between citizens and the news media, as watchdogs, entails a normative conception of good journalism. We have a picture of what good journalism amounts to, on the basis of which we can evaluate and criticize news stories and journalistic practices. The normative picture of good journalism provided corresponds very closely to the traditional one: namely, that good journalism covers what we ought to know, construed in terms of events and policies that affect how we are governed and how our society is governed. The news media guard the public at large from any unwarranted or unwanted incursions by the state into people's freedom or rights. Hence the large degree of coverage given to governmental functions, announcements, elections, policy disputes, initiatives, and politicians' lives. Thus politics and the processes of government are considered a mainstay of good journalism and news coverage.

It also follows that the media's failure to pick up on or cover adequately stories that do have a significant relation to our lives and the way they are governed constitutes a journalistic failure. Of course, it only constitutes such a failure where the story could have been covered or reported on in the first place. If there was no evidence, public or private, concerning some imminent financial disaster then the failure to report on the possible collapse of Wall Street or Lloyds of London could hardly be considered a failure of the news media. But where there is mounting evidence, where sources are available, where events do suggest a given trend with possibly far-reaching implications for the savings or lives of many people, a failure to investigate and report a story constitutes a failure to fulfill the function of the news media and live up to the implied contract. Thus conceiving of the news media as the fourth estate, in contrast to the sociological account, explains both why we value it and what constitutes good and bad journalism.

Nonetheless, there might be worries about such an account. Conceiving of the news media as the fourth estate seems to entail the following: something is newsworthy if and only if the story bears a significant relation to our ability to function as citizens within society. The function is given by a critical analysis of the media's watchdog function in a liberal society. The ordering principle as articulated, that of public significance, also captures the traditional presumption of many journalists that mere entertainment cannot, properly speaking, qualify as news. At best, an entertainment story may serve as a light-hearted leavener between the real news of significant events and disasters. Thus a story about Princess Diana and her children going white-water rafting in Aspen might be a therapeutic sweetener at the end of a bulletin cataloguing the latest serial killing, the day's proceedings of the O. J. Simpson trial, the disasters in Bosnia, or some current dispute between the president and the White House. But at best such a story is deemed parasitic upon "real" news.

But, the objection goes, there is something severely wrong with such a conclusion. For we are naturally interested in, and consider newsworthy, reports concerning the love lives of the rich and famous, from Pamela Anderson, Hugh Grant, and Madonna to Richard Gere and Cindy Crawford. Of course, we do not need to know about such things in order to function as citizens in society. But far from showing that such reports are not real news, this shows rather that the functionalist account of the news media, as the fourth estate, is far too narrow. Indeed, it seems to rest on a distorted understanding of the way the news media evolved. For, if anything, the news media evolved from entertaining, sensationalist scandal sheets and propaganda pamphlets that were far more speculative and loose with the truth than the news media are today.[8] Hence, someone might claim, *Entertainment Tonight* is a great news show providing gossip about the entertainment world, even though no one would ever claim that it provides an adequate representation of people and events that shape the way we are governed.

There is a certain force to this objection. The fundamental flaw in conceiving of the news media *solely* in terms of the fourth estate is that such an account is far too restrictive. We are interested in the juvenilia, interests, passions, and love lives of sports stars, soap stars, writers, actors, talk show hosts, lottery winners, everyday folk who win out against the odds, tales of adversity, glamor, and intrigue, quite apart from whether they have any effect on our public governance or not. Any account that rules out much of what we are interested in, and consequently much of what is included in the media as news, seems to be intuitively false. After all, the audience may not care so much for "significant" events as reports about Pamela Anderson's stormy marriage. Of course it matters as to whether what is reported about Pamela Anderson is true or not, given that the reader wants to find out about what is happening to her. But such information hardly fits in with or is "significant" in the grand scheme of things. Nonetheless, when a football player faces charges for murder, the news media may devote far more space to him than, say, to the Northern Ireland ceasefire or tragic events in Rwanda.

Of course, a hardcore political journalist might retort that we may well be interested in such things but that it is not the kind of thing we should term as news or be interested in hearing about. But then it looks as though an overly narrow evaluative commitment is used to define the category "news" in a way that is inevitably partial. It is not that the presumption of public significance does not highlight a useful and valuable function. Rather it cannot and does not capture the nature of news as a whole.

Moreover, imagine if the news media agenda were wholly driven by the notion of the fourth estate. Presumably the news we would get would be akin to the higher-minded political coverage presented to us by worthy newspapers such as *The New York Times*, *The Chicago Tribune,* or *The Washington Post* in the United States and *The Guardian* or *The Times* in the United Kingdom. The virtues of such papers accord well with the conception of the news media as the fourth estate, detailing and tracking political maneuverings in Washington and Westminster, detailing policy debates, political clashes, public affairs, and scandals. Yet such dull but worthy coverage would hardly be compelling, except to those preoccupied by politics, and we would feel that much of what we value in news had been lost.

Indeed, such news media coverage might effectively alienate us from the political process itself by detailing the minutiae of government in ways too abstract, complex, and tedious to compel our interest. It would tend toward a preoccupation with politics which would be self-defeating, fixating upon an endless litany of detailed facts about particular shifts in policy, endless speculation about political personalities or maneuverings, and the procession of ever more worthy but obscure experts on matters at hand that ordinary people often have no interest in or understanding of. If the sole fare of the news media is politics, and increasingly bears little relation to people's lives, then most people will switch off. This is not merely to say that the way politics is often covered is too obsessive, abstract, and full of jargon. For even if worthy political news were crystallized and conveyed in easily comprehensible ways, as it can and should be, there would still be a lack—a lack of human interest.

However, the objection can be met. Firstly, we should note that the objection does not show that the news media should not function as the fourth estate. After all, consider a news media that consisted solely of gossip, intrigues, and news about the lives of the rich and famous but entirely neglected the workings of government, politics, and public policy. We would, quite rightly, assume that the media was failing us. Thus we may criticize the initial reporting of the Gulf War and Vietnam, prior to and during the early stages of U.S. involvement at least, since it promoted a misconception of what the actual situations were, how they could best be combated, and what the just courses of action were.[9] A more extreme scenario is given in J. G. Ballard's short story, "The Secret History of World War 3."[10] The story effectively points up the absurdity of a news media dominated by prurient human interests at the expense of any understanding of the actual world. The story is narrated by an ordinary surgeon who is the only one among his friends and colleagues who remembers the onset and resolution, within minutes, of World War 3. The reason no one remembers is because the news media have become so focused on the mental and physical health of the president, Ronald Reagan in for his historic third term, that no time and interest is shown in the potentially disastrous tensions between Russia and the United States. In Ballard's story the news media have clearly failed to report on issues and events that affect people as citizens and human beings in the most important of ways. Hence we criticize the news media when they fail to uncover stories, such as the saving and loans scandal, which are important in this way.[11] Quietism and trivialization are blameworthy traits precisely because they constitute a failure of the news media's most important function.

It is part of the very concept "news" that what is reported should be new and significant—significant insofar as such events may or do impinge on how we choose to lead our lives. Within a political state, especially a liberal, democratic state, this entails coverage of political stories and events. Historically it may be true that the news media evolved in relation to partisan polemics, the uncritical acceptance of official versions of events, and sensationalist scandal sheets. However, increasingly we have come to regard the news as our main source of information about events in the world which affect us. Hence we have come to expect journalists and news institutions to cover stories to inform us about the world. This is not to claim that, initially at least, many journalists, papers, and news organizations did so particularly well. Yet as we come to recognize the function of news, and the implicit contract between the news media and its public, we quite rightly come to expect journalists and the media to do a better job in covering the world fairly, accurately, and impartially. Thus we expect journalists not to make quotes up or doctor photographs to give a misleading impression. If journalism is in a better state than it ever was, which is disputable, this suggests only that the news media have come to recognize and carry out their socioculturally evolved function as the fourth estate.

However, what the objection does show is that to conceive of the news media *solely* in terms of the fourth estate is overly narrow and distorting. But it is quite compatible both to claim that one of its primary functions is to act as the fourth estate and to hold that the news media had also better cover stories of human interest. The virtue of such an account is that it both makes sense of our common-sense demand that the news media inform us about events in the world which affect us as citizens and recognizes our deeply human interest in stories about other individual human beings in times of stress, war, hunger, love, fame, death, starvation, abandonment, loss, and suffering. The successes, trials, and tribulations of others fascinate us because they help us to make sense of our own lives. For reports and stories about how people cope with their predicaments, how success was achieved through commitment, determination, or luck, may show us something about our human nature and common lot.

For example the Oklahoma bombing in April 1995 was obviously important in terms of the possible implications for terrorism in the United States. But, in human terms at least, that was not the main focus of the initial story: the main focus was on those killed and wounded, the rescue operation, and the apparently pointless and random nature of the attack on ordinary, innocent people without warning. One of the images that defined the event was of a fireman emerging from the smoke carrying an infant child in his arms. Why was the image so powerful? Because in all its particularity it nonetheless symbolized the horrific nature of the event: the wanton annihilation of innocent life without purpose or explanation.

It is important to realize that such human interest is not, quite naturally, merely confined to momentous events such as the Oklahoma bombing, man-made disasters like the Exxon Valdez, or natural disasters such as drought or earthquakes. Just one look at even the most worthy of newspapers will show that we are, in fact, fascinated by what is often sneeringly derided as the trivia of human life: from how a hostage coped with the ordeal or why a star like Hugh Grant might go to a prostitute, to whether a football star will pull through for his team in the SuperBowl. We find such stories compelling, and, often despite the way such stories are sometimes covered, they certainly do not lack for interest. Even desperately worthy newspapers will cover the human interest stories, though often disingenuously. For example, in the Hugh Grant case, the news angle in the broadsheet papers focused on how the tabloid press covered the story. But there is nothing inherently wrong with wanting to know about events that have a certain human interest, whether in terms of some grand catastrophe or something that touches upon the human condition or concerns the trivia of the royal, the rich, and the famous. If certain events that have no effect on us as citizens nonetheless speak to our natural human interest, then that constitutes good grounds for considering the event newsworthy.

NEWS, ENTERTAINMENT, AND INFORMED INTERESTS

However, considerations of human interest might be thought to lead to a much stronger conclusion—that the implicit contract between the news media and the public quite legitimately allows the news media to focus mainly on entertaining its audience. But we should be wary of presuming that the actual preferences of public audiences should wholly dictate the news agenda, for people's actual preferences may display a marked inclination toward what is entertaining in a way that may come apart from what would normally be considered newsworthy.[12]

Allowing actual audience preferences to dictate entirely the news services provided by the media would inevitably lead to bad journalism, for the drive to entertain would adversely affect not only the kind of stories covered but also the kind of coverage given to them. For example, the spin given to stories would be of an increasingly sensationalistic or voyeuristic bent. Hence even proper news stories might well be approached from an angle that plays upon a parasitic interest or appetite for violence, sex, and death even in the most banal cases.

Oprah Winfrey rushes to Oklahoma to ask people "how they really feel," political issues come to be simplified in terms of the clash of personalities, or ordinary people caught up in extreme events are misrepresented in order to fit certain stereotypes and news categories. Even in cases where reporters or media institutions possess no malice or conscious agenda, the spurious invention of detail or shift in tone would be driven by the desire to discover something interesting and distinctive in order to entertain. For example, in some cases, stories are sold on the basis of stereotypes that play on our fears and worries, such as racism, in a way that can be encapsulated in a single, sharp image, despite the fact that the reality does not conform to such a simple, clear picture.

The essential wrong here concerns how the motivation to entertain may distort news proper. A kernel of truth about certain events may be represented by alluding to key facts, but the emphasis given to the facts concerned—the tone of the report, the terms used, the images portayed—can effectively misrepresent the truth of the matter, often to such a degree that the impression given is the very opposite of the truth. An example from the British press concerns the Taylor sisters, who were sent to jail in 1992 for the murder of Alison Shaughnessy. Michelle Taylor had had a long-standing affair with Alison's husband prior to and some time after the marriage. At the time of the trial the tabloid press used a wedding-video-still headed "Cheat's Kiss," showing Michelle kissing her former lover at his wedding. Moreover, some of the reports contained allusions to a diary full of hate and loathing for Alison. All of these features of tabloid journalism were used to conjure up the picture of a witchlike, jealous harridan of a mistress out to get an innocent bride. The misrepresentation was so great that Mr. Justice Butterfield said that "some of that coverage crossed the limit of fair and accurate reporting by a substantial margin."[13] Even where reports contain a few indisputable facts, the impression given may still be quite the opposite of what was true.

It is important to realize that such criticisms cannot be laid solely at the door of the journalists who actually cover the stories concerned. The increasing importance of the editorial process itself, and thus the power, influence, and autonomy of the editor, has a tendency to exacerbate the problem where news values are entertainment-led. For not only will journalists be sent back to rewrite stories where, though accurate and fair, the news angle is not considered spicy enough, but, increasingly, editors tend to rewrite reporters' stories, often without consultation, according to their construal of reader appeal. Stories downloaded on modems, night editors rushing for the early edition, all kinds of constraints conspire to exacerbate bad practice. Hence an editor who was never there, who has no idea, apart from the piece in front of him, about what actually happened, may rewrite a story to give it a more entertaining inflection and may thus invent quotes that vocalize what he presumes, on little or no evidence, the public would consider appropriate for the subject of the report to feel. Thus the piece may end up distorting the events entirely, especially given the naive public understanding that quotes are verbatim reports of someone's words. Such problems are, in fact, much more endemic to the news process than the public naively presume, especially where an investigative story has been pursued for a long time and people start to lose track of the central chain of events: whether money was offered or demanded, a quote was verbatim or embellished, a statement was gossip or known fact, and so on.[14] The nature of the news process itself, where it is driven by the motivation to entertain, may thus distort even where the initial reporter's story may have been wholly accurate and fair. In the push to entertain, sensationalism tends to predominate over fact in order to speak to the audience's perceived preferences. True, pressure can be brought to bear for a retraction, which U.S. papers are much better at doing than those in the United Kingdom. But harm in such cases has already been done, and the ordinary person—even in a legal system where fees depend on results and the potential strength of a case—stands a far lesser chance of redress. Hence sensationalism is exacerbated in coverage of people otherwise unknown because the media presume they have far greater leeway in this respect.

Where the impetus to entertain in the news starts to take priority over considerations such as whether a story is truly accurate, whether the manner of coverage is warranted, or, indeed, whether it is even in the long-term interests of the news media, then not only is the result an inhuman, damaging disregard for the subjects of such speculation but the intended audience receive a wholly misleading impression of what has happened, one that plays to—because it is closely based on—their often uneducated prejudices about the way the world is.

Moreover the push to entertain distorts not just the shaping of the story and the editorial process but the way journalists are encouraged to behave in "discovering" news stories. Reporters are more likely to face pressure to intrude into the private lives of the rich and famous, to garner unique and compelling exclusives, even where there is no relation to matters of public harm or interest. Indeed, there seems to have been an increasing shift in the nature of news media coverage toward this kind of emphasis in the last decade or more. For example, in July 1995 *The Sunday Times* story about members of Parliament (M.P.s) taking cash for asking questions in parliament, a severe breach of parliamentary etiquette, was not merely a report about an activity that they had discovered going on, independently of their reporting. Rather, they set up a sting operation that offered M.P.s an opportunity it is not clear they would otherwise have had. They managed to entrap two Conservative M.P.s in this manner and then reported the story in terms of outrage at such political corruption. Yet, at the very least, there is no guarantee that without the set-up operation any M.P.s would have been involved in such malpractice in the first place. Moreover, the way the story was reported, at least initially, failed to mention important details about how the story came about and thus elided the *agent provocateur* activity of *The Sunday Times'* reporters, without which there may have been no story. From extreme cases concerning the creation of news or the hounding of the sick and dying to the invention of stories based on mere rumour of events that never occurred, the motivation to entertain corrupts news media practice.

No doubt some may defend such behavior and media sensationalism on the grounds that that is the price to be paid for media freedom. It is usually pointed out that those who complain have a vested interest in so doing. After all, it would be much easier for politicians if their lives were not subjected to close public scrutiny. They would at least be in an easier position to misuse the levers of power for their own benefit or to indulge in the kinds of hypocrisy that betray a craving for power itself rather than a drive to wield influence for the benefit of the common good.

But this claim is disingenuous to say the least. It fails to recognize the obvious fact that much of the criticism is not coming from those with vested interests in protecting politicians but, on both sides of the Atlantic, from members of the ordinary public and from journalists themselves. The increasing distrust by the public of news media who construe news in terms of entertainment values is increasingly registered in public opinion polls and in the number of complaints made concerning the standards and reliability of the news, the way stories are covered, and the behavior of journalists, editors, and news organizations toward the subjects of the news stories.[15] Indeed, highly respected members of the news world are coming to realize that something is fundamentally wrong.[16] As Howard Kurtz, the respected press critic for *The Washington Post*, puts it: "Journalists have become part of a vast entertainment culture that seeks to amuse and titillate and shies away from the risks of old-style muck-raking, as media corporations have grown wary of abusing their influence or offending their audience."[17]

The point is that media freedom to intrude into privacy and to speak freely against politicians, celebrities, and all-comers is granted by society on the grounds that it has a watchdog function to fulfill. Take away the function, or where the news media as a whole fails to fulfill that function, and it is not clear that the news media have any right to behave in such a manner nor indeed that the price is one worth paying. To keep watch over our custodians, to ensure that the politicians are governing in the public and not their private interest, the press may be thought of as possessing certain special privileges as our representatives, just as do politicians, which not every member of the public necessarily has. But intrusions into privacy for mere titillation, regardless of public interest, a casual disregard for standards of accuracy and fairness, often amounting to complete fabrication, and a desire to shock, outrage, and sometimes even offend, amount to a capitulation of the moral high ground that the news media must occupy if they are to possess any moral integrity as the fourth estate. As John Birt, the present director-general of the BBC said, "When Macaulay declared 160 years ago that 'the gallery in which the reporters sit has become a fourth estate of the realm', newspapers were emerging from two centuries of repressive laws, financial corruption and political bribery. In today's fourth estate of the realm, reality often mocks the grandeur of the term."[18]

If a product is paid for and then turns out to be faulty, we normally have a right to demand our payment back: the contract was not fulfilled. If the cost of the implicit contract with the news media is granting warrant to intrude into private behavior in the name of the public interest, then where the media fails to act appropriately we have the right to withdraw the special privileges granted. The special license we afford the media is legitimated by an implicit contract; it is not a God-given right.

The nature of a news media driven by the end-goal of entertainment would inevitably be nonjudgmental. This kind of quietism naturally favors, viciously, the interests of the strong and powerful in society. The whole point of such a conception is to treat the audience's preferences for certain kinds of information as givens which are not themselves open to questioning. The point of the news media is conceived to be predetermined by these preferences. Hence, given the news media report on the preferred information and stories, the very possibility that the news media may fail to cover crucial issues is overlooked. But, of course, people may not have enough or adequate information on which to base their judgments of what they wish to know about. Indeed, how can they, unless reporters and journalists keep their eyes and ears peeled for information that may, potentially, be significant. Conversely, the public may want to know many things, but these might well involve unwarranted intrusion or be inappropriate and unjustified as news stories.

Part of the problem with the HUD scandal was not merely that journalists considered covering such governmental institutions to be tedious journalism but that they perceived the public to be wholly uninterested in such matters. But even if most people do not care about so-called minority issues, the issues nonetheless ought to be reported where events concern the construal of and application of justice in society. Hence in the 1950s, despite a lack of much public concern, the U.S. media rightly and in some cases gallantly covered the birth of the Civil Rights movement. Public lack of interest may arise not just from a lack of information but a failure to understand why such information might be important. Yet good journalism should not merely track audience interest but seek to show the public why they ought to be concerned about such matters, whether in terms of their own self-interest or in terms of human empathy, even though as a matter of fact they happen not to be.

So journalistic judgment is required to recognize what, ideally, people should know about: namely what, under conditions of adequate information, reasonable education, and given a reasonable amount of moral compassion, an audience would be interested in. Hence, even if an actual audience does not care about the HUD or a war in Bosnia, they should be told about such cases precisely because they ought to care about them. Thus news reports ought to highlight just why we ought to care, whether on grounds of prudence or humanity, and should be assessed accordingly.

GOOD NEWS AND INFORMED UNDERSTANDING

We have seen that news is an inherently evaluative term. For in identifying something as news we are effectively stating that this story possesses something of interest or value to us. In one sense this is to go beyond the traditional hard-news conception of journalism. Reporting is a value-laden method of enquiry which aims at obtaining information and knowledge about contemporary events in our world. This is not straightforwardly to assimilate news to forms of propaganda. For news, as distinct from propaganda, aims at truth via the impartial description of events. But we should recognize that impartiality does not entail value neutrality because reports seek the appropriate description of important events. Hence judgments as to whether something should figure in the news agenda, how it should be described and interpreted, are implicitly value-laden. Relative to this aim we evaluate news reports as good or bad. Good reporting aims at the truth via truth-promoting methods. Conversely, bad reporting is truth-indifferent.

Consider the infamous case of Janet Cooke, a reporter at *The Washington Post*. In 1980, 26-year-old Cooke wrote a story, for which she was awarded a Pulitzer Prize, about "Jimmy," an 8-year-old child who led his life on the streets.[19] But subsequently the prize was withdrawn and Cooke sacked because *The Washington Post* discovered, and to their credit publicly exposed, the fact that the child featured in the story did not exist.[20] Janet Cooke had intentionally made the character up for the sake of a sensational story and thus, presumably, a name for herself. Quite apart from the deceit of her editors and public, Cooke's intentionally fictitious story is bad journalism precisely because truth-promoting methods were abandoned and the truth was not sought. Moreover, it is important to realize that bad journalism does not necessarily arise from such intentions. Bad journalism can arise from sloppy methodology, a failure to check sources and quotes, or lack of critical judgment—things that Janet Cooke's editors may have been guilty of when approving her story despite nagging doubts about its veracity. The point is that both honesty and discipline, among other things, are required to be a good journalist. The value of truth must be respected in journalism, and this entails respect for certain values and principles required to arrive at it faithfully.

Hence the practice of fact- and source-checking by most magazines in the United States constitutes good practice, one that the media in the United Kingdom would do well to follow. Moreover, it follows that the correction of errors, with apologies where appropriate, is important. It is interesting to note the difference in practice here between the United States and the United Kingdom. The news media in the United States tend to correct errors, even the most trivial of cases, quickly and appropriately. The correction is given space and prominence in the erroneous paper in proportion to the offense. If it is merely a name correction, then the correction takes up only a small column, but a major error is treated as such and often put on the front page. By contrast, the British press, if they do apologize for errors, tend to put the apology in a tiny box a few pages in. Similarly, the U.S. press took up the idea of ombudsmen or readers' representatives way before the British print media. Such a figure serves not merely to represent readers' interests and the public in matters of accuracy but also as a semiautonomous adjudicator in matters of offense, decency, the kind of news covered, and even as an outlet for journalists under editorial pressure to slant a story. Such good practice is in the long-term interests of the media, since the news media are more likely to be trusted if they are known to check their facts and apologize for errors. At least in this respect the U.S. press manifests a greater commitment in its public practice to fulfilling the obligations of the implicit contract.

Moreover, as we have seen, the value of a particular news story is not reducible to truth narrowly conceived: many stories may well be true but irrelevant or insignificant in relation to readers' interests and values. After all, what is news for one community may well not be news for another in this sense. Hence what constitutes a large proportion of the news for a broker on Wall Street may be completely irrelevant to a waitress in New York, a blue-collar worker in Detroit, or a potato farmer in Idaho. Hence it is crucial to bear in mind the ways in which particular stories are relevant to the interests and needs of audiences addressed. For example, President Clinton's renewal of a commitment to affirmative action would obviously be national news because it concerns a substantive policy interpretation over questions of fairness which would affect U.S. citizens and reveals commitment to a particular conception of justice. Many other news stories will inevitably be far more parochial. Hence certain news reports are considered significant because of varying concerns, cultural assumptions, beliefs, or values that many people in a region or particular culture share.

For example, in France it was common knowledge among journalists and politicians for many years that President Mitterand had a daughter from a long-standing relationship outside his marriage. No doubt in the United States and the United Kingdom such a fact, at least nowadays, would have been reported almost immediately it was known, with Mitterand exposed rather than protected by the press.[21] In part this reflects a rather different cultural attitude toward private affairs of the heart and their interrelation to politics and public affairs. In Britain and the United States the implicit presumption is that unethical behavior in private life may manifest a character flaw that may carry over into the performance of public duties. In France the implicit presumption appears to be that private and public lives are more radically separable in this regard. Hence, as with Bill Clinton and Gary Hart, such a story would merit major media coverage in the United States but was left uncovered in France for many years. But it is consistent to hold that what qualifies as news in a particular community might well not be newsworthy elsewhere. Hence there is a distinction to be made between stories that address our more general sociocultural needs and interests and those that are more specific.

Still, our evaluative conception of news implies that reports had better be factually oriented, impartial, and relevant to our governance or human interests. So if political representatives were taking money for asking particular questions in Congress or claiming expenses for fictitious trips and activities, it should obviously be headline news, and the rationale we have outlined accounts for why this would be so. In the case of payments, we have politicians—elected to represent the interests of their constituents and enact legislation for the benefit of society—who are apparently acting in their own self-interest at the expense of those they were elected to serve. In the case of travel expenses, even though there is no apparent direct harm to constituents' interests, the fact that a political representative is prepared to lie for his own personal gain might suggest that he would be prepared to do the same in his role in public office. Hence it is important for people to know these facts so that they can judge whether or not the character concerned should remain in public office. The point is that such cases of corruption and malpractice, along with issues of public policy and legislation from abortion, welfare, business regulation, legal redress, and criminal justice, have a significant effect on who governs in our name and what is enacted on our behalf in shaping society. Thus shifts, changes, distortions, and corruption in public policy and personnel must constitute news.

Obviously, on this model, reporting must be factually accurate because people's judgments about what is happening, which provide the basis for their evaluation of what ought to be done, rely on accurate information. Similarly, news coverage had better be impartial in the sense that personal prejudices, bias, or vested interests had better not influence the way a particular story is covered. Otherwise we are far more likely to end up with a distorted and thus misleading impression of the way things really are. If the basis for a given judgment is false, then we are far more likely to make a mistaken judgment about what we think ought to be done. Hence speculation presented as fact is morally bankrupt because it misrepresents to the reader what is actually so and thus breaks with the implied contract between the news media and the public.

Indeed, as an unofficial estate of governance, journalists, the press, and news media had better be, in a significant sense, outsiders to the political process. For they should have no vested interests in keeping the workings of government opaque or conspiring to distort the political process. Thus, in principle, journalists should be free from the kind of temptations and influences to which those inside government might, by virtue of their position, be open. Of course, given that the press is in the position of the people's watchdog regarding government, journalists and the media are themselves, to the extent they perform their job properly, in a position of power. For, if taken as trustworthy, press reports about government policies, maneuverings, and corruption obviously have a strong determining effect on how people understand politicians and their policies. But given such a position of influence the media themselves will be open to lobbying by politicians and vested interest groups and to pleas or bribes from the subjects of various stories, events, and investigations. No one expects that journalists will prove to be infallible or, necessarily, moral saints. However, as outsiders to the political process who do not directly have any hold on the levers of power, we should expect the press to be less susceptible to the kind of corruption politicians are open to: the perversion of justice in the name of the people.[22]

We have defended a broad conception of the naive view of journalism's proper function. The core function of news is to be informative about significant events and stories of human interest. Of course, what counts as significant is in one sense communally relative, and we should be careful to distinguish the kind of reporting appropriate to different news genres, from quick news bulletins to in-depth investigative journalism and documentaries right through to feature articles that are more partial, speculative, and evaluative. Hence the context of a claim makes a difference to its appropriateness. We all understand, rightly, that speculation has its proper place in feature articles but should not be constitutive of hard news bulletins.[23] But overarching all our own particular interests and the varying constraints of distinct news genres is the goal of promoting a greater sound understanding of significant events and human issues.

Given our account of news we can pick out certain minimal ethical constraints to which good journalists ought to adhere. For example, we can make sense of a journalist's duty to report events that it is in the public interest to know in order to function as citizens in society. Of course it might be thought that the advent of ever more versatile computer technology will ease editorial pressures and proprietorial control. Indeed the ability of ordinary people to capture news events that remain uncovered by major networks will certainly enhance the possibility of broadening out the news agenda. But such utopian aspirations should be tempered with the recognition that, in fact, the opportunities such technologies offer us still depend to a great part on the capacity for the news institutions to stand apart from major proprietorial control.[24] Moreover, independently of such questions, the need to exercise judgment regarding what is newsworthy and whether reports are truthful and impartial will never go away. Though technology may afford us many new opportunities, it is, in this sense, neutral.

Yet the minimal ethical constraints do not just concern factual accuracy, impartiality, source-checking, record-keeping, and ombudsmen but, just as importantly, entail a responsibility to set the context within which a news story occurs. For the public need to gain a sense of why an event is happening and what is significant about it. Hence we rightly criticize news programs that place too heavy an emphasis on striking images and soundbites at the expense of explanations concerning why or how an event occurred. A news service that consists entirely of bulletins and striking images and is entirely event fixated is a perver sion of good news practice because it manifests an inherent bias against under-standing.

The news media's job is to cover stories that, under conditions of ideal information, reasonable education, and compassion, we would want to know about. It is this basis that provides the justification for conceiving of the press as the fourth estate. Moreover, it entails that journalists and the news media have a strict obligation to ensure that the stories they are reporting did in fact happen as they are represented. These are, minimally, the news media's ethical obligations, which they must live up to in order to fulfill their part of the implied contract. Good or ideal journalism would do more. The distinction between what is ethically obligatory and what is good, admirable, or ideal is quite a basic one. For example, we normally recognize that we are ethically obliged not to harm others. However, though this might be admirable, we do not normally consider ourselves to be ethically obliged to give away all our possessions to support those in need. The distinction applies similarly to journalism. To be ethically adequate, journal-ists must live up to the implied contract and report fairly and truthfully on events that are of importance for our lives. However, rather than merely react to and report on episodic events, good journalism also seeks out, uncovers, investigates, and explains fundamental or social shifts underlying episodic events. Thus good journalism not only reports on but also investigates and may even campaign for injustices to be righted. Take, for example, the reporting of the U.S. civil rights movement in the 1950s.[25] Journalism that merely reported on the particular events as they happened would not be unethical in breaking an implied contract between the public and the news media. However, reporting on and campaigning against the underlying structural injustices and progress of the civil rights move-ment certainly constituted morally admirable journalism and ideal practice.

Thus the traditionalist conception of the media as the fourth estate actually gives us quite a substantive, discriminating, normative conception of the duties and ideals of the news media. Such a conception, and the ethical critique that it suggests of the state of the contemporary news media, accords with the intuitions of many practicing journalists and the public at large. Journalism that involves presenting speculation as fact, placing entertainment above significance, and proliferates sensationalism, voyeurism, and celebrity gossip constitutes an abro-gation of the purpose of the news media. But we can only justify this judgment if we recognize what constitutes the right kind of news coverage and journalistic values required by the media to fulfill their obligations as the fourth estate to be an essential component of free and democratic government.

NOTES

1. Lewis Carroll, *Sylvie and Bruno Concluded* (London: Macmillan, 1893).
2. Gaye Tuchman, *Making News* (New York: Free Press, 1988), John Fiske, *Television Culture* (New York: Routledge, 1987), pp. 281–308, and Tom Koch, *The News as Myth* (New

York: Greenwood, 1990), are good examples of work that presumes that narrative form and institutional relations make something news.

3. Howard Kurtz, *Media Circus* (New York: Random House, 1994), pp. 37–52, details with insight the ins and outs of both the scandal itself and the failings of the news media.

4. *The Sunday Times*, 19 February 1995, broke the "story" as a full exclusive alleging Foot had been a KGB "agent of influence" at the peak of the Cold War. On 7 July 1995, *The Sunday Times* published a minimal page-two apology and paid substantial undisclosed damages to Michael Foot.

5. See Lucas A. Powe, Jr., *The Fourth Estate and the Constitution* (Berkeley and Los Angeles, CA: University of California Press, 1991).

6. "No one pretends that democracy is perfect or all-wise. Indeed, it has been said that democracy is the worst form of government except all those other forms that have been tried from time to time." Winston Churchill speech, *Hansard*, 11 November 1947, col. 206.

7. See, for example, John Locke's *Two Treatises of Government* (New York: Cambridge University Press, 1963), in which he stresses that citizens entrust political power only on condition that it will be exercised according to the public good. But those in power will be tempted to abuse their position. Thus, especially in his *A Letter Concerning Toleration* (New York: The Library of Liberal Arts, 1955), Locke emphasizes that the citizenry need to know the basis and workings of their government in order constantly to judge the actions of those to whom power has been entrusted, so that the people can exercise their own political power when that trust has been abused.

8. See Anthony Smith, *The Newspaper: An International History* (London: Thames and Hudson, 1979).

9. See Marianne Fulton, "Changing Focus," in *Eyes of Time: Photojournalism in America*, ed. Marianne Fulton (New York: New York Graphic Society, 1988), pp. 208–220, and Kevin Williams, "Something More Important than Truth: Ethical Issues in War Reporting," in *Ethical Issues in Journalism and the Media*, ed. Andrew Belsey and Ruth Chadwick (New York: Routledge, 1992), pp. 154–170.

10. J. G. Ballard, "The Secret History of World War 3," in *Best Short Stories 1989*, eds. Giles Gordon and David Hughes (London: Heinemann, 1989), pp. 1–12.

11. A similar story could be told about the 1980s savings and loan scandal, which only indirectly started to emerge in July 1989 through Charles Babcock's reports in *The Washington Post*. See Kurtz, *Media Circus*, pp. 53–75.

12. See, for example, P. Clarke and E. Fredin, "Newspapers, Television and Political Reasoning," *Public Opinion Quarterly*, *42* (1978): 143–160; and J. B. Lemert, *Criticizing the Media* (Newbury Park, CA: Sage, 1989).

13. *The Guardian*, Tuesday, 1 August, 1995, p. 3.

14. See Tom Goldstein, *The News at Any Cost* (New York: Simon and Schuster, 1985), pp. 200–227.

15. A Gallup poll in 1991 conducted across six EEC countries revealed that public confidence in the press was lower than in most other social organizations, including the legal system and police. Indeed, only 14 percent of those surveyed expressed confidence in the British press. See Raymond Snoddy, *The Good, The Bad and The Unacceptable* (London: Faber, 1993), p. 11.

16. See, for example, Joan Deppa, *The Media and Disasters* (London: David Fulton, 1993), Mark Pedelty, *War Stories* (New York: Routledge, 1995), and Mort Rosenblum, *Who Stole The News?* (New York: John Wiley, 1993).

17. Kurtz, *Media Circus*, p. 5.

18. John Birt, The Fleming Memorial Lecture at the Royal Institution, April 1988, as quoted by Snoddy, *The Good, The Bad and the Unacceptable*, p. 12.

19. The story ran in *The Washington Post*, 28 September 1980, and was awarded the Pulitzer on 13 April 1981.

20. Bill Green, "Janet's World," *The Washington Post*, 19 April 1981, pp. A1, A12–A15.

21. I say nowadays because once upon a time such facts would not have been reported in either the United Kingdom or the United States. For example, the British prime minister Lloyd George was a well-known philanderer, but such things were never reported in the British press earlier this century, and John F. Kennedy's promiscuity was of legendary proportions, yet the U.S. press at the time never passed comment upon it.

22. Thus, for example, we should have strong reservations about the kind of relationship that Ben Bradlee describes as existing between himself and John F. Kennedy in his *Conversations with Kennedy* (New York: Norton, 1975). Of course the bonds of friendship and the payoff in terms of information otherwise inaccessible to the journalist seem great, but there is something highly corruptive about the terms of the relationship laid down by Kennedy, including, for example, the requirement to submit stories first to the president for his personal approval.

23. Hence we also recognize that the New Journalism of the 1960s or George Orwell's literary journalism is valuable in promoting our understanding of the kinds of people and events they are about while recognizing that, were they presented as hard news stories, they would be deeply flawed, since the form combines elements of fact and fiction and is not obviously directed toward truth in terms of facticity.

24. The increasing drive toward mergers in the media world, with, at the time of writing, Time Warner chasing Turner, Disney chasing ABC, Westinghouse after CBS, not to mention the global expansion of Rupert Murdoch's media empire, suggests that the technology may be harnessed in favor of increasing media conglomerate control rather than decentralization.

25. See Juan Williams, *Eyes on the Prize* (New York: Viking Press, 1987).

3 *Impartiality as a Regulative Ideal*

INTRODUCTION

We have seen that adequate news journalism must aspire to the goal of truth and, moreover, in such a way that what is reported is set in context and promotes the audience's understanding of why the event reported is significant. It is this conception that, properly speaking, underwrites the conception of the news media as the fourth estate, but more broadly it includes stories of human interest and concern. The point of the implicit contract between the public and the news media is to achieve knowledge and understanding of current events and developments in the world around us. Hence the news media's duty is to provide true reports that enable us to get a quick but informed grasp on happenings to people and institutions which not only directly affect our functioning in society but are of social, cultural, or human interest. We have dwelt briefly on constraints and measures that such a conception might entail for good journalistic practice. However, if the notion of an implicit contract between the news media and the general public is a useful one, it ought to supply us with the basic regulative ideals to which good journalistic practice ought to adhere.

REGULATIVE IDEALS

Given the point of the implicit contract, journalists must shape and phrase their report according to the level of understanding of the intended audience. It is important to bear in mind that typically this means nonspecialists. The point of reporting the news is to convey the essence of what has happened in a way that can be easily grasped and thus constitute a basis from which to assess what has happened. Thus the level of comprehension that a story presumes is of the essence. A story filled with scientific or bureaucratic jargon, for example, will obfuscate the supposed interest for and significance of a story for the general reader. Hence the reader will be unable to judge on any basis what is happening, never mind being able come to the appropriate judgment. The crucial thing to bear in mind is that the news media must provide news bulletins and radio and television programs that any reasonably literate nonspecialist can comprehend. Of course, there will be a basic range over which this is true. Hence different papers will typically aim at a generally presumed higher or lower level of understanding and interest in particular kinds of stories. Thus what one may legitimately presume in terms of comprehension, on the basis of vocabulary, about a reader of *The New York Times* may not be legitimate in terms of *U.S.A. Today*. Moreover, there will be a range of feature journalism, magazines, and current affairs programs that go in for in-depth explanation of context and critical analysis and, as such, play an integral role in both supporting and contributing to the news agenda. But the bare essence of news must be, if nothing else, addressed to the general audience, who may not be particularly interested. Therefore the story's significance must be made clear and require little specialist knowledge: presumptions, jargon, and motivations should be stated in as plain a language as possible while still retaining the appropriate tone and emphasis for the report.

Bear in mind that this does not mean that the news media must pitch their journalism at the lowest level of comprehension. There are threshold constraints in terms of the information required by any reasonably informed person.[1] Indeed, certain basic information and understanding must be presumed in order for the reporter to be in a position to communicate anything at all. But different audiences do entail distinct levels of understanding to which the story should be pitched. Furthermore, there are institutional constraints of space, time, the editing process, the need for pictures, and so on. Nonetheless, within such constraints, the journalist must gear the story to the intended audience in order to communicate effectively.

Focusing on the understanding of the intended audience as a regulative ideal encapsulates the point of journalism: to render complex events comprehensible, within given time constraints. What is required of the journalist will obviously vary according to both the audience addressed and the nature of the story covered. For example, covering a war story such as Bosnia will obviously require reference to a wider context. In the case of the war in Bosnia only a very limited understanding could be presumed. For example, many Americans and a surprising number of Europeans would have been hard pressed to locate Bosnia on the map before the war started. Moreover, as Bosnia, Serbia, and Croatia had formerly been subsumed peacefully under Tito's Yugoslavia for four decades or more, even a minimal awareness of the history and nature of the ethnic animosities could not be presumed. Hence merely episodic coverage of the Bosnian war, focusing just on UN troop movements, the shelling, skirmishes, and battles, was obviously inadequate if unsupplemented by explanations as to why Serbia was seeking to expand and why the animosities were so complex. Moreover the constant pressures of deadlines and time constraints of rolling news services can exacerbate the tendency merely to report without really finding out and conveying what exactly is going on. CNN may have congratulated themselves on their coverage of Bosnia because of the talent and technology they had at their disposal. But what good are such things when Peter Arnett was forced to do fourteen live shots in a day, using only news agency reports to convey to his viewers what was going on at the battlefronts? The nearest many reporters in Bosnia came to eyewitness reports was the rooftop perch of their accommodation. When the longest period of time that journalists are allowed to foray into the actual situation is forty minutes, it is not surprising that the result is news agency patter giving the appearance of news while failing to convey any deeper understanding of the war.[2] If the backdrop against which events are happening is not sketched out and reporters are restrained from finding things out for themselves, then obviously we cannot expect a general audience to understand how things are, and thus the contract between the public and news media remains unfulfilled.

Of course, there may be an immensely complex chain of events leading up to the news story itself. But it does not follow that journalists should devote as much time and space to the background events. Rather they should seek to flag or reveal the practical media, political, policy, and human interest aspects of the story in ways that do not oversimplify. Hence we can make sense of the demand that the news media should not concentrate on the human drama at the expense of promoting an adequate understanding of the complex issues involved. Moreover, if the story is a long-running one, over time a certain basic understanding of aspects of the story can be built up and assumed. An obvious example is the coverage of the O. J. Simpson trial. From the run-up to the trial to the verdict itself, the news coverage was intense. The opening of the trial was covered live by at least five national television networks, and polls suggest that 82 percent of the U.S. population followed the trial fairly closely.[3] Thus a cumulative understanding of the basics of the case could be built up and fine details examined. Moreover, as the court case proceeded, different aspects of the case itself could be examined and the questions it touched off—from issues of race, domestic violence, money, and justice to the power of media fame and the role of the media in the process of justice. Understanding what is going on is not merely a matter of providing ever more factual information. Rather we need the relevant background understanding required to make sense of what the significance of the facts of the case are.

For example, imagine a reporter covering the purported disregard for elderly patients without health insurance in public hospitals. A reporter might include the fact that some of the more seriously ill patients in such hospitals had, unbeknown to them, been marked down as patients not to be resuscitated should they suffer another heart attack. Phrased like this, without further explanation, such a fact seems to reveal the callous practice and cruel treatment of the poorest and most vulnerable in society. However, the fact looks far more innocuous when conjoined with the explanation that, in fact, the rationale involved explains why it is a common part of medical practice. For patients who have suffered a number of heart attacks and whose condition gives them no chance of reasonable recovery it is usually considered preferable if they are not perpetually resuscitated only to suffer more pain, consuming greater resources, and culminating in eventual death from an irreversible heart attack weeks later. Thus, if a patient is unable to express his or her own wishes and where there is no family to act by proxy, doctors commonly agree on an order not to resuscitate.[4] Looked at in this light, the use of such notices in hospitals is, of itself, innocuous. If a fact is cited where the appropriate understanding cannot be presumed, then the rationale should be explained. Thus the selection of details and the representation of their significance must be geared toward the presumed understanding of the intended audience.

The second regulative ideal generated by the implicit contract is that of the impartial reporter. Remember that the point of the contract is to enable the general public to have a fair and accurate account of events so that they can judge situations for themselves. Thus what should be distinctive of a journalist or news story proper must be a certain kind of detachment. One way to grasp what is involved is to imagine what might distinguish a reporter of a demonstration from, say, a participant in the demonstration. Whatever the reporter's beliefs about the validity of the demonstration concerned and the behavior of those involved, the reporter should aim to maintain a professional distance from the issues involved to portray them accurately and dispassionately for all. This stands in marked contrast to the partial, evaluative concerns, prejudices, or emotions that a participant in the demonstration would be likely to convey. After all, the very reason that demonstrators are there is because they feel passionately about the cause on behalf of which they are demonstrating: they believe their viewpoint to be the right one and will naturally represent it as such. The reporter's duty is to convey their viewpoint, but in a balanced fashion, so that the considerations of others who feel differently are presented in the fair and appropriate light.

This is not to deny that a journalist may be motivated to cover a story because he or she thinks that one side is right or has initial prejudices. Hence a journalist's initial prejudices may ultimately be falsified, which can be infuriating when you have spent time and effort chasing what turns out to be a nonstory. But the point is that the intrinsic goal of journalistic activity is to report what is true and not what we might wish were the case. So rather than merely cast events in a light that confirms the reporter's unreflective suspicions, he or she has an ethical obligation to investigate whether those suspicions are well founded. Of course, journalists do typically start with implicit assumptions and possible hypotheses that may explain an event.[5] But a good journalist will always remain open to the possibility that the true story may involve a completely different explanation from the one, preinvestigation, that they would have been inclined to give.

The regulative ideal of the impartial journalist enables us to pick out a significant flaw in unethical journalism: a disregard for the truth in favor of the values, prejudices, or beliefs a journalist or news organization merely presumes to be true. The fabrication of the boy "Jimmy" by Janet Cooke for her "exclusive" is thus flawed even if, as a composite fictional character, it conveyed something of what it was like on the streets of Washington.[6] The impression that Cooke's story gives might be wholly accurate in terms of substance, and the sense of what is "reported" may in fact be true; but whether it is or not is a matter for empirical verification. The problem with Cooke's "report" is that it presents itself *as* empirical verification: a story that refers to actual people and events on Washington's streets. But it is, in fact, a speculative, imaginative hypothesis. It is presenting fiction as fact because Cooke was either committed to the idea that Washington's streets were like this or because she wanted an explosive story in order to make her name—or, of course, both. Cooke abrogated a fundamental ideal of ethical journalism: she disregarded and invented facts for her own purposes. If her story had not been presented as factual, but rather in the style of New Journalism, an imaginative re-creation of what life might be like on Washington's streets, then there would not have been such an outcry. But the point is that she presented as fact what was not, in order to suit the particular line she was taking. Reporters who take bribes from political parties, or papers that skew stories to fit archetypes because this will help sell papers, are guilty in a similar respect.

The ability to weigh up the evidence impartially, to write a story open to confirmation or falsification by the evidence, and to draw out reasoned conclusions rather than being led by mere intuition, feeling, or commitment, is the essence of good journalism. The ideal of impartiality helps us to pick out what we should be wary of when considering the danger of reporters and journalists getting too close to their sources. The danger is an ever-present one, especially in the field of political journalism, as there is often the lure of access to privileged information offered by those figures with a particular viewpoint to push. The danger of being drawn into the same circles, the feeling of privileged access, the attraction of the personalities and even friendships can lead to professional failure because a journalist thus drawn in may be emotionally too close, too secure, and have too much vested interest in maintaining a relationship to report things objectively when these rub against the account proffered by a favored source.

A suitable analogy here might be the kind of professional distance that teachers ought to maintain regarding their students. However well-intentioned, building up close personal relationships with students whose papers a teacher has to mark can ultimately place the teacher, psychologically, in an extremely difficult situation, fraught with dilemmas in a way that may distort his or her ability truly and fairly to judge the student's performance and level of attainment. Hence emotional ties and commitment on the personal, social, and professional level can, in this manner, obstruct proper investigative reporting precisely because the ability to take up an impartial stance is lost. In the same way, an over-reliance on "official" sources of information, due to political, social, or personal inclinations, can be distortive. For example, the unquestioning stance adopted by segments of the press early on toward Joseph McCarthy's charges concerning the supposed communist infiltration of U.S. government and culture in the 1950s clearly constitutes a failure of impartiality. It is not that the facts they reported were inaccurate, nor would anyone think that such charges should be left unreported;[7] for the description of McCarthy's speeches and charges of treason and communism were accurate. Rather the reports failed to question whether the charges being made were themselves plausible, had any basis in fact, and thus were fair or not. Given that impartiality is a question of what the truth of the matter is, an unreflective deference toward assertions made by those in authority thus constitutes an abrogation of good journalism.

The point is that the ideal of the impartial reporter enables us to make sense of and criticize journalists and media institutions whose reporting of world events is contaminated by or pressed into service for the furtherance of their own personal, political, or social agendas. In the above case a particular reporter was seduced into taking a particular version of events and omitting facts that did not fit with it, in return for professional favors and social prestige. But a failure in impartiality need not be reducible to the personal integrity of a given journalist. An entire news structure may be geared in such a way as to preclude impartiality. If we look at a Leninist conception and use of the news media in early twentieth-century Russia, we see the information communicated by the media conceived wholly in terms of propaganda.[8] Indeed, until recently, news in the Soviet Union consciously strove not to cover industrial disputes, crime, AIDS, poverty, and even disasters such as Chernobyl until the last possible moment. Even when such stories were covered, the underlying rationale was that failing to cover a huge story like Chernobyl would have brought the news service manifestly into disrepute and revealed it explicitly as an arm of government propaganda.[9] The purpose of propaganda is to advocate a particular world view, regardless of the facts, and deride the enemy unconstrained by fine distinctions such as truth, falsity, fiction, rumor, and sensationalism. In propaganda, a story need only contain enough recognizable truth to persuade people of a given viewpoint. The point of news is to report the truth, irrespective of what a given viewpoint might wish were the case. Vehicles of propaganda, such as *Pravda*, have no such aim. Thus in George Orwell's *1984,* newspapers are continually written and rewritten without any relation to what in fact happened.[10] Rather, what is reported is what the Party wishes to have happened in a way that renders its actions most consistent and coherent with its ideology. The Ministry of Truth treats truth as instrumentally valuable rather than as an intrinsic goal, and the use of the term "news" is merely honorific.

The recognition of impartiality as a regulative ideal does not just enable us to criticize personal bias or political propaganda. It provides a basis from which we may criticize any feature that distorts or inhibits the function of journalism: to communicate the truth about significant events in our world. For example, where the intrinsic goal of newspapers and news programs is conceived of solely in business terms, the truth may be conceived merely as an instrumental goal for the accumulation of advertising revenue. Hence a fundamental problem with news programming in the United States is the fact that television programming evolved to maintain viewers' interest between advertising breaks.[11] Thus rather than emphasizing the important or significant aspects of the news, the emphasis can sometimes, falsely, incline toward entertainment.

SUBJECTIVISM

However, there is a rather general form of skepticism that would preclude the ideal of impartiality from having any normative force. The basic idea is that what constitutes news, and thus what is significantly true, is itself radically dependent on the media's or viewer's world view and understanding of events. Essentially it amounts to the claim that all news is inherently subjective. At its most extreme, such a position leads to Baudrillard's infamous claim that the Gulf War only happened on television.[12] In one sense the claim is obviously ludicrous: battles occurred, people died. But the point underlying the rhetoric is not. When we think about a description of an event, the report is obviously driven by the interpretation and evaluation of the events concerned. Reporting is an inherently value-driven process. Thus it is hard to separate clearly between pure description, interpretation, and evaluation. Since different individuals, groups, and societies interpret and evaluate their world differently, this suggests that what constitutes news must be relative to the particular communities involved in any given context. Moreover, for any one news event, there will be a multiplicity of divergent interpretations and evaluations open to potential reporters.

Take a trivial example, such as a football game. Different reporters from different towns might describe the same game differently. A reporter from the home team may describe their leading striker as having a poor game, the defenders as lacking co-ordination, and the opposing team as very lucky. Based on the same evidence a reporter from the visiting team's town may emphasize the skill of his defenders in freezing out a great striker and their striker's verve in outwitting a plucky defence and praise astute play in taking the scoring chances created. The nature of the game seems very different depending on which side one is reporting from. More radically, whether an event is news or not will itself be relative to the interests, values and concerns of the news media concerned.

The interesting claim is that unless an event speaks to our particular interests and concerns, which themselves determine the significance and thus the nature of the event, then it might as well not have happened. This is not a straightforward denial of an event's occurrence. Rather it is to say that events do not have any significance unless they fit into our subjective, and culturally variant, attitudes, interests, and concerns. Thus the meaning of a given event—whether it is news or not, what kind of news it is—depends on and is constituted by the activities of the relevant interpreting journalists, news media, and general culture.

The claim is stronger than the recognition that we may not be in a position to know the truth about particular events. For example, before the Gulf War we were not in a position to know the true scale of the massacre of the Kurds, because of lack of access to the area and local information. This involves only the trivial recognition that we cannot always have access to the facts that would alert us to a news story and set the record straight. Nor is the claim just about the indeterminacy of meaning—that a given event may be open to different possible interpretations regarding its significance. For example, one may quite consistently interpret a sharp rise in violent crime as the result of increasing drug use, the proliferation of guns, the increase in poverty, the retreat of the middle classes from the cities, the dissolution of civil society, and so on. One could imagine articles that approached an announced increase in violence from each of these distinct perspectives. Rather the thesis more radically denies that there are stories or facts that constitute news out there in the world independently of the media's construal and representation of them. What is true of the event itself, and thus whether it is news, depends on the categories, concepts, and values brought to bear by, in the first instance, the media. The basic argument stems from the recognition that the meaning of an event is dependent on context. An obvious example will do to show this.

On 30 August 1994 on the announcement of the ceasefire in Northern Ireland there was a rush of calls for stories covering the ceasefire and the symbolic hopes for the future of the Northern Ireland peace process.[13] One of the larger issues raised by the ceasefire was how to cover Northern Ireland when it was no longer the threat of violence, bombings, and disturbance that predominated. But on the day of the ceasefire itself the important goal was to capture something about the hopes and promise of peace in the province. Crispin Rodwell from Reuters walked around Belfast and finally came upon a slogan freshly painted on one of the walls: "Time for Peace, Time to Go." So he chose a spot some distance back and photographed the slogan while old ladies walked by and a boy played ball against the wall.

Rodwell sent a batch of photographs through to Reuters, including a photograph of the boy knocking his ball against the wall in front of the slogan "Time for Peace" with the "Time to Go" half of the slogan cropped off. The executive editor of Reuters then telephoned Rodwell to check that it had not been set up in some way by getting someone to paint the slogan or that he had not paid the boy to play against the wall. Once Reuters were reassured, the photograph was syndicated around the world and used on the front page of most British papers. The point here is that, as Rodwell and the Reuters editor both knew, the slogan "Time for Peace, Time to Go" was in fact a familiar Sinn Fein slogan that had been used for years to express the view that British troops should withdraw voluntarily from Northern Ireland. But, Baudrillard would claim, the meaning of the slogan is transformed by the journalist's clever cropping and the placing of the photograph on newspaper front pages next to lead stories on the ceasefire, above one-line frames, suggesting that the photograph manifested a new hope for people in the province. The photograph as published was taken to express the new hope for peace and mutual understanding. The same slogan under different contexts is actually taken to manifest and symbolize quite distinct sentiments and hopes. The presumption is that the journalist and media community generally determine the relevant context and thus the meaning and significance of an event as news. What enables the slogan to express the symbolic hopes of the community for a fresh peace is the fact that the photographer, Reuters, and the papers who used the photograph have, with a little cropping here and there, framed it as such. Therefore the nature of an event as news is determined by the media community.

But despite the apparent ease with which the argument may be applied, there is something deeply counterintuitive about the conclusion. Why is it so obvious that the meaning or context of an event is appropriately fixed by the media? If anything, surely we want to say that the use to which the media have put the slogan has prised it apart from its original meaning. After all, typically at least, the media come along to an event, to photograph an event afterwards or as it happens and the event itself remains independent of the coverage. Of course, the media can and often do have a more mediating influence. But unless there is a special story to be told about the distorting effect of the media's presence—from staging events for the camera to interest groups attempting to manipulate the media—then the basic case shows the general skeptical thesis to be false. In the specific case discussed, most local people would hardly have seen the slogan as an expression of new hope in the light of the ceasefire. If anything, given the intended meaning of the Feinian slogan, it is a deep irony that it was presented as symbolizing a new departure in the sad history of Northern Ireland's troubles. Hence we ought to feel rather uneasy when photographs are cropped in ways that only partially represent, and thus distort, what is being represented. Although the editor of Reuters rang up to see whether the photograph had been staged, he ought to have been concerned with whether the picture actually misrepresented the assertion of a familiar and highly partisan viewpoint as if it manifested hopeful and tolerant sentiments, thus possibly misrepresenting how those at the heart of the conflict apparently feel. Indeed, in the long run, such coverage may be vicious through painting a false picture of changes in attitude which suggests that only good will is required, something that is far from obviously true.

Someone might ask whether it matters that a particular picture is misleading in this way if it expresses the general sentiments at the announcement of the ceasefire. But, at least here, the point is that whatever else is true, it certainly amounts to falsification, by omission, of the true nature and meaning of the painted slogan. Had the slogan been pictured in full, then, more appropriately, it would have emphasized the wishful euphoria at the time of the ceasefire less and intimated the hard work that still needed and remains to be done. It is only because the nature of an event is significantly prior to and independent of the media coverage of it that we can make sense of the way the media can and often do misrepresent events—from factional reconstructions that present as facts speculative reconstructions and dramatic moments, down to the outright falsification of facts.

The fact that the Northern Ireland photograph distorts the nature of the slogan pictured brings out the most radical consequence of the subjectivist's thesis. If the subjectivist were right, then we would have no possible grounds for claiming that a report misinterprets a particular event. The news media of Germany, the United States , the U.S.S.R., and Britain all framed the lead-up to World War II, the nature of the war itself, and its progress rather differently. Yet they are not necessarily equally true. Of course, many reports were partial and biased. But this is a criticism. For how a report is framed may be inappropriate, especially if it is false. Falsity arises from a gap between the way an event is and the way it has been represented to be. Hence, conceptually, we think it perfectly possible for the media to misconstrue the nature of an event. Just consider how many have reacted within the news media to the coverage of the Gulf War. Retrospectively many in the media consider the primary focus on the Allies' technology to have been grossly misleading.[14] In part this is because the journalists allowed themselves to be misled by the official framing of the events concerned. But the point is that in both cases it is possible for the media to misconstrue and thus inappropriately frame how things in fact are.

The conclusion that the media determine the nature of an event contradicts our common recognition that context cannot be the sole determinant of meaning: the event itself and the language, concepts, and understanding available to us are important constraints too. But even the categories or values we bring to bear upon an event are not themselves wholly relative. After all, it is possible for an entire set of interpretative categories and values to be mistaken. Generally, it is quite possible that Freudians are almost wholly mistaken in construing the fundamental motivations of human action in sexual terms. They have a conceptual scheme, in the light of which they interpret and evaluate human action. But it may be that the underlying beliefs and values they use to explain the meaning and significance of human behavior are mistaken. The general conceptual point brings out the fact that it is quite possible for the news media to misconstrue the nature of an event. Hence reporters may use the wrong words or focus on the wrong aspect of a story. If the radical theory is merely a thesis about the meaning of a report, then the thesis is trivial and must be supplemented by a theory about an event's significance and how it relates to the world rather than just refer back to the media context. To conceive of certain reports as mistaken is to commit ourselves to the claim that things were and thus should have been represented differently. Hence we cannot be subjectivists about news reporting.

OBJECTIVITY AND THE IDEAL REPORTER

It is crucial to realize that stories, events, people are not infinitely malleable according to the slant a reporter or news organization wishes to give to a story. Indeed, it is a lack of commitment to reporting the way things are or may be that leads to the worst excesses of unethical journalism. The flawed idea that news is merely subjective in the radical sense discussed serves only to lend false credence to such moral degeneration.

The best way of articulating how truth can be both subjective, in the sense that it depends on human experience, and yet objective, in the sense that we can be mistaken about how things are, is to think of secondary qualities such as color.[15] Colors are obviously subjective in the sense that they are necessarily connected to our experience. Nonetheless, we obviously do not count every experience of seeing blue as necessarily an accurate experience of a thing's being blue. For example, we consider certain people to be color-blind precisely because they have the sensation of one color when, by contrast, everyone else sees it as, under standard conditions, another color. This may be due to nonstandard lighting conditions, genetic defects which explain congenital color blindness, or even disease. When we suffer a fever, our taste buds are often distorted, and food can be tasteless or taste quite different. Hence we may be mistaken about tastes and colors even though the sensation we have is, subjectively, unmistakeable. We can be mistaken about whether something is blue or is bitter, because of body malfunctioning or nonstandard conditions of perception. We rely on a normative conception or model of the standard observer: what the standard observer unobstructed by physiological distortions would see or taste under normal conditions.

In the case of the good reporter, though, the secondary-properties analogy stretches even further. Far from relying merely on what the standard observer might perceive, we trust that the good reporter's sensibilities are more discriminating than that of the standard observer. The analogy is not merely that, ordinarily, our judgments are not interfered with by genetic or physiological distortions; for even where there are no such distortions, standard observers can be wholly mistaken or only partially grasp the state of affairs concerned. Journalistic judgment may be flawed because it simply is not as sensitive as it needs to be to appreciate the relevant event properly. Just as binoculars enable us to see more perceptively, so a journalist's training and experience hones his ability to pick out the nature of political maneuverings, motivations, and events. Hence the ideal of the impartial reporter relies on a conception of the ideal observer. Of course there are problems in identifying whether a reporter qualifies as an ideal observer or not. But we can at least spell out various criteria, none of which will alone be sufficient, but possession of a cluster of which will certainly indicate good journalistic judgment and discrimination.

Firstly, a good journalist must have had experience of covering various human tragedies, social issues, or political events. With little or no previous experience a journalist obviously does not have a basis upon which to make the necessary comparisons, because, especially in the coverage of political stories, there is necessarily a comparative element in the interpretation and evaluation of events and characters. Moreover, we would expect the journalist to have had at least some degree of formal training. Training in technical skills—from how to acquire information to writing, filming, and editing—enables the reporter to be proficient in the means required to fulfill his job. Moreover, through developing an understanding of the skills required, training can develop a finer and more discriminating appreciation of what can be achieved, from how to get hold of government information to the use of alliteration and photograph framing to enhance the impact of a story.

An ideal observer of events should lack ingrained prejudices or commitment to pushing a given agenda. This is not equivalent to saying that a reporter should not possess any prejudices, sentiments, or views concerning a particular story. The crucial point is that the reporter should be open to the possibility that the prejudices he has may be mistaken; hence, he or she should look to see whether the story confirms or falsifies his prejudices rather than viewing the story as an instantiation of them. Different ideal observers may vary in their prejudices and presumptions, but they will all be intent on finding out what is the case rather than directed toward confirming their prejudices through covering the story. One way of bringing the contrast out is to consider the case of a reporter who is not politically committed and thus is freer and more able to discern problems in the maneuverings and manipulations of all political parties. By contrast a reporter ideologically committed to the Democratic party may well find it more difficult to subject Democratic politicians to the same kind of critical scrutiny to which he subjects Republicans. For natural psychological reasons our critical gaze tends as a general rule to fail more when directed toward favored causes, and such a failure in journalism leads to a kind of critical myopia.[16] Of course, such journalistic myopia need not be the result of an intellectual or ideological commitment; it may result merely from a susceptibility to the latest fad or fashion. Hence to uncover the truth it is important for the ideal journalist to be able to distance himself or herself from received wisdom or contemporary orthodoxies. A reporter who remains uncommitted in this sense is freer to subject all to his critical gaze and speak out concerning how he finds things to be, independently of favored attachments. A reporter should also be of a composed character, self-disciplined and able to maintain a cool character in the face of great excitement, panic, or danger, so that he can observe details and aspects of an event which others might miss. For example, Philip Jones Griffiths, who worked for *Life* and other magazines while in Vietnam, describes the way he achieves his fundamental aim of encapsulating the truth, in the following terms; "The way my brain works and my body works is to take a long, calm look at things and try to answer and assess ... [putting] it together so that under your arm you can have a document that will tell you clearly, truthfully, and as meaningfully as possible what actually happened there."[17]

An important feature of a good journalist is the ability to set aside potential distractions. The failure of the news media coverage of the Gulf War arose partly from the distractions of the warfare technology knowingly displayed by the military. In some ways this distraction led the main focus of the coverage to shift from the war itself to the pyrotechnics of military technology. Similarly, it is familiar for journalists to be tempted by social favors, political power, and financial incentives away from the true nature of a story or from acting with due journalistic integrity. For the allure of power and influence can viciously blur people's sense of what their job as a journalist is and why they are doing it. As John Yang of *The Washington Post* states with regard to journalists who cover Washington: "A lot of guys over there are so self-important. ... Their entire existence is based on the fact that they're White House reporters. They've got T-shirts and luggage tags that say 'White House' and have the presidential seal. It makes you look like you're on the team, and a lot of people feel that way."[18]

A different kind of example may help to bring out the distortions that financial incentives and temptations can bring with them. In March 1984 the Securities and Exchange Commission (SEC) started an informal and then formal investigation into one of the reporters and the editors of *The Wall Street Journal*. The *Journal* had a long-running column, "Heard on the Street," which was an amalgam of gossip, rumors, and stock market analysis: a positive mention in the feature could raise a company's stock markedly. So obviously anyone with foreknowledge of the column could make a large sum of money, and the SEC had reason to believe that someone was doing just that. The essence of the case turned out to involve the writer of the column, Winans, and his roommate, Carpenter, who were indicted for conspiring to profit from their advance knowledge of the *Journal* articles. Obviously such a lack of journalistic integrity can start to skew exactly what rumors are written up and why. One might also have doubts about placing Winans in sole charge of such a column and at such a poor rate of pay, as Winans apparently complained, which thus exacerbated the obvious temptation.[19]

The importance of avoiding distractions and resisting temptation is really the upshot of the requirement to make sure that as journalists we can focus on the appropriate object of a given story. In investigating, attending to, and reporting a story the journalist must always keep in sharp focus the point and purpose of the report concerned. Too often journalists are seduced into explaining the mechanics of a given political policy and its genesis, giving commentary about the political context, personalities, and critics without making clear why this is directly relevant to the policy announcement concerned. Indeed, quite generally, it sometimes seems as if journalists are writing with their peers in mind rather than for a general audience, often leading toward long-winded descriptions and a preoccupation with jargon.[20]

It is also important to note a journalist's track record: whether he or she is consistently right and whether people tend to agree with his or her analysis of a given situation over time. Agreement among journalists is often a good indicator that a particular report is fair; of course, it is not sufficient, as the whole press corps may be hoodwinked in a particular instance. But over time the track record of a journalist will speak for itself and is a useful indicator. But the real mark of a good journalist concerns the reason we would expect such agreement: because a journalist's judgment, description, and analysis are reasoned and finely tuned.

The final feature of a good journalist, and the one usually most underrated, is a certain empathy or delicacy of imagination. A good journalist will always have a sense of why people might have acted in a certain way—their possible emotions, motivations, and intentions. Through exercising the sympathetic imagination, he or she will be able to understand characters from the inside. Thus a good reporter should be able to take an audience to the heart of the matter through describing the sights, sounds, and human nuances that we might otherwise miss. But it is important not to confuse understanding with assent. A journalist might, through grasping the pressures and motives involved, understand why a person acted in a certain way and yet still appropriately condemn the resultant action, say corruption, for what it was. Of course one of the problems is that we trust the journalist, often without independent means of verification. Nonetheless, there are clear cases or paradigmatic reports where we can say that they exemplify the properties that we value in good journalism. Hence when difficult or complex matters are involved, where appearances may be tricky or deceptive, we tend to look to what these journalists have to say.

It is important to recognize that despite the emphasis on confirming hypotheses, good journalism is more of an art than a science. For observation, subsequent reportage, and commentary on an event is directed toward how we should conceive of and understand the events concerned. This explains the need for journalistic discrimination, because, though subjective, like autobiography it is an art constrained by truth. We can evaluate journalism objectively in the sense that the ideal observer clearly gives standards that enable us to determine whether a report is appropriately considered and reported and whether or not it is likely to be true.

A CULTURE OF TRUTH AND IMPARTIALITY

Yet there remains a nagging doubt. What is so peculiarly disinterested about journalism? If we take a look at most newspapers, even excluding the feature columns, the reports use pejorative, evaluative language and opinions all the time. The conventions and genres of news reporting all shape and form the events covered in particular ways, and the interests and values presupposed are what determines whether an event is newsworthy.[21] Furthermore, even where different papers cover the same story, they often cover it from entirely different angles. Surely any news media, by virtue of having to select and interpret events as newsworthy, are necessarily biased? Hence what gets reported is a function of the media's principles of salience rather than any intrinsic features of the events concerned. The news genre, the story of characters and events in the world, seems necessarily to be crisis-driven. Hence bad news is good news. Indeed, we might follow Paul Weaver and suggest that not only is bias inevitable but the media disingenuously presents itself as neutral—for the media's news agenda and coverage of events are biased in favor of their own interests. This is a vicious problem because it leads to the falsification of real world. We are presented with a picture of the world as being in a perpetual state of crisis, as if there are tragedies of epic proportions every day:

As officials and journalists adapt to the news story's preconception of ordinary events as crises and the front page's preconception of ordinary days as times of great excitement and historical consequence, the actions they undertake and the stories they tell become fabrications. What's actually going on in the real world is the ordinary business of ordinary institutions. What officials and reporters converge on, therefore, are travesties, not real events. The news stops representing the real world and begins to falsify it. The barter transaction between newsmaker and journalist degenerates into an exercise in deceit, manipulation and exploitation.[22]

Hence we end up with an endless round of press conferences, press releases, and "performances" by political, business, and media personalities to gain news coverage favorable in some way or other to their own interests and agendas. Thus, taking up this kind of analysis, it might be objected that the impartiality ideal rests on a crude and flawed distinction between neutral facts and partial values. The very process of selection and the differing emphases given to the same facts bear out the point that, far from being disinterested, reporters, papers, and the news media generally cover stories on the basis of their own values and interests. Value-neutral reporting is a myth, and thus the regulative ideal of impartiality is unrealizable. Therefore, impartiality and the underlying notion of the ideal observer cannot be a requirement of ethical journalism.

Moreover, we might go further and suggest that the impossibility of value-neutral reporting is a virtue. After all, we typically buy a particular newspaper or watch a given news channel because of the way it represents the world to us.

Journalism as a form of advocacy is hardly a recent turn in journalism. If we look back, journalism tended to be far more partial and adversarial than it is today. Winston Churchill's reporting of the Balkans war was motivated by a compassionate contempt for the inadequacies of British foreign and military policy, and paper proprietors typically used their papers to promulgate favored political or business interests.[23] Different reports represent events differently, and we seek that which we judge to be the most appropriate—which is itself an interested, evaluative judgment. Thus the reporter, when judging how to report an event for his intended audience, must report it in the appropriate light. So the same journalist reporting the same event for two different newspapers would skew his article differently.

Looked at in this light, the regulative notion of the common reader actually clashes with the ideal of impartiality. Any reasonable reader wishes a news report to make sense of and structure the events in order to explain their significance in terms of society. Different readers buy different papers because they differ over how or what enables us to make sense of society. Hence a liberal will more naturally buy *The New York Times* because he or she expects them to understand and represent events such as increasing divorce, crime, and poverty in certain ways, whereas by comparison *The Washington Post* is more likely to focus on business issues and perspectives. Indeed the differences in the United States are ones of mere degree and nuance by comparison with the gulf in world views that separates papers in Britain, from the deeply conservative *Daily Telegraph* to the progressively liberal *Guardian*. So, someone may claim, meeting the requirements of the common audience entails journalistic partiality toward the world view favored by the intended audience. Hence even if impartiality were realizable, journalists should not seek to achieve it. Thus the ideal of the impartial reporter may seem an impossible myth, sustainable only given a naive understanding of the history of the media and the pragmatics of the news business and journalism. At best the ideal of impartiality might be useful in clarifying the putative goal of truth, but it is certainly not a normative ideal that applies to all good journalism.

Now we might be tempted to reply that the ideal of impartiality does not so much pick out an aspect of a journalist's story as the way he approaches it. Thus whether a journalist is impartial or not depends on the purpose for which he or she investigated and wrote up the report. If I interview someone in order to find out the truth about a particular story, then that qualifies as impartial journalism. Conversely, if my motive in interviewing them is to further my financial, sexual, or social standing, then my intention in acting is far from impartial—for the end goal of my action is not the truthful reporting of a given story, but to extract certain favors for myself. What is important is the basic motive, whether I am writing a story because I want to get at the truth or for the furtherance of my own personal interests. So, one might argue, the ideal of the impartial journalist concerns how one attends to or covers events. Thus the distinction is a motivational one, rather than one based on claims about reporting events or facts in terms of objectivity.

But, important as motives are, this is certainly an inadequate response, for it is quite compatible with my motive of furthering my own personal interests that I cover a story in a faithful and true manner. My motive may be to cover a story for my own advancement, and yet, in writing a given story, I may write it with the intention of presenting things as they really are. Indeed, any decent news media organization ought to be structured in such a way that the two are harmonized— so the best way of personal advancement in journalism is to report things as they are. The really crucial thing is that the motive—whether purely one of aspiring to portray reality, personal advancement, or a mixture of these and other considerations—does not pick out good journalism as such. Rather, good journalism is constituted by the achievement of the end toward which the motive should be directed. Thus the intention involved in investigating and reporting should involve a commitment toward reporting the objective truth of the matter.

A stronger response is to point out that the interpretative nature of journalistic reporting does not preclude objectivity. It may preclude disinterest, where the term is construed as meaning journalism that is independent of value commitments, prejudices, and presumptions. But where objective is taken to mean explanations that are intelligible, consistent, and coherent and fit with the facts independently of particular prejudices and values, then this remains an appropriate ideal. Hence we distinguish impartial journalism, which may entail taking a stance on particular issues, from biased journalism, in the vicious sense of distorting and falsifying the way things in fact are. Impartiality is thus compatible with a partisan approach, where, for example, what may best explain particular events is in fact the unjustified racism, cruelty, and inhumanity of certain sections of society, something that ought to be chronicled to show it for what it is. But bias in its significant pejorative sense means a commitment to a particular interpretation or presumption independently of the facts. Thus bias in the vicious sense is quite rightly condemnable because it involves an imperviousness or disregard for the facts and true nature of a story in favor of whatever values or prejudices are held.

Consider what renders a report propaganda, as distinct from good journalism. Editorials by proprietors, wartime reports, or even news organizations toeing a government line may all constitute propaganda where they involve the deliberate misrepresentation of how things are in order to portray the world in a way that best fits with the proprietor's, nation's, or government's plans, interests, or wishes. But we can only properly recognize such reports as propaganda if, at the same time, we recognize that good journalism is not and should not be like this. That is, irrespective of the particular prejudices that we might have, we should only interpret and report a story in a way that is most consistent with what actually happened: the facts. Of course, there may be and often is, especially in complex matters, more than one possible interpretation that is consistent with the facts. Hence a news event may legitimately give rise to a number of different interpretations and reports. If they are all consistent with the known facts, then all well and good: journalists cannot necessarily know which one is in fact true, given the mutual consistency. But, as with all stories, journalists are under an obligation to make clear in what way they are interpreting the event concerned, and they must remain open to the possibility that their interpretation may not be the right one. Thus it is imperative for good journalists to articulate clearly why they think that their interpretation most appropriately fits the story concerned and what the actual or possible anomalies in such an interpretation are.

The ideal of the impartial reporter is not a chimera, where we understand it in terms of appropriately describing events in the world rather than as an isolated detachment from our interests, values, and beliefs. The fact that we cannot obtain an Archimedean point outside our beliefs and values does not preclude the ideal of objectivity. Rather, it is a matter of remaining open to a healthy skepticism about whether events, people, and stories are as we presume them to be, a commitment to checking and evaluating other possibilities and making clear to the reader the basis and reasons for representing the events in a particular way. Good journalists should always remain open to the possibility that any one of their presumptions or beliefs may in fact be mistaken, even though we can never examine them all at the same time. So an impartial reporter is always open to the possibility that his or her original intuitions and opinions about a given case may be wrong in a way in which a biased reporter would not be or a propagandist would not care. Thus the ideal of the impartial reporter does not, as is often falsely presumed, rule out personal interests and the possibility of a multiplicity of interpretations and evaluations of particular events. Nonetheless, the recognition that we cannot be "disinterested" in any radical sense does not entail the denial of a motivating journalistic ideal that should be cherished: impartiality and the journalistic aspiration toward truth.

Through clarifying what the ideal of the impartial journalist amounts to we have reached very particular requirements that, at least in much contemporary practice, are not lived up to sufficiently. Weaver is right to condemn aspects of contemporary journalism, but not because the ideals themselves or the nature of the newspaper process, when properly understood, are flawed. Rather it is because the pragmatic practices of much contemporary journalism do not, in fact, square up with those very ideals. Journalists often make up quotes, present their interpretations as the only possible ones, fail to highlight possible anomalies, and talk up nonnews stories just to manufacture material for air time or column inches. Hence, unsurprisingly, journalists often present a far more certain and definitive view of events to their public than may be warranted by their own research. The moral problems in such a state of affairs are not only inherent in the possible misrepresentation of a particular event but also lie in the consequences: the audience is given a far more simplistic black-and-white version of how things are than is in fact the case. Hence the problematic but contingent political bias of much news media. The results are damaging because such oversimplification fosters a false basis on which the public makes its judgments as citizens. Indeed, in a democracy the problem becomes particularly vicious since politicians are dependent on public favor and support, and they may thus pander to and reinforce the simplistic world picture of the audience. But garnering support for domestic and foreign policies based on a distorted and simplistic world-picture is a dangerous business, often with far-reaching and hideous results.

Commitment to the ideal of impartiality is not to deny that journalists and news media reports may be biased or, through drafting the first sketch of history, fundamentally mistaken. However, as initial sketches, news aims to describe and explain how events happened and analyze the relevant causes appropriately. Sometimes, through no fault of their own, journalists can be mistaken, and occasionally the reasons they articulate for attributing certain causes to an event may not be good ones. Yet it does not follow from this that we should not expect reporters to describe, investigate, and analyze events and their explanations. Journalists can and do seek to report events impartially, and, over time, the important question to be asked is whether a reporter has described the events and attributed the causes as they turned out to be.

It is true that current affairs, especially political and social ones, are often intricate, convoluted, and hard to disentangle and that reporters will typically diverge over which aspects are the most significant. Hence we often have fundamentally distinct representations of the same news story. But this is not because impartiality is an impossible ideal. Indeed, experts in many fields, from science to sociology, where there is a truth of the matter, often disagree about diagnoses, explanations, treatment, and even whether a certain phenomenon constitutes a problem or not. Of course, journalists may not be able to find out the truth of a particular matter, but it in no way follows that there is no fact of the case. Perhaps only in time may we be able to sort out what the likely truth of a particular event was. But the essential point is that journalism, from bombings in Oklahoma and famines in Ethiopia to unrest in Russia, should aim to be impartial by reporting the facts of the case and explaining events clearly and rationally, based on the way the world and events within it are found to be.

NOTES

1. See C. Berry, "Learning from Television News: A Critique of the Research," *Journal of Broadcasting 27* (1983): 359–370; S. Iyenger and D. R. Kinder, *News that Matters: Television and American Opinion* (Chicago, IL: Chicago University Press, 1987); and V. Price and J. Zaller, "Who Gets the News? Alternative Measures of News Reception and Its Implications for Research," *Public Opinion Quarterly 57* (1993): 133–164.

2. Martin Bell, *In Harm's Way* (London: Hamish Hamilton, 1995), pp. 207–209.

3. Ian Katz, "Juiciest of Tales," *The Guardian*, Monday, 23 January 1995, Tabloid Section, pp. 2–3.

4. Tom L. Beauchamp and James F. Childress, *Principles of Biomedical Ethics*, 3rd edition (New York: Oxford University Press, 1989), pp. 148–150.

5. See S. Holly Stocking and Nancy LaMarca, "How Journalists Describe Their Stories: Hypotheses and Assumptions in Newsmaking," *Journalism Quarterly 67* (1990): 295–301.

6. Bill Green, "Janet's World," *The Washington Post*, 19 April 1981, pp. A1, A12–A15.

7. As George Reedy, press secretary to Lyndon Johnson, stated, "The objective reporting standards of the day held that if a Senator was going to make charges of treason, espionage and communism in high places, that in itself was news." As quoted in the *Columbia Journalism Review 24* (1985): 36.

8. For according to Leninism, as Kautsky encapsulates it, the governing elite should "strive to enlighten and convince the masses by intensive propaganda before we can reach the point of bringing Socialism about." K. Kautsky, *The Dictatorship of the Proletariat* (Ann Arbor, MI: University of Michigan Press, 1964), p. 95.

9. See Brian McNair, *Glasnost, Perestroika and the Soviet Media* (London: Routledge, 1991).

10. George Orwell, *1984* (London: Secker and Warburg, 1974).

11. See Robert W. McChesney, "The Battle for the U.S. Airwaves, 1928–1935," *Journal of Communication 40* (1990): 29–57.

12. In his original article, a few days before the Gulf War, Baudrillard claimed that there would be no war and, even if there were, the mass media coverage and simulation of it would be what our judgment of reality was based on and, therefore, there could be no basis upon which to distinguish the "real" from the "imaginary." See Jean Baudrillard, "The Reality Gulf," *The Guardian*, 11 January 1991. Even in his second article, written just after the cessation of the war, "The Gulf War Has Not Taken Place," *Libération*, 29 March 1991, Baudrillard still adheres to the claim that the war was a fabulous simulation involving a conflict between distinct imaginary realms not open to investigation in terms of rational assessment and questions of truth or falsity.

13. *Decisive Moments,* BBC 2, January 1995.

14. At the time of the war most of the information about casualties, intimations concerning disingenuous motivations for going to war, and facts suggesting that Saddam Hussein could hardly pose a strong military threat were all available, but the media were seduced into covering the war almost solely from the official military perspective of the Allies. See Douglas Kellner, *The Persian Gulf TV War* (Boulder, CO: Westview Press, 1992), and Mort Rosenblum, *Who Stole the News?* (New York: John Wiley, 1993), pp. 118–128.

15. See, for example, C. L. Hardin, *Color for Philosophers: Unweaving the Rainbow* (Indianapolis, IN: Hackett, 1988), and R. M. Boynton, *Human Color Vision* (New York: Holt, Rinehart & Winston, 1979).

16. See, for example, R. E. Nisbett and L. Ross, *Human Inference: Strategies and Short-comings in Social Judgment* (Englewood Cliffs, NJ: Prentice-Hall, 1980), and Miles Hewstone and Charles Antaki, "Attribution Theory and Social Explanations," in *Introduction to Social Psychology*, ed. Miles Hewstone, Wolfgang Stroebe, Jean-Paul Codol, and Geoffrey M. Stephenson (Oxford: Basil Blackwell, 1988), pp. 111–141.

17. Philip Jones Griffiths, interview with Marianne Fulton, 20 February 1987, quoted in *Eyes of Time: Photojournalism in America*, ed. Marianne Fulton (New York: Little, Brown and Company, 1988), p. 212.

18. As quoted by Howard Kurtz, *Media Circus* (New York: Random House, 1994), p. 303.

19. See Tom Goldstein, *The News at Any Cost* (New York: Simon and Schuster, 1985), pp. 248–252.

20. Kevin Catalano, "On the Wire: How Six News Services are Exceeding Readability Standards," *Journalism Quarterly 67* (1990): 97–103.

21. See, for example, Ronald N. Jacobs, "Producing the News, Producing the Crisis: Narrativity, Television and News Work," *Media, Culture and Society 18* (1996): 373–397.

22. Paul Weaver, *News and the Culture of Lying* (New York: Free Press, 1994), p. 2.

23. See Anthony Smith, *The Newspaper: An International History* (London: Thames and Hudson, 1979), and Anthony Smith (ed.), *Television: An International History* (Oxford: Oxford University Press, 1995), for the distinct but related evolution of television as a news medium.

4 Deceit, Lies, and Privacy

TRUST

Without trust the news media cannot fulfill their function of conveying significant events and stories of human interest to the general public. This is especially important given that most of the information we acquire about the world is gleaned from the media. If the public do not trust the media's reports, if editors distrust the journalists, if journalists cannot trust their sources, then reliable news coverage is difficult to achieve, and, even where a report is trustworthy, the public will dismiss its veracity. We discussed earlier the case of Janet Cooke, the ambitious young journalist on *The Washington Post* who won a Pulitzer prize for her piece "Jimmy's World" about the plight of a drug-abusing 8-year-old boy on Washington's streets. It subsequently turned out that Jimmy was a fabrication. Aspects of the story—from the problems of drug abuse and poverty to the social deprivation depicted—were true. However, the central story around which these themes were highlighted was a fiction, but one represented as fact. When *The Washington Post* found out, her prize was returned and the paper commendably ran its own investigative article about the whole affair.

The point is that not only did Cooke break a bond of trust with the readers of *The Post*, she abrogated the trust placed in her by her colleagues and editors. An editor must be able to trust that journalists have done the relevant research, are quoting their sources faithfully, and, at the most fundamental level, are motivated to tell the truth. Without such trust, any newsroom would break down.

A news service that consistently falsifies information, as *Pravda* did for ideo logical reasons, or ignores certain kinds of stories, say because covering cancer research would upset a channel's tobacco sponsors, will hardly be trusted by its public. Furthermore, if news sources feel unable to trust reporters regarding their anonymity or depiction, then obviously the media's ability to uncover exploitation, corruption, and fraud would be severely curtailed. For people in fear of their jobs or very lives will not trust journalists lightly. If broken promises, the endemic misuse of unattributed sources, trafficking in rumor or speculation, and intrusions into privacy in pursuit of a "good" story are perceived to be the journalistic norm, then the very people the media depend on to uncover stories will become uncooperative, and the public they are attempting to inform will be deeply skeptical. So when the news media intrude upon the grief of people caught up in human tragedies like Lockerbie or the massacre of schoolchildren in Dunblane, the fact that we remain shocked but unsurprised is a reflection of just how much our trust in the news media has been eroded.

Yet, paradoxically, journalists, editors, and producers would not be carrying out their jobs properly if they were too trusting. Investigative journalism is predicated on the assumption that all things are not as they appear to be. Although initially we should take politicians, figures of authority, and people generally at face value, it may turn out that our trust is not justified. Indeed, the fact that authority figures and social institutions wield great power entails the need for critical scrutiny. Milgram's experiments from the 1950s, where unknowing subjects were instructed to electrocute someone supposedly in the next room, show that it is all too easy to abuse positions of power and influence for corrupt ends.[1] So it is crucial that the motives and actions of those in power are scrutinized, and the media have a positive duty to do so. Without a healthy skepticism journalists would be more open to manipulation and less likely to get at the truth of the matter. Furthermore, uncovering instances of corruption may require a journalist to manipulate, lie, or intrude into someone's privacy. Similarly, there may be a strong public interest in tracking down a source whose anonymity a journalist had promised to protect. So to fulfill their function, journalists may have to break the very bonds of trust upon which they depend. Hence journalists need to think carefully about when, where, and why, if at all, it may be morally permissible for them to lie, deceive, or intrude into someone's privacy and break promises they have made.

LIES, DECEIT, AND BROKEN PROMISES

Paradoxically, we demand that journalists tell the truth and yet, to get at the truth, they may have to lie. Similarly, journalists often promise sources that remarks will remain off the record or their anonymity will be protected, yet sometimes there is a strong public interest in breaking such promises. Failure to keep promises and tell the truth supposedly gives rise to the public distrust of journalism and the media in general. Hence promises of confidentiality and truth-telling are often considered sacrosanct rules of ethical journalism. But what is the underlying presumption here? The basic thought, as articulated by Kant, is that if we do not always abide by our word and tell the truth then the social practices of honesty and promise-keeping will inevitably break down and the media will be unable to function.[2] Furthermore, as Anselm and Barth would suggest, possessing moral integrity surely means that we do what is right despite the consequences. Thus the most "innocent" of lies is morally corrupt.[3] To lie to expose wrongdoing involves the vice of hypocrisy; it is to perform the very thing that is being condemned.

Consider a recent *Sunday Times* investigation into whether British M.P.s were asking questions in the House of Commons for financial inducements rather than on behalf of their constituents. Although there were rumors, and various lobbying groups had been making inflated claims about their influence, there was little hard evidence to suggest that such practices were going on. *The Sunday Times* decided to blanket target a number of M.P.s from all parties, and two responded to this initial approach.

A journalist then met up with the two M.P.s—Graham Riddick and David Tredennick, both Conservatives—pretending to be the chairman of an arms company wanting information that might affect a possible arms contract. For a fee of £1,000, they initially agreed to ask questions in the House.[4] It seems, to start with at least, that the public interest justifies the deceit and lies required to uncover the story. Yet if we look a little more closely, the obviousness of this conclusion is questionable.

It could be claimed that *The Sunday Times* investigation did not prove that the bribery of M.P.s was taking place. It only proved that, offered this financial incentive, a couple of M.P.s were prepared to ask questions in the House of Commons, and subsequently they were suspended for so doing. The real question concerns whether anyone else is going around offering such inducements. For if the answer is no, then *The Sunday Times* investigative team is creating a state of affairs for its own news scoop. The success of their investigation could thus shed little light on whether these activities were actually taking place independently of their operation. In aiming to get a news scoop, the investigative journalists used deceitful means—the very accusation laid at the feet of the M.P.s in *The Sunday Times* report—to create a news story that picked out an activity that might not otherwise be happening.

This is not to absolve the M.P.s of blame for their actions, but it is to recognize that without the deceit in the journalistic investigation such a state of affairs might never have arisen. The use of checkbook journalism to elicit testimony from those caught up in criminal trials, the deceitful setting-up of journalistic scoops or lies told in order to get confidential information under false pretenses, journalists seeking to create, talk up, or distort events to create ever more newsworthy stories seems hypocritical and fosters a journalistic climate in which lies and deceit are deployed to create "news" and will naturally lead the public to distrust what is reported. The picture of the world presented to the public becomes a highly distorted and harmful one. To the extent that such reports are trusted, the public's opinion may be framed on a false basis; in a democracy where many public and foreign policy decisions are driven by public opinion, this is highly damaging.

However, there was, in fact, evidence that M.P.s were abusing their position. So the journalists did have some reason to believe that the activities they were "investigating" were going on prior to their subterfuge. Moreover, the report did succeed in turning the spotlight onto an area where political procedures were, at the very least, open to abuse. Nonetheless, aspects of *The Sunday Times* report were dubious. For example, they failed to report both that the question of payment was raised by their reporters and not by the M.P.s, and that one of the M.P.s, Graham Riddick, had returned his £1,000 check prior to their exposé. Moreover, quite what was actually proved by their investigation, in terms of actual abuse, was fairly negligible.

But, must lying lead us down such a slippery slope, and does deceit necessarily compromise our moral integrity? Imagine that a journalist is secretly investigating a case of political corruption. She attends a political function to see what kind of terms certain figures, whom she suspects of corruption, are on. The central figure of her investigation jokingly enquires whether the journalist is investigating his political and financial affairs. Kant's argument apparently requires the journalist to tell him exactly what she is doing, which would be both imprudent and scupper any chances of finding out at what level, if any, corruption was taking place. Yet, under such circumstances, to the extent that the journalist's investigation concerns a matter of crucial public interest, we should consider her to have a moral duty to lie. So, at least under exceptional circumstances, lying is not only permissible but morally required.

Just think how impossible journalism would be if journalists and news programs were, under all circumstances, committed to telling the truth. No journalist would ever be told anything, and it would be nigh-on impossible to uncover stories of public interest. In cases of war or extreme national interest we are prepared to accept that information may justifiably be witheld or that we may be lied to in the interests of protecting the public or the strategy of our troops. Thus we would censure a television network such as the CBS—which broadcast a report regarding the Unabomber suspect hunted by the FBI—if their report leaked information that could hinder a police enquiry, or a newspaper that published secret military strategy plans during the Gulf War. As long as we recognize that deceit and lying are justified only under certain strict conditions, it is far from clear that the social practices of truth-telling and promise-keeping would break down.

Good journalistic judgment is required to know exactly when and where the relevant conditions apply, a matter about which we may be mistaken. But, as with truth-telling and promise-keeping in everyday life, we naturally accept that under certain circumstances lying may be permissible and, less frequently, a moral duty. Kant's objection to lying and deceit fails to discriminate between different kinds of promises, deceits, and manipulations. There is a vast moral difference between telling a white lie for the sake of a friend or the public, and a vicious lie designed to cover up evil, corrupt actions that should be uncovered. Morally discriminate lying has not undermined the general practices of promise-keeping and truth-telling.

Telling white lies does not inevitably lead to the dissolution of the trust required for the media to function. Of course it might be suggested "that keeping the public's trust is such an important consideration in journalism that responsible editors can validly put trust in the balance with a possible risk to human life and come out on the side of doing what is required in order to retain the public's trust."[5] But this must be wrong if we are supposed to assume that the truth must always be paramount. The public is unlikely to trust the media if they always reveal the identity of anonymous sources, give details of rape victims, or confess to the nature of their investigations when pressed to do so. So, far from compromising their moral integrity, journalists may have a positive moral obligation to lie if, by so doing, they are able to uncover instances of public corruption, harm, or wrongdoing.

The argument so far might be thought to entail that the end justifies the means. If the end is justified, then the means required to achieve it are morally permissible if not obligatory. Consider a case like that of Robert Maxwell. Here was a man who was swindling, among other things, large amounts of money from the investment funds of pensioners who had worked for various companies that he owned. Through abusing his position and coercing others to do his bidding, he stole from large numbers of people who had entrusted their money to his companies and ultimately his stewardship. Obviously the last thing Maxwell wanted was to allow prying journalists access to accounts that would incriminate him. Perhaps the only way a journalist could get the evidence to substantiate claims of Maxwell's wrongdoing was, at the very least, through lies, deception, and possibly acting illegally. Where the public at large, or certain members of the public, are being harmed, then it seems reasonable to hold that the unfortunate means required for journalists to unearth and prove the scandal are justified.

MOTIVES AND INTENTION

Appealing though such a doctrine is, it cannot be the whole of the story. Consider again the case of R. Foster Winans, who used information acquired in his capacity as a *Wall Street Journal* reporter to profit himself privately.[6] His motives in pursuing confidential information were impure. He sought information not just to report financial stories but to make money for himself as any insider trader might. The point is, we condemn not just his actions but his motives and intention in acting the way he did.

Consider Robert Capa's famous image from the Spanish Civil War, published by *Life* magazine on 12 July 1937 under the caption "Robert Capa's Camera Catches A Spanish Soldier The Instant He Is Dropped By A Bullet Through The Head In Front Of Cordoba" (more commonly known as "The Death of a Loyalist Soldier"). The photograph shows a soldier falling backwards, apparently from the impact of a bullet. The photograph is blurred and slightly out of focus, perhaps due to the soldier's and Capa's speed of movement. The soldier is caught on the left-hand side of the picture frame, arm thrown back, rifle in hand, suspended in the air. No one else is in the picture, and the soldier's shadow reinforces the dramatic image. There is a fair amount of controversy surrounding this photograph because, it is alleged, the shot was posed and thus constitutes a deceit. If true, this would be deeply ironic, since Capa was a cofounder of the photojournalist agency Magnum, whose reputation for integrity and authenticity is renowned the world over. True, the very allegation may constitute a scurrilous imputation of Capa's moral and journalistic integrity. Nonetheless there is some evidence to suggest that the photograph is not quite what it seems.

As the historian Phillip Knightley points out, the photograph's blurring and lack of focus is consistent with the image having been taken from the frame of a cine film, possibly shot while a platoon of Republican soldiers was on a training exercise in 1936.[7] Far from the soldier being pictured in the moment of death as *Life*'s caption would lead us to believe, the film shows the soldier falling back and then getting up again. Knightley suggests that Capa's agent sold the pictures to *Life*, possibly without Capa's knowledge, while Capa was away covering the war. Bear in mind that the invention of details and events in the Spanish civil war was not the rarity one might imagine. Arthur Koestler wrote fictional stories about it from Paris, inventing plausible events and battles on the grounds that such deceit was justified because it helped "the right side." But the morally important question here, quite apart from whether such an end is justifiable, is whether Capa intended such deceit when he took the pictures and gave them to his agent.

For the sake of the example we will assume that, though debatable, Knightley's description of Capa's photograph is the correct one. Crudely, there are two basic possibilities. Firstly, Capa could have asked Republican soldiers in training to pose for him and have shot the film to pass it off as scenes from the midst of the war. His intention in taking the film and passing it on to his agent could have been to deceive. If so, then we would rightly consider him to be guilty of lying about the context of the photograph; for he then intended to, and was successful in, passing off easily shot pictures from training maneuvers as images from the very heat of a major and important battle. Conversely, Capa may have had no such intention and filmed the training exercise for its own sake or to practice his filming. He could then have passed the photographs on to his agent without even thinking that they might be used a year later by *Life* to represent scenes from some future battle. He may not have intended or given the impression that the photographs were as captioned by *Life*. If so, Capa would bear no direct responsibility for the deceit since he had not intended the photographs to be presented as images of something they were not. In this case the deceit, if it is one, was unintentional on the part of Capa, and morally speaking he could not be held to blame.

Matters may be more complex than the two possibilities discussed. It is possible that Capa ambiguously titled the original photograph so that his agent could, if the opportunity arose, sell the image for the kind of use made of it by *Life*. But we would still think Capa bore some responsibility for the deceit then, even though he did not straightforwardly lie: the intention under which an act is performed is partly constitutive of and thus determines the nature of the action concerned. The same actions performed under different intentions may morally differ.

Now, in this light, consider the well-known case of Watergate. Woodward and Bernstein, reporters for *The Washington Post*, had been chasing a story alleging that President Nixon's chief of staff was involved in subterfuge and spying activities.[8] The possibility was even raised that the Watergate break-in had been initiated by Nixon himself. But the reporters' primary source then denied his previous testimony. So, at a crucial stage in their investigation, it looked like there was no story after all. The pressure was on for the reporters to rescue themselves and unearth a decent story to justify their reports. As it turned out, through approaching, lying to, and pressurizing grand jurors, they found out about Nixon's attempt to corrupt the democratic process. So most people are inclined to think that this is a paradigm case of good journalism that, unfortunately, required the use of manipulation, deceit, and lying. But what they discovered was purely as a result of luck. Woodward and Bernstein had no real inkling of what was actually going on, and it was pure coincidence that they stumbled across the story. Any doctrine that renders the morality of journalistic action a matter of pure moral luck can only be hopelessly inadequate. For such a view cannot take account of one of the primary determinants of ethical action: intention.

Woodward and Bernstein were not pursuing their story because they believed the public interest was at stake. Rather, they wanted to revive their journalistic reputations and that of their paper. Given what they uncovered, we can only be glad that they stumbled across what they did. But the end result of an action does not transform it from an immoral act into an ethically admirable one. For Woodward and Bernstein had no idea of what they would find. Journalistic integrity requires that the intention behind action had better be to achieve the morally admirable end. The difference between blamelessly killing someone and murder is not the end result of an action but the intention under which the action was performed. Similarly, there is a crucial moral difference between a journalist who exposes a politician's affair merely in order to gain personal revenge, discredit the political party, create a "good" story, or for financial gain alone and someone who does so in order to inform the public about a possible case of hypocrisy that they ought to know about. So it is important to discern not only what end was achieved by a report but also the intention under which the journalist's actions and report were formed.

Even in cases where journalists' reports are a matter of public interest, their actions are not necessarily ethical. For the intention and underlying motive in getting the story or making the report may be dubious. Certainly in the Woodward and Bernstein case the motive for lying and misleading grand jurors seemed to concern self-protection rather than any notion of the public interest. Deception and lying are not justified whenever they happen to suit the furtherance of our own careers or personal ends.

Moreover, this is not a point that merely applies at the individual level. For the news media have a public duty, as the fourth estate, to strive to report on and protect the public interest. Hence where the motive for news stories, programs, or institutions perverts the fulfillment of this goal, there is something fundamentally wrong. To the extent that a proprietor's political views or business interests dictate the kind of news coverage that a paper or channel affords, then—insofar as the paper or channel conceives of itself as a news institution—there is something wrong. Where sensationalism, business interests, or ideological commitments are given priority ahead of the duty to inform, then good journalism is perverted; for, whether at the structural level or in the case of an individual journalist, where the intention is primarily directed toward ends other than the public good, there is a vicious disjunction between the goal aimed at and what the true goal of professional journalism is. The morally respectable journalist is not one who merely, as a matter of luck, happens to stumble across a matter of great public interest, which retrospectively justifies his immoral activities and subterfuge. Rather he is someone whose motive is to uncover the harm that he has good reason to believe is being perpetrated, and his sole intention in lying is to uncover that harm. Thus deceit and lying in journalism are permissible where the matter is one of strong public interest *and* the journalist's motives and intention in lying are the right ones.

Note, however, that lying and deceit must be the only means by which the morally respectable journalist could achieve his justifiable goal. There is a general, strong *prima facie* presumption in favor of truth-telling: we need never justify ourselves in telling the truth, except in extreme circumstances; but we must always justify lying or deceit. Hence if the well-intentioned journalist could achieve his end without such devious means he should do so, even if this involves much greater time and effort. There is a useful analogy here to the taking of human life. Allowing others to live and not harming them need never be justified, but killing them always requires justification. Although we may recognize that killing someone else in self-defence is justifiable, it must always be the last resort. Hence, though more difficult, if I could have prevented an assault on me by pinning my assailant down rather than killing him, then the act of killing remains morally unjustifiable.

It is crucial to stress that investigative journalists must have reasonable grounds for supposing that wrongdoing is going on. Moreover, good journalists should always be aware that their sources may have disreputable motives for making allegations. Perhaps the source is trying to manipulate the journalist rather than being a straight-up whistle-blower. Hence a journalist should always check what grounds there are for suspecting dubious practice before investigating further, let alone use measures involving deceit, lying, and the breaking of promises of confidentiality. The public are more likely to trust reporters who make clear what their sources are, what the basis for their conclusions is, and what the grounds were that suggested that an investigation was appropriate.

Cases of journalists lying, deceiving, and promise-breaking are, *prima facie,* wrong. But where there are no other means of investigating a matter that a journalist has good grounds to believe is one of great public interest, then such typically dubious means are justifiable. Indeed, where these are the only means open, the journalist has a moral duty to adopt them where the public interest is strong enough to trump the harm done in its name—the significance of the story must outweigh the *prima facie* presumption against lying and promise-breaking and the potential side-effects on journalistic practice and the public's trust in the media. For example, lying to or deceiving Robert Maxwell to substantiate allegations about thousands of pensioners being stolen from is justified, whereas doing so merely to find out about the theft of an office pencil would not be. We must recognize that matters in which there may be a public interest are not automatically strong enough to warrant such behavior.

For example, *The Guardian* newspaper thought it had good reason to believe that a then British government minister, Jonathan Aitken, had stayed at the Ritz Hotel in Paris and had this and various other "gifts" paid for without having declared them as such to the House of Commons.[9] Given the possible bribery of a government minister there was obviously a strong public interest in discovering whether these allegations were true. However, to substantiate the allegations the *Guardian* journalists needed proof not only that Mr. Aitken had stayed in the relevant hotel but how much his bill was and by whom it had been paid. Obviously the hotel would not give them details if requested on the grounds that they were investigating Mr. Aitken's possibly improper conduct. So the journalists sent a fax on House of Commons notepaper requesting a copy of the relevant bill, which they duly received. Such deception appears to be the only way they could possibly have substantiated their claims impartially.

In a similar light, consider remarks that Jesse Jackson confidentially made off the record to Milton Coleman of *The Washington Post* during the 1984 presidential campaign. He referred to New York as "hymie town" because he believed that New York was basically run by Jews. Precisely because the public has a crucial interest in understanding the nature of Jesse Jackson's character, as he was running for the presidential nomination, the *prima facie* presumption in favor of confidentiality is outweighed, for such comments not only reflect an aspect of his character but one that had, thus far at least, been kept well-hidden. It is crucial that the public see the attitudes that are part and parcel of a man seeking to become president, who could potentially wield immense power and influence in their name; so, in reporting these confidential remarks, *The Post* fulfilled its moral obligation, as did Milton Coleman.[10]

THE NATURE OF PRIVACY

Our conclusions concerning deceit and lying naturally lead us into the matter of privacy. For if the *prima facie* presumption against lying can be overridden in the name of the public interest, then perhaps the same applies to our right to privacy. But it is crucial that, first of all, we develop some sort of understanding of just what privacy is and why it is important. Of course, most people naturally value their privacy and think it important that certain areas, activities, and information about their lives should remain private. Hence we naturally think that one of the great evils of a totalitarian state is that it does not consider individual citizens to have any sphere of privacy that ought to remain outside its jurisdiction. Similarly we tend to presume that invasions of privacy, without the subject's consent, by journalists, newspapers, and media programs are morally wrong. The burden of justification stands in favor of those who wish to have their privacy respected. For intrusions into the private areas of our lives constitute a harm or failure to respect our rights as individuals. Thus the law tends to protect us from intrusions into our home, private papers, the public disclosure of embarrassing private facts, or publicity placing us in a false light. But quite why we have a right to privacy needs to be articulated.

One thing we commonly recognize is that revelations about ourselves are a matter within our gift: not just anyone has a right to know anything about us. Hence friendship is partly a matter of how much we are prepared to reveal about our private selves to another, as opposed to what we are indiscriminately prepared for everyone to know about us. This already tells us something about privacy. It is partly constituted, as Parent puts it, by "the condition of not having undocumented personal knowledge about one possessed by others. A person's privacy is diminished exactly to the degree that others possess this kind of information about him."[11]

In other words, the kind of information about ourselves that we choose not to reveal to others—as distinct from information that is publicly available—is private. The value of privacy, according to Parent, is that it prevents anyone else acquiring power over us to our disadvantage. Such a bulwark against the state is required if we are to be free from threats of manipulation and coercion regarding our behavior. As rational, free agents we have a right to consider areas of our lives to be closed to others, and so doing reduces the possibility of our being manipulated or coerced into behaving in a way that we would not otherwise choose. So, for example, our sex lives ought to be considered private, since shielded from the social pressures of prurience, blame, and condemnation we are much freer to pursue our sexual desires as we would choose.

However, what Parent fails to notice is that it is the *areas* where we typically choose not to reveal information about ourselves, or do so only very discriminately, that mark off the private aspect of our lives. It is not merely particular information about our lives that is private but those areas of our lives that the information concerns. Hence an intrusion into privacy is not merely where someone has obtained, without our consent, information about us. Just as a burglar can break into our house and fail to get any goods or information about us, so a journalist may intrude into our privacy, without our consent, and yet fail to find out anything about us. For what is intruded into are certain areas of our lives which are intrinsically private. That is, relationships, activities, and concerns that we consider not to be the business or concern of anyone else except ourselves and those with whom we choose to share these aspects of our lives.

Furthermore, we do not consider the value of privacy to lie solely in the way that it protects us from manipulation by others. Rather we consider privacy to be intrinsically valuable since it allows for intimacy and thus the space within which certain personal activities, relationships, and goods can flourish. First, a realm of privacy enables us to consider, test out, and develop interests, activities, and beliefs that we would not be prepared, at least initially, to commit ourselves to or pursue in public. Thus the protection offered by the private sphere enables us to test and develop our identity and character as a person.[12] Secondly, and interlinked with the first consideration, a realm of privacy enables us to cultivate and pursue meaningful familial relationships, friendships, and loves. After all, if we indiscriminately told everyone everything about ourselves or acted the same way with strangers, colleagues, friends, and lovers, then the symbolic significance of many acts and confessions we normally consider private would evaporate. We choose to reveal intimate aspects of our selves, and so trust in others, and through so doing cultivate particular, intimate relationships without which our lives would be much impoverished.

Privacy involves not so much the right to be left alone, since we can be harassed in many ways that do not intrude into our privacy, but delineates a sphere within which we are free to be intimate with others and pursue goals and interests we have without being subject to the public gaze. As James Rachels articulates it: "If we cannot control who has access to us, sometimes including and sometimes excluding various people, then we cannot control the patterns of behavior we need to adopt . . . or the kinds of relations with other people that we will have."[13] Indeed, gossip and slander can be harmful precisely because they feed on, and may damage, a person's ability to pursue valued private goals and friendships. Moreover, the very act of publicly revealing private peccadilloes, relationships, or activities can even harm someone's ability to pursue his or her public goals. For example, a doctor revealed without his or her consent to be homosexual may find it much harder to work with many patients due to their reactive prejudices. So privacy is also required to protect us from the irrelevant and slanderous judgments of others that may prevent us from pursuing and attaining public goods. Individuals require privacy to grow and develop as autonomous individuals with meaningful personal relationships, which is why we condemn societies that fail to respect people's privacy.

A right to privacy is based both on the recognition of ourselves as rational free agents and on the psychological importance of a sphere of privacy for certain fundamental human needs, desires, goals, and relationships to flourish. It is important to note that the right to privacy, so construed, is not merely an extension of property rights, as it is so often assumed to be.[14] It is odd to talk of intimate exchanges and activities being owned or possessed by particular individuals. Moreover, private conversations and exchanges often take place in public areas, from parks to restaurants and bars. Yet we may still rightfully object to someone eavesdropping on an essentially private conversation in a public bar. We can imagine a person attempting to take his life in a public place being filmed by close-circuit television cameras, and the resultant film being broadcast on some "real life" crime show or documentary to an audience of millions. The cameras themselves might not constitute an invasion of privacy, and may lead to the man's life being saved, but broadcasting the film would constitute a gross invasion of privacy.

However, although we do have a right to privacy, it can be overridden where information or activities that an individual would choose to keep private should be placed in the public sphere. Where what is being carried on in private is a matter of central public interest, then the individual's right to privacy dissolves away. As Belsey puts it: "Where some information about an individual that he or she would prefer to keep private *should* be in the public domain, then putting it there is not overriding that individual's right to privacy because no such right ever existed concerning this aspect of the person's life ... all invasions of privacy are unjustifiable."[15]

To put it in more concrete terms, a politician's right to privacy has not, strictly speaking, been invaded if a journalist investigates instances of corruption in the politician's political affairs, even though he or she may have sought to keep them private. Indeed, if a right to privacy were considered absolute, then this would provide the conditions under which corruption and vicious hypocrisy can flourish since many people's public facade, behavior, and roles could not be held to account. Thus a journalist's delving into a politician's private papers, which details his or her corruption, does not constitute an intrusion into privacy but a justified investigation into an essentially public matter. For political corruption is not something that is or should be considered an essentially private matter.

Given that the *prima facie* right to privacy can be outweighed by considerations of the public interest, we need to clarify when, where, and under what conditions the right is trumped. A different way of putting it is to ask where the right to privacy, based on recognizing its contribution to our well-being, outweighs apparent public interest in a particular story. The relevant considerations ultimately depend on the status and role of the person at the centre of the news story.

DISTINCT RIGHTS TO PRIVACY

The first and easiest category to consider is that of politicians, businessmen, and those who occupy positions of power and influence in society. Politicians are elected to represent their constituents in a democratic process; therefore, any actions of theirs that give us good reason to believe that they are involved in a corruption of that process justifies investigating their private matters where these touch on the possible area of corruption. So where it is suspected that a congressman or congresswoman is taking money in exchange for the use of his or her political powers, say to push a government grant toward a particular firm, then the media are justified in investigating the relationship between possible payments, "gifts," and the member's political actions.

The public need to know if their representatives are representing their interests fairly and well. Similarly, where civil servants, businessmen, doctors, and teachers are not acting in the best interests of their government, shareholders, patients, or students but abusing their position for personal gain in some way, then they have no right to privacy concerning such matters. The public needs to know if their investments are being defrauded, if their government functionaries are corrupt, if doctors are going against their code of practice, or teachers are abusing the welfare of their pupils. Indeed, as the fourth estate, the media have a moral duty to investigate such matters. Because such figures exercise power on our behalf and significantly shape our lives, the media, on our behalf, has a duty to examine their conduct where it is relevant to their exercise of power.

But even here things are not quite as straightforward as they may appear, for although the inability of politicians to perform their job—due to private vices such as alcoholism or corruption—should clearly be exposed, a much more difficult matter concerns the gap that sometimes emerges between the private character and public persona of a powerful public figure. It is perfectly possible to say one thing that we genuinely believe to be right and yet act in another way that we genuinely believe to be wrong. For example, a politician who sincerely espouses family values may fail, in a particular instance, to live up to them; through weakness of will he lapses into a brief adulterous affair, and yet he still genuinely wishes he could have controlled himself more, because he considers his actions deeply wrong.

We are all fallible, and it is not clear that the public good is served in unearthing such cases where the person concerned is truly penitent in his private life and consistently carries on espousing family values in public. Perhaps the person best qualified to warn us of the dangers of excessive drinking may be a deeply regretful alcoholic; similarly, the politician who moves to outlaw prostitution and yet visits prostitutes may be consistent—he wants to outlaw prostitution because the mere possibility offers a temptation to which people such as himself may, wrongly, succumb. Of course, such lapses may show flaws in a politician's moral character which could go on to manifest themselves in public life. If a man cannot resist temptation in his private life, in the face of what he knows to be wrong, then perhaps he is more likely to be as corruptible when pursuing public business. If as a public figure he is prepared to be duplicitous in his private life then he may be prepared to be duplicitous in his public life. Hence, of course, public figures place much store on presenting their private lives in as admirable and stable a light as possible. But this suggests that we ought to be very careful to distinguish a truly momentary lapse, which the individual is deeply repentant about, from consistent failure to fulfill publicly articulated ideals in ways that do suggest a general weakness of character.

There is a typical journalistic presumption that where there is a gap between the ideals that a public figure espouses and his private conduct, the public interest overrides his right to privacy; however, this presumption is flawed. Such hypocrisy, if it is such, is not clearly wrong, and it would constitute a far greater social ill to reveal it as hypocrisy in the way that the media undoubtedly would: exposure may only serve to undermine the argument being made, say concerning family values, which should be assessed on its merits rather than being presented as false because of a gap between ideals espoused and human failure to live up to them fully.

However, cases of human failure and genuine repentance should be clearly distinguished from forms of vicious hypocrisy, where public figures cynically use their publicly declared aspirations as camouflage for actions that do not even truly aim at their professed goal. The mismatch here is vicious because people in positions of privilege, influence, or power are not even attempting to live up to their publicly professed goals and political or business mandate but, rather, are seeking to corrupt it. Thus they abuse the trust placed in them by others and very often harm particular individuals, constituents, or shareholders. Such forms of vicious hypocrisy are clearly a matter of public interest and distinctly newsworthy, and thus they are strong enough to outweigh any *prima facie* right to privacy. One has only to look at figures such as Kennedy, Nixon, or Robert Maxwell to see how a public persona can mask deep, vicious inconsistencies that are clearly contrary to their publicly professed goals and, even, what is legal.

Consider the case of the once highly promising congressman Mel Reynolds, who at the time was one of America's fastest-rising black politicians. It emerged that he was clearly involved in soliciting child pornography and was eventually charged with seducing a 16-year-old campaign worker, Beverly Heard, and obstructing the course of justice by possibly trying to bribe her.[16] Similarly, consider the media coverage of the sexual life of Gary Hart when he was running for the Democratic presidential nomination in 1988. Not only were the stories about his promiscuous womanizing taken as legitimate targets of investigative journalism, but Hart himself effectively challenged the media: "Follow me around. I don't care . . . about the womanizing question. I'm serious. If anybody wants to put a tail on me, go ahead. They'd be very bored."[17] Quite apart from the naively bad judgment shown by Hart in issuing this challenge, such sexual excesses and the drive to pursue them, even at the cost of harming others—and, in the Reynolds case, perverting the course of justice—betrays a character flaw that is deeply worrying in anyone wielding political power. Stories concerning church figures abusing children or conducting affairs, police corruption, state deception, and political shenanigans are all a matter of immense public importance and thus outweigh any right to privacy: in their different ways, all involve a vicious and harmful betrayal by particular individuals of the public trust placed in them. Hence journalists may intrude into their privacy in order to investigate and expose the harmful contradictions, negligence, and hypocrisy of those in positions of power and influence.

It must still be stressed that apparently similar kinds of cases may, morally speaking, have to be treated differently; in part, the harm and possible public interest involved depends on the nature of the publicly professed goals. For example, imagine two politicians from different parties, both of whom are homosexual and live with their lovers. One of the politicians is a spokesman for his party, and it condemns homosexuality as a vice and would seek to outlaw it. The other politician is also a spokesman, but his party deems sexuality an essentially private matter unless harm of some significant kind is involved without meaningful consent. Only in the first case would the media be justified in intruding into the politician's privacy in seeking to root out, prove, and report on the politician's sexuality, because the disjunction between what he professes as a matter of public policy and what he does suggests a form of vicious hypocrisy: he is trying to enact measures that will deny to the public the very choice he wishes to exercise. Thus the public should know about such an anomaly and the politician asked to account for such an apparent inconsistency. But in the second case the politician's private conduct has no direct bearing on what his publicly professed goals are or the measures he is attempting to bring about on behalf of the public. Hence, in the latter case, any journalistic intrusion into privacy would not be justified.

The second relevant category of persons we should consider are those, such as public celebrities, who do not straightforwardly exercise positions of power and influence but whose lives are, by their very nature, much lived in the public eye. Film stars, television celebrities, society figures, and sometimes journalists themselves come into this category to varying degrees. In essence such figures and their careers are, to a large extent, created by their public persona and often involve the exposure of many intimate details concerning their lives. Hence the media often cover scandals or stories concerning the love lives of such people, from Cindy Crawford to Hugh Grant. It is important to recognize that such stories involve normally private affairs and should properly remain so if we were talking about the love life of an ordinary person. But we should appropriately draw the boundary between the public and the private in a different place when we are considering people whose career and success are dependent on the publicity that to a large extent they seek.

In some ways we should think of the trade-off in terms akin to a Faustian pact. It is hard to see how many of these celebrities would have the career they have without publicity concerning their private lives, which is often cultivated or played to by the person concerned. If, for example, Pamela Anderson or Heather Locklear make much of their sexual nature and talk freely in public about their love lives, then they have placed that aspect of themselves in the public domain. Effectively they have given tacit consent to the media to be interested in and cover these aspects of their lives. So though they may be right to complain about media intrusion in particular cases, they certainly cannot justifiably complain about the media attention devoted to their sexual affairs, and this cannot, as such, constitute an invasion of privacy. By pursuing the very profession they have chosen, they are in a significant sense public property. Similarly, if Sarah Ferguson or Diana Spencer pose for *Hello* magazine and talk about intimate aspects of their lives for the public, then they cannot justifiably complain when the media seek to examine critically, reveal, or chase up these aspects of their lives: they have, in effect, invited the audience in and declared that these parts of their lives are public. They sought to create the public demand or interest in them and use it for their own advantage. The need for and use of the media by such figures entitles the media to cover normally private aspects, whether they actually consent or not, in ways that could not be justified regarding an ordinary, private figure.

Furthermore, we should recognize that the category of public figures does not merely include "media personalities" but those who become public figures by virtue of the extreme, immoral, or antisocial actions that they perform. Someone who commits an act of terrorism, is a serial killer, or traverses society's legal and social norms in an extreme way is a perfectly legitimate focus of public interest. The nature of certain crimes—Jeffrey Dahmer's,[18] for example—are such that the perpetrators effectively forfeit all rights to consultation and privacy. The public interest here obviously lies in obtaining some insight into how such dark deeds can come about: what motivations, upbringing, social conditions, and even biological factors may affect people in such a way as to cultivate their delight in the depraved infliction of violence on other adults and children. Moreover, where the parents or friends of such people may appear to be partly culpable, then their rights to privacy are partially forfeited and certainly not as strong as they would otherwise be.

The last category we should look at are those people who are thrust into the limelight of media attention for no reason other than their accidental involvement in a particular tragedy or news story. An ordinary person's right to privacy should be considered to be very strong indeed here, unless they freely consent to publicity about a private aspect of their lives or seek to use the resultant publicity for their own advantage in a way that brings them into the category of public figures. True, in the United Kingdom the right to privacy is not enshrined in law, and, in the United States, "People who are catapulted into the public eye by events are generally classified with elected officials under privacy law . . . the courts have ruled material as newsworthy because a newspaper or station carries the story."[19] The mere fact that people are interested in something, and thus can be dressed up as newsworthy, is presumed to override the ordinary individual's right to privacy.[20]

But the underlying rationale is inadequate because it fails to recognize the possibility of being mistaken and thus does not match up to what our moral rights are. The media and the public at large have no interest in and thus no right to know about personal aspects of an ordinary citizen's life, except where these bear on significant public harm or relate directly to how a tragedy came about. The mere fact that a private citizen becomes caught up in a road accident, earthquake, terrorist bombing, or protest march does not, of itself, bear in any way on the media's obligation to respect their privacy. If a teenager dies of a drugs overdose it is clearly relevant to ask where and when she took the drugs, whether she had a habit, and what her parents' attitudes and advice had been. But it is completely irrelevant, and of no public interest, to pry into the teenager's love life in the way the media might regarding a public celebrity. The fact that intruding into the private life of someone caught up in a news story may make for more entertaining or compelling news bears no ethical weight at all.

Let us return to the news media coverage of the bombing of Pan American Flight 103 over Lockerbie, Scotland, in 1988. As we saw, one particular couple arrived at the airport not knowing about the tragedy and approached a Pan Am official to ask what had happened to the flight. The woman was told that the flight had gone down and that all on board had been killed. Her immediate response was one of hysteria, and she collapsed in a public exhibition of grief, rage, panic, and despair. The instantaneous reaction of all the journalists and camera crews present was to crowd round her while she was writhing on the floor; the footage was relayed to various news stations and was broadcast fairly quickly on CNN.[21]

Obviously such images make for compelling news broadcasts. Yet capturing her hysterical, essentially private grief on film and displaying it for all to see constitutes the grossest violation of her privacy. The fact that this occurred in a public place is beside the point, for, as Sissela Bok points out, what is private is not necessarily secret and what is secret may not be properly considered private at all.[22] Private lives are rarely secret but mark out a sphere in which our most personal, intimate relations and activities are not properly considered—unless we so choose—the business of others to know, see, display, comment on, or judge. The horrific grief and loss of self-control concerns a deeply intimate, private relationship, and loss that is nobody's business but her own and that of those nearest and dearest to her. The only appropriate public reaction is one of comfort, kindness, and efforts to find her a private space in which to come to terms initially with what has happened. Broadcasting the images of her grief serves no public interest and tells us nothing new about the nature of such tragedies and the loss of a loved one. For the public interest, what we need to know to function in a democratic, civil society should not be confused with whatever the public may be interested in.

The mere fact that we may be interested in knowing or seeing something does not give us any right to see or hear about it. The only form of interest in such images can be the prurient gaze of someone compelled by others' horror and misfortune. Such a voyeuristic form of interest can never justify such gross intrusions into privacy. This is significant because many dramatic reconstructions, documentaries, and news images broadcast in the name of the public interest amount to no more than a predatory feeding of our more voyeuristic interests in the horror and misfortunes of ordinary people's private lives,[23] something that the media—at least without due consultation and consent—have no right to do. Indeed, the exploitation of the misery of others for public consumption and pleasure is, irrespective of whether consent has been given, itself morally dubious. Moreover, where the media's primary interest lies in pandering to such interests, as opposed to what the public need to know, they are, appropriately, open to the charge of media hypocrisy themselves.

A report that condemns a murder as inhuman and yet dwells salaciously over the intricate minutiae of the killings betrays a vicious form of hypocrisy: the form of interest taken is one that delights in the very thing that is supposedly being abhorred. The rhetorical mask of "the public interest" slips to reveal the real interest, which, when we look at the ways in which such stories are often covered, involves a prurient delight in the misfortune of others. The use of "the public interest" to justify that which is clearly designed to pander to our baser lower pleasures is itself hypocritical and constitutes an abuse of the media's power, influence, and moral duties.[24]

Indeed, it is of the first importance that we know about instances where the news media are themselves guilty of sleazy journalism, and this is especially true where issues of justice are involved. The soliciting by the media of witnesses' testimony for large sums of money inherently lends itself toward a corruption of the impartiality and fairness of the judicial process. Witnesses may be tempted to talk up their testimony, emphasize sensationalistic aspects, and even present speculation as fact where so doing may greatly enhance the amount of money and media attention that they are likely to receive during and after the trial. Indeed, as we saw from the O. J. Simpson trial, the level of television punditry, from lawyers to psychologists, the dramatization of witnesses into media celebrities, and the kinds of interests in the case often pandered to may undermine the public's faith both in the judicial process itself and in the impartiality of the media's reporting of it. The last thing the public need is for the news media's coverage or practices such as checkbook journalism, which is endemic in the United Kingdom, to intrude on and effectively distort the course of justice and the political process.

Thus the media have an enormous moral responsibility arising from their privileged function and role in a democratic society, and the dangers suggest that we should play close attention to the procedures under which justifiable intrusions into privacy may take place. For an intrusion to be a justifiable one, we must already have good reason to believe that what is being kept secret concerns a matter of public harm, abuse, or interest. This links to the requirements outlined earlier concerning commitments to telling the truth, checking putative facts, the trustworthiness of sources, and so on, because the very act of investigation itself is based on the premise that there is, at least, a *prima facie* charge to be answered. Furthermore, the intention in pursuing an investigation must be laudable and not marred by the pursuit of false self-promotion or pandering to gratuitous public interests. Only then may we consider the journalist who intrudes into a figure's privacy to be justified in so doing: unlike *The Sunday Times* story about Michael Foot (see Chapter 2), the journalist should not be open to the accusation that appropriate safeguards and interests were not followed.

Moreover, we should also recognize that even when all the constraints have been followed sometimes journalists can be, perhaps through no fault of their own, genuinely mistaken. It may turn out that though evidence pointed to possible corruption, and thus a journalist felt justified in intruding into a figure's privacy, there turned out to be nothing of significance going on. In such a case it is crucial that we recognize that such an invasion of privacy turned out to be unjustified, and the media should apologize appropriately.

The three primary categories we have discussed, and the relative weight of their right to privacy, are not exhaustive. But what they do illustrate is the need to recognize that the right to privacy is not absolute and does not apply uniformly across cases. Rather, we should think in terms of a sliding scale that seeks to weigh up news figures' political, economic, and public power and influence, their celebrity status, or their rights as an ordinary citizen against whatever public interest and considerations of harm might speak in favor of intruding into their privacy. Especially in the case of political and public figures, where private hypocrisy may manifest character flaws with potentially disastrous results in public life, the right to privacy is extremely weak indeed. Conversely, for an ordinary, private citizen the right to privacy is so strong as hardly ever to justify intrusion except where the public interest is very great indeed.

The need to recognize the sliding scale of our right to privacy also indicates that different treatment by the media is appropriate to figures who fall into different places along the scale. At one extreme, that of the ordinary citizen, the right to privacy is so strong that if any program, documentary, or news report is being made about them, then their rights of consultation are very strong indeed, and consent is required if the program is to possess moral integrity. Moreover, where an ordinary citizen's rights to privacy have been invaded, there are grounds for presuming that they ought to be compensated by the offending paper, channel, or, more substantially, by a media self-regulatory body funded by the industry for just such a purpose. At the other end of the scale, where the politician entrusted by the public is furtively attempting to cover up his wrongdoing, the rights of consultation are far weaker—though he should be consulted and given an opportunity to rebut the charges made—and the need to obtain consent does not apply at all.

NOTES

1. Most subjects were prepared, under the authority of the instructing experimenter, to electrocute the person supposedly in the chair next-door to well past fatal levels. See Stanley Milgram, *Obedience to Authority: An Experimental View* (New York: Harper & Row, 1974), and Eddy Van Avermaet, "Social Influence in Small Groups," in *Social Psychology*, ed. Miles Hewstone, Wolfgang Stroebe, Jean-Paul Codol, and Geoffrey M. Stephenson (Oxford: Basil Blackwell, 1988), pp. 372–380.

2. Immanuel Kant, *The Philosophy of Immanuel Kant*, trans. L. W. Beck (Chicago, IL: University of Chicago Press, 1949), pp. 346–349.

3. See Anselm's *De Veritate*, included in *Truth, Freedom and Evil: Three Philosophical Dialogues*, trans. and ed. Jasper Hopkins and Herbert Richardson (New York: Harper & Row, 1967), p. 110, and Karl Barth, *Church Dogmatics*, Vol. IV, Part 3, ed. G. W. Bromiley and T. F. Torrance (Edinburgh: T. and T. Clark, 1961), Section 70, "The Falsehood of Man," pp. 451–453.

4. "M.P.s, Cheques and Honey Tea on the Terrace," *The Sunday Times*, 10 July 1994, p. 1.

5. Stephen Klaidman and Tom L. Beauchamp, *The Virtuous Journalist* (New York: Oxford University Press, 1987), p. 157.

6. Howard Kurtz, *Media Circus* (New York: Random House, 1994), p. 126.

7. See Phillip Knightley, *The First Casualty* (New York: Harcourt, Brace, Jovanovich, 1975), pp. 209–212. It is interesting to note that though he talks about many of his other photographs, Robert Capa never mentions this one in his autobiography, *Slightly Out of Focus* (New York: H. Holt, 1947).

8. See Carl Bernstein and Bob Woodward, *All The President's Men* (New York: Secker and Warburg, 1974).

9. See *The Guardian*, Thursday, 3 November 1994, p. 1.

10. See Milton Coleman, "18 Words, Seven Weeks Later," *The Washington Post*, 8 April 1984, C8, detailing the ins and outs of the case. It is also discussed by Klaidman and Beauchamp, *The Virtuous Journalist*, pp. 167–168.

11. W. A. Parent, "Privacy, Morality, and the Law," in *Philosophical Issues in Journalism*, ed. Elliot D. Cohen (New York: Oxford University Press), p. 92.

12. See Andrew Belsey, "Privacy, Publicity and Politics," in *Ethical Issues in Journalism and the Media*, ed. Andrew Belsey and Ruth Chadwick (New York: Routledge, 1992), pp. 77–92.

13. James Rachels, "Why Privacy Is Important," in *Philosophical Dimensions of Privacy*, ed. Ferdinand D. Schoeman (New York: Cambridge University Press, 1984), p. 296.

14. See, for example, Samuel Warren and Louis Brandeis, "The Right to Privacy," in *The Journalist's Moral Compass*, ed. Steven R. Knowlton and Patrick R. Parsons (Westport, CT: Praeger, 1995), pp. 84–87.

15. Belsey, "Privacy, Publicity and Politics," p. 77.

16. Although Heard admitted that their sexual relationship was consensual, sex with a 16-year-old is illegal in the state of Illinois.

17. See Jeffrey B. Abramson, "Four Criticisms of Press Ethics," *in Democracy and the Mass Media*, ed. Judith Lichtenberg (New York: Cambridge University Press, 1990), p. 234.

18. See Clifford G. Christians, Mark Fackler, and Kim B. Rotzoll, *Media Ethics: Cases and Moral Reasoning*, 4th edition (New York: Longman, 1995), p. 116.

19 Jeffrey Dahmer was discovered by police in 1991 to have dismembered body parts in his apartment, including a head stored in his icebox, and in 1992 he was convicted of cannibalism, necrophilia, and fifteen counts of murder.

20. See Brian Winston, "Tradition of the Victim," in *Image Ethics*, ed. Larry Gross, John Stuart Katz, and Jay Ruby (Oxford: New York, 1988), pp. 46–48.

21. See Joan Deppa, *The Media and Disasters: Pan Am 103* (London: David Fulton, 1993), and Saul E. Wisnia, "Private Grief, Public Exposure," in *Impact of Mass Media*, ed. Ray Eldon Hiebert, 3rd edition (New York: Longman, 1995), pp. 113–118.

22. Sissela Bok, *Secrets* (New York: Pantheon, 1982), pp. 10–14, 249–264.

23. See Plato, *The Republic*, trans. D. Lee, 2nd edition (Harmondsworth: Penguin, 1974), Book IV, 439e–440a, pp. 215–216, where Plato describes Leontion's base delight in dwelling on the spectacle of maimed corpses.

24. See Plato, *Gorgias*, trans. D. J. Zeyl (Indianapolis, IN: Hackett, 1987), 491e–497a, pp. 64–71, where Socrates shows that the cultivation of our baser appetites can only lead to an impoverished life and is to be distinguished from a truly good life.

5 *Sex and Sexuality in the Media*

INTRODUCTION

One of the most contentious issues in media ethics concerns the representation of sex and sexuality. Obviously the use of sexual imagery and the open discussion of sexual matters in the media are of great interest and help to sell newspapers, boost television ratings, promote films, and sell consumer products. Hence *The Sun* newspaper, the most popular newspaper in the United Kingdom, still has its topless models adorning page three. Indeed Kelvin Mackenzie, *The Sun*'s one-time editor, once said "I've thought about scrapping it. But people expect it— Page Three is *The Sun*."[1] Although the news press in the United States is rather more restrained than its U.K. counterparts, it remains commonplace to see news stories cast in terms of sexual stereotypes and features salaciously "investigating" the sex lives of various public figures or cultural groups. Moreover the portrayal of sex has become a staple part of media culture. From the sexual ideals in billboard advertisements to the deliberate sensationalism of chat shows and drama documentaries, sex is used to further commercial ends. Moreover, especially in Hollywood films, the depiction of sex often amounts to an end in itself rather than an intrinsic part of the plot or characterization. The extreme of this spectrum obviously leads into the spheres of pornography. The fundamental question is whether, why, and, if so, how representations of explicit sexual behavior may be immoral.

The reasons why many people object to sexual representations in the media differ. Often, it is just that someone feels embarrassed or offended. But mere embarrassment or offense is not, of itself, reason to find images ethically dubious. After all, the offense taken or embarrassment caused may reflect something peculiarly sensitive about the person who feels it, rather than stemming from the nature of the image concerned. Offense and embarrassment are sometimes misplaced. That an advertisement or a film offends against what is taken to be common decency may just mean that the program causes embarrassment or, more fundamentally, that it offends against certain deeply held moral views about the nature of sex and sexuality. Typically such objections are couched in terms of obscenity and degradation. But it is important to ask just what is meant here. The reason sometimes given is that obscene images focus on people as significant by virtue of their sexual characteristics and endeavours. The thought is that a certain kind of sexual delight is taken in the representation of another's body. What constitutes the degradation is the delight taken in another person merely as a sexual object and what makes the image obscene is the fact that it is directed toward arousing such delight in us. Thus the objection seems to rely on the Kantian thought that treating others merely as sexual objects is fundamentally dehumanizing. We depersonalize another human being in order to focus on that person's appearance as a sexual object, as if his or her sole function were the satisfaction of our sexual desires and appetites.[2] Yet we often treat people with sole regard to particular aspects of them: as a porter, taxi driver, waiter, cashier, or student. We do not ordinarily think that doing so is itself immoral. Indeed, if we did, it would begin to look as though nearly all our interpersonal relations are morally dubious. There must be something more specific going on if the objection is to retain any force. We sometimes do want our partners to look at us as sex objects, while recognizing that that is not all that we or they are.

Perhaps the strongest line of argument rests on the idea that representing sex in certain ways may constitute a harm in some significant sense.[3] Obviously if something is harmful to others we naturally think we should not pursue that action without good cause. True, the painful loss of my leg may be the only way to avert the onset of gangrene. But inflicting pain or chopping someone's limbs off is obviously immoral unless there is some further end in view that justifies it. Inflicting gratuitous pain without my consent, preventing me from pursuing my life as I choose and marring my capacities to do so is a basic wrong. If we have reason to believe that certain representations of sex or sexuality are harmful, then we obviously would have reason to think them, under normal circumstances, immoral.

THE ARGUMENT FROM DIRECT HARM

The simplest form of the harm argument asserts a direct causal link between looking at certain kinds of sexual representations, paradigmatically pornography, and actions held to follow from repeated exposure to them, such as sexual harassment, mutilation, and rape. If true, this would not only render many media representations of sex ethically dubious but would also constitute a strong basis from which to argue for increased social control and regulation—the increasing amount of pornography and Hollywood's apparent obsession with sex would be partly to blame for sexually dubious or criminal behavior. Images of sex and female sexuality are thought causally to incite men to commit acts of sexual violence and indecency. Indeed, the perpetrators of sexually motivated crimes often themselves claim that certain kinds of pornographic material led them to commit their crime. Catherine MacKinnon refers to the case of Thomas Schiro, who battered and murdered a woman in Indiana in 1981 because, in his defence, he claimed that he got so "horny from looking at girly books and watching girly shows that I would want to rape somebody."[4] Thus, arguing along the same lines, Andrea Dworkin claims that "pornography functions to perpetuate male supremacy and crimes of violence against women because it conditions, trains, educates, and inspires men to despise women, to use women, to hurt women. Pornography exists because men despise women, and men despise women in part because pornography exists."[5] Given that men cannot control their sexual urges, which may be inflamed through watching suggestive and explicit sexual material, the media should not produce or use such material in order to protect women from harm. Moreover, such a position entails that those who have been under the influence of pornography should not be held to blame or even punished since they could not have acted in any other way.

Yet we have strong grounds for presuming that the link cannot be quite so straightforward. The fact that the empirical evidence for such a strong claim is fairly indecisive should give us pause for thought. If there were a direct link we should expect a fairly high level of conclusive proof. The empirical evidence does, however, at least give us some reason to believe that there is a significant probability that watching pornography and related representations can affect the way we feel and think about sex. But it does not follow from this that media representations directly affect our actions in the way that the strong causal thesis presumes. For there is a deep fact about human psychology that the direct-harm thesis fails to take into account. Namely, that the link between what we are exposed to, what we think and feel, and how we act is far more complicated than adherents to the direct causal claim can allow.

For it to be true that exposure to pornography inevitably leads to sexually motivated and harmful behavior, it must be true that we necessarily imitate the behavior of what we are most frequently exposed to. But what fundamentally distinguishes humans from animals is our self-consciousness. Hence we can choose how to act in a way in that animals, who merely behave, cannot. Whereas animals naturally follow by instinct and example, as can be seen from Pavlovian conditioning, human beings are able to think about, understand, and thus come to modify the nature of their actions. Of course, those who have been brought up badly, in dysfunctional and abusive households, may be more likely to be incited by pornography to view women in a certain way and act upon that understanding: the lack of social skills, low self-esteem, and lack of any other paradigms for the expression of their natural human desires and appetites may render them more vulnerable to such influences.[6] Nonetheless, we would still hold the individuals concerned responsible for their heinous actions, even though their perpetration of them may be more understandable given their social environment and upbringing. To put the point another way, animals merely behave, but human beings act. Hence sex in both cases has a function, propagation of the species, but only in human beings can it be understood as the entwining of two individual selves whether for pleasure or as the manifestation of love. The nature of the act involved depends on our underlying understanding of it. Hence it is not mere exposure to pornography that counts but how we understand what we are exposed to. Sexual representations cannot, of themselves, cause people to commit sexual crimes; it is our understanding that determines whether and how we react to what we are shown. I may be repeatedly exposed to many forms of explicit and sadistic pornography, but because I have reason to believe that the acts portrayed are wrong, in the sexual violence directed toward women, they may only serve to confirm my understanding that sex is and should not be primarily a matter of power relations and violence. Hence, if anything, such movies may reinforce rather than undermine my ability to order my sexual desires and actions appropriately. For the movies may confirm my understanding that such forms of sexual relations are harmful and that we do not normally act to realize a goal unless we conceive it to be good.

There may be a weak causal link between what we watch and how we act. But the causal connection will itself depend on what we believe and thus judge ourselves to have reason to do. Hence even if we judge we have reason to do something because we watched a certain program, the responsibility for what we do lies with us and not the television program. The mere representation of females or sex or the discussion of sexuality may be blamed by some for playing a causal role in sexual crimes. But this may be a reflection of the criminal's disturbed state rather than the harmful nature of sexual representations, whether they be pornography, sex manuals, commercials, safe-sex posters, nude portraits, or classical sculptures. Hence we tend to look back at the Victorians, who covered up nudes and lopped off the private parts from classical statues, with a mixture of ridicule and bewilderment. The argument from direct harm depends on a basic misunderstanding of the relationship between human desires and action. Furthermore, the attempt to protect women not only cossets them but renders any comment and imagery of a sexual nature inherently suspect. Thus the natural consequent is ridiculous policies that presume we have no moral responsibility and control. For example, at the University of Nebraska at Lincoln a graduate teaching assistant was asked to remove a photograph of his wife in a bathing suit from his desk because such images created a "hostile-environment [of] sexual harassment of female faculty, students and staff."[7]

Consider the case of the person who shot Ronald Reagan in an attempt to prove his love for Judie Foster. Now, let us say, unless he had watched the movie

Taxi Driver he never would have been "in love" with Jodie Foster or attempted to kill the U.S. president. But the fault does not lie with the film; rather, the fault resides in the person who attempted to shoot Ronald Reagan. Similarly, without the Bible many acts of undoubted evil might not have been committed, but we do not automatically think that the Bible is therefore intrinsically immoral. Rather, many evil acts are due to the morally reprehensible character or possible mental illness of the perpetrators. The Bible or *Taxi Driver* have played a causal role in bringing harm about, but the causal role arose only because of the mental state of those concerned—which is where the problem lies. Causal responsibility is not the same as moral responsibility. Someone may commit murder when he sees the color red. But we do not thereby conclude that painting things red is immoral. Perhaps a reddist cult group brought him up to believe that red exuded killer rays. Thus the morally significant factor is not the color red but the far more significant variables concerning his upbringing as a child with the inculcation of certain false beliefs. Conversely, and more likely in this kind of case, he may just be mentally unbalanced and unable to control his irrational urges.

Still, admitting the possibility that people can and sometimes do act irrationally allows the argument from harm a significant toehold: recognizing the possibility of irrationality means recognizing that people may understand what is good and yet still act in a contrary manner. I may know that having another drink will be really bad for me and yet still choose to drink it. Thus even though I may possess an appropriate understanding of sex, in terms of the importance of consent and reciprocity, exposure to pornographic films may nonetheless cultivate my nonrational desires and appetites. If the film concerned does not merely serve to trigger these appetites arbitrarily but is directed toward them, then the nature of the film may itself be morally problematic.

Nonetheless, the mere recognition that certain kinds of representations do speak to our nonrational sexual appetites and desires is insufficient to establish the direct-harm thesis.[8] Films that speak to this aspect of ourselves may contain, cathartically release, or sublimate our baser sexual desires in ways that are socially useful rather than harmful.[9] Perhaps without sexually explicit representations there would be far more sexual crime about. Representations of sex might contain and sublimate the kinds of sexual desires that we ought not direct toward other people. Indeed, in countries where sexually explicit material is widely available, such as Sweden, Denmark, and Japan, violence against women is comparatively rare, whereas in other countries where such material is extremely difficult to get hold of, such as China, Iran, and Saudi Arabia, violence against women is comparatively common.[10] So even if there is a causal link, it is not clear that it only runs in one direction. Even if certain kinds of sexual representations do speak to certain nonrational desires it does not follow that harm must result.

Consider the case of alcohol. Obviously there is a causal relationship between how much alcohol one drinks and the way that one behaves. Yet since harm does not necessarily result from drinking it, drinking alcohol per se is not clearly immoral. But it does not follow that harm results. Of course some people have a tendency when drunk to go out and about looking for a fight. But, conversely, other people become more vivacious or just plain soporific. Representations of sex in the media and their causal effects are diverse and need not manifest themselves in harmful ways. Sexually explicit material might liberate the sexually repressed and thus enhance the lives of many. Thus although there may be a weak causal link, we have good reason to believe that the direct-harm thesis is false. Rather, it is certain uses to which sexually explicit films or alcohol are put, the kind of person involved, and their characteristic tendencies that are morally problematic. If I know I am likely to become aggressive when drunk, I should not drink. If I know I am likely to want to act out violent fantasies if I watch pornography, then I should avoid it. But the link is not necessary, and, in both cases, the moral flaw inheres in my character and not in the alcohol or pornographic representation of sex.

THE ARGUMENT FROM INDIRECT HARM

The argument from harm appears implausible if one considers it purely in relation to explicit material such as pornography, which is usually heavily regulated, because we can choose whether to expose ourselves to it, just as we can choose to drink alcohol or not, and thus the responsibility for our character, however modified by such exposure, remains our own. But if we step back a little, a significant problem arises. For the argument from harm need not rely solely on the pornographic nature of the material concerned. Of course, certain explicit depictions of various forms of sexual activity will speak to certain sexual desires. But the argument from harm arose from a quite general consideration: namely, that the way people are typically represented can come to affect the way they are understood and thus treated. In fact it is on this basis that the Canadian Supreme Court in a landmark ruling accepted a link between pornography and the way women are treated in society. In *R v. Butler* (1992), a criminal statute outlawing violent or sexually degrading material was declared constitutional because such material constituted a kind of "hate-speech" that threatens women's right to equality.

Although arguments over sex in the media are typically discussed in relation to pornography they apply quite generally to media representations that would not qualify as pornography at all: many news stories, advertisements, television programs, and films may represent women in ways that tend to suggest that they possess certain characteristics, such as being sexually submissive, docile, fragile, emotional, intuitive, irrational, intimate, domestic *ad infinitum*. Indeed, many women feel aggrieved at the way that they are ordinarily portrayed on television or in the movies: average plots often lack strong female parts, with women being forced to play simple-minded male-dependent characters. The point is that media representations may inculcate and promote false stereotypes that could be harmful to women, from the extreme instances in pornography of women "enjoying" rape to the staple ideal housewife or the svelte paradigms of beauty adorning billboards. Although we can choose whether or not to indulge in pornography, we obviously cannot escape the media's representations of sex and sexuality in news stories, soaps, cartoons, dramas, and the billboards that surround us day and night.

So there remains the possibility of a much more subtle link between representations of sex and harm. Even though no one repeatedly exposed to pictures of waiflike fashion models in magazines, glamorous blondes on advertisement hoardings, or the depiction of stereotypical gender roles on television will automatically try to harm particular women, such material may be indirectly harmful. These images may reinforce and encourage certain attitudes toward the opposite sex, possibly cultivating a sense of low self-esteem, inferiority, or humiliation in those who fail to match up to the ideals represented. The way that sex, gender roles, and women are depicted in media representations may shape the way most people in society, including women themselves, think about sex and gender roles. Repeatedly seeing women represented as naturally submissive objects of male desires and requiring a male lead may influence our conception of women generally. Hence our thoughts, attitudes, and dispositions toward women may be affected, and thus people may come, indirectly, to suffer as a result. It is a commonplace of contemporary psychology that the more times an assertion is repeated the more likely people are to believe it, for both cognitive and social reasons, no matter what the lack of apparent justification for the statement is.[11] It would be unsurprising, especially given the power and vividness of media images, if the same did not hold true for the ways in which we tend to think about sex, sexuality, and gender roles.

Consider the case of someone interviewing candidates for a job, or a journalist writing up a news story. Their general conceptions of women may play a role in determining which candidate gets the job or how the story is written up. If the presumption that women are not natural leaders and managers leads to the woman candidate for the job not being taken seriously by the interview panel, then it would appear that she has been harmed, albeit indirectly, by our repeated exposure to certain kinds of media representations—she certainly has not been afforded the equality of opportunity that she might fairly expect and have the right to demand.

Nonetheless, the argument from harm remains dubious. For although indirect harm may result from representing women in various ways, such results do not show the representations themselves to be inherently immoral. Rather, at best what has been shown is that we should all be aware of the way in which categories, images, and representations can shape and modify the way that we may come to conceive of ourselves, the world, and others. But this works both ways. After all, depicting women in this way and allowing for free sexual expression may promote rather than undermine women's rights. Perhaps the last thing women need, if they are to be treated as equals in the public sphere, is the idea that women need to be protected from or cannot cope with sexual imagery. Indeed, presumably women are more likely to be excluded from positions of influence if men in positions of power are made to feel increasingly paranoid about how they may behave toward and interact with them. If we cannot relax and act naturally with someone, then we are less inclined to want to work with them. We are responsible for what we think and do. If there is no direct harm in the making and showing of media programs and films that represent women in various ways, then there can be no moral wrong in so doing. The wrong inheres in someone prepared, uncritically, to accept dubious representations of female sexuality or gender roles as authoritative.

EQUAL REPRESENTATION

However, objections to media representations of sex as degrading are not wholly reducible to the causal thesis that, thereby, particular individuals will subsequently be harmed. Sometimes the objection relies on the idea that certain depictions of sex are directed toward lustful appetites. Now, we should be wary of allowing free rein to puritanical zeal. Lust is a common human appetite and not necessarily bad. Sexual lust is bad only when it is manifested in particular kinds of acts, such as rape or adultery, as distinct from others, such as making love with our partner. Nonetheless, many moral conservatives and radical feminists would all agree that even if there are no causal consequences for someone's behavior, to seek out and delight in images and stories that focus entirely on the sexual aspect of a person is degrading. The thought is that certain sexual representations are immoral, by virtue of the delight the perceiver takes in a wholly inappropriate way of looking at the human body. Thus an image need not be pornographic to be immoral since the image may not be at all explicit and yet be directed toward an inappropriate way of viewing another person. The harm does not result from looking at such images but is itself constituted by the degrading nature of those images and our subsequent delight in them.

So part of what might be degrading is the nature of what is expressed in depicting women pornographically. For, paradigmatically, pornography involves representing sex and the play of sexuality as a question of male power and the desire to possess and control women. Hence, independently of a causal relation, what is degrading is the nature of what is expressed. Pornography and related images are taken to be immoral because they are abusive of or express a disdain for women. Consider, by analogy, the objection that some people have to the traditional courtesy of men opening doors for women or always paying the bill. No one objects to doors being opened or restaurant bills being paid per se. It would be ridiculous to claim that such acts are intrinsically immoral. But what is morally problematic is the underlying understanding, whether conscious or not, that women are fragile by nature and lack financial power, and hence they need protecting from the physical and commercial realities of a harsh world. Similarly pornography may not itself be bad but becomes so when it seeks to rob women of their individuality apart from their sexual aspects, and thus transform them into mere sexual ciphers whose sole purpose is to please men. It is important to recognize that such a fault is not peculiar to pornography but may itself be endemic to the presentation of sex in quite ordinary films, television programs, and advertisements. What is objected to is not merely explicit sexual detail but the understanding expressed—that women are interesting solely by virtue of their sexual nature, rather than the myriad ways in which we are and ought to be interested in persons.

It is important to see that the explicit intention of the filmmaker is not required for an image to be problematic in this way. Of course, if the motivating intention is to express this understanding, then the producer will himself be open to censure. But the image itself, independently of intention, may be directed solely toward eliciting a sexual interest from the viewer. Similarly the motivating intention in opening a door may not be to express a paternalistic attitude toward women, but nonetheless the fact that I only open doors for women may express this understanding. For how the image or convention may reasonably be under-stood does not merely depend on the motivating intention but the nature of the action or image produced. In both cases the nature of what is expressed is taken to be insulting to and thereby degrading of women. It is to treat women in ways that imply that they are not as competent, autonomous, or worthy of respect as men.

A standard argument takes off from the assumption that pornography and related depictions of sex constitute a form of woman abuse whose motivation is to subordinate women: "Pornography is the institution of male dominance that sexualizes hierarchy, objectification, submission, and violence. As such, pornography creates inequality, not as artifact but as a system of social reality; it creates the necessity for and the actual behaviors that constitute sexual inequality."[12]

The basic idea is that many media representations portray women as sexually submissive victims of male lust and, as such, are immoral. But it should not go unremarked that women are not always portrayed merely as passive subjects of sexual aggression. They are often portrayed as sexually predatory themselves both in pornography and in films like *Basic Instinct, Aliens,* and *Disclosure*. Similarly, though there are genre and cultural variants, we can see from the Wonderbra series of ads or Marky Mark's Calvin Klein ads that representations of gender in relation to sex and sexuality can work in many ways. It is intellectu-ally disingenuous to claim that, as a matter of definition, pornography *necessarily* involves female oppression. Men can be portrayed as objects of female desire in just the same way or as sexual victims in pornography or films like *Disclosure*. Indeed, perhaps the increasing demands made on men's physical appearance partly stem from an increasing focus on male bodies as objects of desire with legs and pass to match. If pornography is degrading and harmful, it is not necessarily true that just women suffer. Rather than constituting a case of woman abuse, it should more appropriately be considered a case of person abuse.

If the objection amounts to the claim that pornography constitutes a form of woman abuse, then it seems that there is nothing apparently unethical about media representations that speak to our sexual interests per se. It is far from clear that pornography even typically involves the portrayal of violence against women that many seem to presume. The wrong inheres in the understanding implicit in certain kinds of pornography—that women should be pliant and subject to men's violent sexual desires. But this does not show that pornography is inherently immoral. We do not think that opening doors or paying dinner bills is wrong per se, only where it is used as a vehicle for an ethically dubious understanding of women. The answer is to reform the conventions and representations respectively. We should open doors for anyone behind us, alternate paying for dinner, and redress the balance of certain kinds of images of women in pornography and the media generally. Hence, as some feminists have argued, rather than consider all pornography to be immoral, it may be that what should be aimed for is nonsexist pornography.[13]

OBSCENITY, DEGRADATION, AND INHERENT WRONG

We have seen that considerations of harm cannot wholly pick out what might be considered morally wrong with degrading representations of sex and sexuality. However, a different kind of argument, based on a marked distinction between imagination and fantasy, may prove more fruitful. One way of glossing the distinction is to refer to the way we sometimes talk about art. When we talk about a great play like Shakespeare's *King Lear* we tend to say not merely that it is beautiful or imaginative but true to life. Through the way we are directed to imagine the fictional characters and plot, *King Lear* can show us something about the nature of human folly, envy, love, and the way we are. Thus good art engages and promotes our imaginings in a way that enables us to understand human reality more deeply. By contrast when we call works like Tolkien's *Lord of the Rings* fantastical, the thought is that it may be highly entertaining but, essentially, it bears no significant relation to reality. A fantasy, in essence, constitutes a flight from reality and thus threatens to become vicious where the fantastical is used as a substitute for reality. To watch *Rambo* as a piece of escapism is one thing, to watch and treat it as if such characters significantly relate to the way that we should understand ourselves and our world, as people like Jeffrey Dahmer might, is to make a serious mistake. The thought that certain media representations are inherently fantastical and thus debased might be connected to a causal thesis: namely, that exposure to sexually explicit representations tends to undermine our capacity for deep human sexual relationships. Nonetheless, the obscenity does not primarily consist in the effects of such images but in the degrading nature of the image themselves.

To draw the argument out a little, following Roger Scruton we should distinguish between two fundamentally different kinds of desire satisfaction.[14] To start with, there is the satisfaction of a desire itself, which amounts to the fulfillment of what motivates us. For example, my desire for a cigarette is obviously satisfied when I light up and inhale. But the mere satisfaction of a desire is not to be equated with the fulfillment of the person who desires. For something to fulfill us, it must satisfy our well-being or fundamental interests. Of course, whether a desire satisfies our well-being is a matter of degree and presumes an understanding of what is good for us as human beings.[15] Note that we are concerned with the person as a rational animal; hence, a person's well-being is not to be identified straightforwardly with an entity's biological interests or the satisfaction of occurrent desires. Rather, we must recognize that certain kinds of capacities naturally aim toward a certain kind of realization. The absence of such a realization constitutes a decline in or corruption of the person as a whole. Thus, as a rational being, to the extent that I fail to develop and realize my rational capacities and thus remain wholly unreflective I lack well-being.

A slightly more simplistic way of making the contrast is to draw a distinction between that which we merely happen to desire and that which we need to flourish as human beings. Obviously what I desire may not coincide with what I need. So the mere satisfaction of a desire is not necessarily equivalent to the satisfaction of our well-being. For example, I may desire a cigarette, want to get drunk, and wish I could be distracted from my work, but to fulfill these desires would not necessarily contribute to my fundamental well-being in the way in which completing my work or remaining healthy and *compos mentis* would.

More importantly, satisfying desires that we happen to have may undermine our personal satisfaction or well-being.[16] For example, alcoholics and crack addicts obviously satisfy certain desires but in so doing come to undermine their capacity to function coherently. Satisfying one of their desires undermines their ability to maintain and develop some of their most basic human interests, from personal relationships to pursuing social activities, goals, and projects that they would otherwise choose to have. In a rather different way, satisfying our lustful desires may undermine our well-being. If someone is married, then satisfying a desire for some other relationship obviously corrodes the commitment that is constitutive of marriage, even if the partner never finds out. The point is that many of our desires are basic, are nonrational, and need to be ordered according to our basic human interests and needs. A perverse desire to inflict gratuitous pain on the helpless is obviously a desire that we should never seek to fulfill and something that we should strive not to possess. Thus, Scruton claims that "whatever persons are, they have reason to avoid both the fulfillment, and also (if possible) the possession, of corrupt desires."[17]

Scruton's claim is that the satisfaction of a sexual desire through fantasy not only fails to satisfy our human well-being but actually undermines our capacity to flourish. To see how this is supposed to be so we must clarify what it is that renders something fantastical. According to Scruton, fantasy is a property of a desire if the desire conforms to the following conditions. First, the object in thought is not equivalent to the object toward which the desire is expressed or pursued. For example, in the British television drama series *A Band of Gold* one of the central characters, a prostitute, is employed to walk up and down dressed in a pair of rubber cleaning-gloves, black stockings, and high heels while the man masturbates. The desire here is fantastical because although the woman concerned is the object in thought, the desire can only be expressed or pursued through the paraphernalia of the gloves, shoes, and stockings. Second, the object pursued acts as a substitute for the object in thought. Hence, in the *Band of Gold* case, the man could not get sexually aroused without the prostitute walking up and down in the relevant state of dress or undress. Last, the pursuit of the substitute is to be explained in terms of a personal prohibition. In the *Band of Gold* case this remains unexplained, but we could easily imagine a story about why someone should become so fixated on cleaning gloves and stockings as a substitute for sex: perhaps they grew up in a family where sex was considered deeply corrupt.[18] So he internalized a prohibition against sex and accepted it as just and appropriate. Hence such a character would feel bad if the prohibition were broken. The internally accepted prohibition forms part of his deliberation and is self-imposed. Thus the relevant desire comes to be transferred onto a substitute that is not itself forbidden: "So we could define fantasy, briefly, as a real desire which, through prohibition, seeks an unreal, but realized, object."[19]

What is sought is not sex itself, which is prohibited, but a substitute for it. In sexual fantasies the experience desired is experienced through the fantasy object that we become attached to by fixating activity. The desire is fantastical because sexual desire is pursued through delight in the substitute paraphernalia rather than through fulfillment of the desire itself.

Of course this is not yet to say anything about the nature of media representations that satisfy fantastical desires. After all, documentaries, magazines like *Vogue,* and films like *9½ Weeks* can all be used as fantastical objects of desire in the way identified. But explicitness is an important element, for the fantastical desire is unconcerned with questions of truth or artistry since its primary concern is for explicit detail. Those who devour pornography derive pleasure and delight from enriching their lives vicariously. What they delight in is the explicitly sexual, shocking, repulsive details, and paraphernalia that act as a substitute for the inability to confront, pursue, or appropriately suppress what their desire in thought is actually directed toward. Hence we often tend to draw a distinction between art that has sexual content and pornography, where the detail is incredibly explicit and the focus is primarily on sexual features and actions for their own sake. Nonetheless, mere explicitness is not straightforwardly what identifies a media image as a fantasy object. Rather, a fantasy object is a substitute whose character is determined by circumstances that generate the fantasy. Hence, in the case of pornography, explicitness is obviously symptomatic of its fantastical nature, but images can be fantastical without themselves being explicit; for example, soft pornography, with women in various states of undress or dressed up in various costumes, remains fantastical. Such representations are directed toward encouraging the transference of the original desire in thought to the fixation on the representation as a substitute through which the desire is pursued and expressed. We are encouraged to seek out explicit imitations rather than engage with our sympathetic imagination or focus on matters of artistic style.

Now that we have a conception of a fantastical desire and what a fantasy object is, we need to step back and question what is so vicious about fantasy objects. Realism involves the attempt to represent the world as it is and thus deepen our understanding of it. Of course, we do not believe that what we actually see is what is happening. We see actors on the screen and imagine them to be particular characters and events. The image is taken not as a substitute for the object of a real desire but as something that may deepen our understanding of events and people of the kind depicted. This is not to say that realistic media images are imitative, but rather that they should operate according to a reality principle: this is how such a person might believably be or act. Hence there is an objective constraint on what we imagine and how we respond emotionally to the image.

By contrast, fantastical representations do not attempt to show us how the world is or might be. Rather, they seek to present the world in a way that matches up to our preexistent desires and interests. Thus the image is taken as a substitute for what we desire, and its significance is determined by the desires that we project onto it. So the image is designed to speak to and gratify our desires without any reference to how things might or would actually be. A fantastical image is a pure imitation of the object that gratifies our projected desires rather than of a reality that is independent of our projected desires. Hence questions arising from the reality principle—whether things would in fact be like this— tend to undermine or corrode the fantastical. We have only to look at the highly stilted dialogue, characters, and plots of pornography, as distinct from art that has sexual content, to see this.

Fantasy itself is necessarily a bad thing because it does not promote, and may even mar, our personal well-being. The pursuit of fantastical objects requires little effort and little interaction with or transformation of the world. Hence gratification is easy. Sexually obscene representations are those directed solely toward sexual arousal in a way that does not aim at its realization in union with another person but mere gratification from an impersonal viewpoint. The sexual desire here is unfettered by and uninterested in encountering another person as a subject with beliefs, desires, and appetites of their own; rather, the interest is in the object of the fantasy, whether the costume or the image of a person, which is wholly shaped by the fantasy of the image's perceiver and cannot itself shape the perceiver's responses. Fantastical images are obscene because it is not really a person who is the object of our sexual desire but rather an object or image of a person. There is no subject-independent significance to the fantasy since its nature is determined by the subjective passion that we seek to realize in it. The image has no potential to resist, control, or engage with us precisely because its purpose is to occlude in fantasy the personhood of the individual depicted.

A rather different way of articulating the same thought is via Robert Nozick's experience machine.[20] Imagine that we could plug ourselves into something like a virtual-reality machine in which we could realize our every sexual wish, want, desire, and goal. A special feature of the machine, moreover, is that once plugged in, we think we are in the real world. Thus our experiences in the machine are not even undermined by the thought that this is only a simulacrum, and we would feel as though we had achieved all our sexual aspirations. Given that our real sexual encounters may be much more complex, difficult, and mundane, would we plug ourselves into the machine? Presumably not.

Why? Precisely because, though we would feel as if our sexual desires had been fully satisfied, the point is that they have not been satisfied at all. The sense of realization that we would arrive at would be a false one: we would not, in fact, have actually experienced sex with or reacted to anyone. It is not the mere lack of participation that is problematic about obscene sexual images; it is, instead, the fantastical nature of desires that seek solely to derive pleasure from an objectified image that supplants the personhood of the individual toward which sexual desire should properly aim. Fantastical images are an evasion of the objective world, and our place in it is subsequently diminished. Real achievement and well-being comes from the actual realization and pursual of goals and not the mere feelings that might arise from a falsely deluded sense of satisfaction. It matters in a very deep sense that what we pursue is real and that our normal passions are directed toward an objective subject-independent reality. Hence we naturally draw a distinction between mere sexual fantasizing and truly reciprocal sexual relations.

What is wrong with certain kinds of sexual representations is both the direction of the sexual desire—toward a mere object or image, rather than a person—and the fetishization of women's bodies, which reduces the significance of women to their sexual features. Hence both the subjects of such images and the viewer are degraded.

FANTASTICAL MEDIA?

However, Scruton goes on to argue that television and film are inherently fantastical media because they use explicit imitative images rather than utilizing the conventions that art uses to direct our imaginings toward a deeper understanding of the world and others. Fantasy is prior to and veils the world in its use of the image concerned rather than seeking to promote an understanding of it. The difference between pornography and art with sexual content is instructive. Pornography possesses all the character and explicit detail of the event depicted portrayed in a banal, lascivious manner, aiming to be a substitute for sex, whereas art prescribes our imaginings in a way that deepens our understanding of sexuality. But the consequence of this argument, Scruton suggests, is that all photographic and televisual media representations of sex and sexuality are inherently immoral.

However, we can retain the distinction between fantastical and proper representations while rejecting the implausible claim that filmic media are inherently obscene. First, the claim that film and photography generally lack artistic conventions, in contrast to theater or the visual plastic arts, is straightforwardly false. We can see why someone might be misled into thinking this. We look at a Sherlock Holmes film and we see a street that looks just like the original Baker Street and may think the image a guileless perceptual substitute; by contrast, we see props in the theatre and have to imagine that they represent a street. Yet one has only to look at the use of various film techniques such as montage to see that this claim is far from being the case at all.

In the early days of film, the Kuleshov experiments described by Pudovkin using creative montage point up the use of artistic conventions to shape the viewer's imaginative engagement with the series of images in a film. They took a close-up photograph of a famous Russian actor and interspliced it with images of a bowl of steaming-hot soup, a corpse, and a playing child.[21] The audience's response to the edited film was to proclaim what a great and subtle actor the man was. But the actor's facial expression, being a photograph, had been identical in all cases; the conjunction of images merely served to encourage the audience to project their feelings about the still-life objects onto the unchanging expression of the actor. A different kind of case is the chilling shower scene from Hitchcock's *Psycho*. Shot from seventy or more camera angles, with jagged, discordant music, it shows a deft mastery of the highly conventionalized nature of film, to incredibly imaginative effect. If you look carefully we never see the knife go in. Film is not merely imitative but utilizes artistic conventions to prescribe our imaginings. Moreover, in addition to filmic conventions arising from editorial techniques, our imaginings are guided by the use of lighting, set design, filmic genres, the use of hand-held cameras, particular character actors, and so on *ad infinitum*. The claim that televisual media are inherently fantastical cannot rest on the thought that such media lack artistic conventions.

A second, distinct consideration suggests that film and television are inherently fantastical because of the identification of the realization of our desire with the camera as distinct from reality. The cinematic apparatus presupposes a voyeuristic gaze, resulting in the fetishization of sexual body parts. For example, we may derive pleasure from watching the camera sadistically following screaming females as they run from threatening monsters, delight in seeing stories of female characters imperiled and saved by masculine heroes, or identifying the camera with the viewpoint of the tormentors in *Carrie* or when Jodie Foster's character is raped in the bar-room in *The Accused*. The fantastical experience afforded by television and cinema may be explainable in terms of provoking and sating our prurient curiosity via a confirmation of patriarchal or gendered schemas. More particularly, in pornography what is shown by the camera is so explicit that the sexual act is realized imitatively rather than shown imaginatively. Hence, as with fantasy generally, we are faced with a gratuitous realization that undercuts the possibility of imaginative understanding. The possibility of innocent pleasures afforded by films that represent sex is thus denied.[22]

But though such claims may hold in relation to particular films, as a general critique of televisual media they are false. Whether a film gratuitously realizes imitatively explicit sex is a matter of how and why we are shown certain images—to direct and shape our understanding, or with the sole aim merely of explicit revelation. The difference is that sexual sensationalism has no purpose except merely to draw attention to the explicitly sexual features of the female character and body. But, as can be seen from a film such as Buñuel's *Belle de Jour*, a film or a television program can deal very seriously with the nature of sexual relations, motivations, and fantasies without itself reducing the interest of the characters and the point of it merely to the imitative explicit revelation of sexual detail.

Furthermore, the idea that film and television elicits an inherently gendered gaze must be false, given that we complain when a movie that conforms to the relevant patriarchal categories just is not interesting enough. Indeed we can and do derive immense pleasure from films, such as Ridley Scott's *Thelma and Louise,* that consciously subvert or violate what are taken to be standard gender schemas. We can and do value conflicting representations of sexuality, from the representation of women in *Nosferatu* as passive, chaste, and helpless victims to films like *Alien* where the strongest characters, and the most predatory, threatening ones, are female.

Scruton's argument presumes that the media of television and film necessarily pander to the fantastical, which imitatively seeks to realize transferred, preexistent desires rather than constituting true representations that seek to deepen our emotions and understanding: "For many interests in the cinema involve no imaginative effort, and have no imaginative reward; and many films are made precisely as the objects of such interests."[23]

But the assumption is false. Film and television do utilize artistic conventions and do not presuppose the identification of desire realization with the camera. That many films, television programs, and photographs are produced for obscene interests does not entail that these media are inherently fantastical. True, televisual media do lend themselves to explicit use because they involve imitative images and sound in a way that mere words or paint marks do not. But it does not follow from this that film and television are inherently fantastical and pornographic. Televisual media can be used in particularly vivid ways both for the promotion of fantasy and for the realistic representation of sex and sexuality in imaginative ways that are not reducible to mere levels of explicitness.

It is also important to recognize that a substantive theory of human sexual relations forms the backdrop to Scruton's claims. Scruton holds that human sexual relations should necessarily be intentionally directed toward "a significant other." Desires not directed toward a specific individual as a person are thus considered perverse. This is to treat another person solely as a means to our own ends rather than as a person in his or her own right. Hence what is wrong with lechery, voyeurism, and the images that respond to these kinds of interests is that they publicly foreground a person's sexuality at the expense of respecting him or her as a person.[24] But it is far from clear that our more general sexual desires and lusts, given they do not manifest themselves harmfully, are immoral. What is wrong with taking a wholly sexual interest in the appearance of another person? After all, my focusing solely on another person's sexual aspect in no way entails that I view her as nothing more than an object for my sexual pleasure. To be interested in only one aspect of a person to the exclusion of almost everything else is not automatically to fail to treat them as a person. When I buy my train ticket, my newspaper, pay my shopping bill, or ask for service in a restaurant, I may not be in the slightest bit interested in anything else apart from an individual fulfilling a certain function. To fail to ask about the functionary's interests, pastimes, hopes, fears, and aspirations is not itself objectionable. Why should taking a sexual interest in someone, or an image that speaks to that kind of interest, be any more objectionable? Someone would only think this if they thought, falsely, that sexual interest is necessarily a form of domination involving the desire to possess, control, and subjugate another. Yet sexual interests constituted by this kind of desire to dominate are, rather, sexual desire gone wrong.[25]

Nonetheless, what our argument does show is that whether an image that speaks to our lascivious interests is degrading depends both on certain features of the image involved and on the context within which the image is shown. In engaging with an imaginative film that explores sexuality, such as *Belle de Jour*, we are interested in the characters, events, and world as we are directed to imagine them by the representation. By contrast, in a film that is directed toward our fantastical desires we are only interested in the spectacle of the actual people and objects seen in the film; hence our interest is fixed not on a fictional character as portrayed but, as in the case of hard-core pornography, on the sexual parts and actions of the performers concerned. The explicitness in such images is symptomatic of, but not required for, an image to be fantastical. The element of degradation enters in where that interest is played to through plots, dialogue, abuse, and sexual intimations of a degrading nature: for example, where women are displayed as commodities, no better than animals, as if they only desire control and the infliction of pain by men against their will. Such fantastical representations are immoral precisely because they encourage us to look at individuals as objects to be treated with force or brutality to make them conform to our sexual desires. Moreover, they are not true representations since they do not aim to enhance our understanding of the world, others, and ourselves.

Secondly, the context of images that are not inherently degrading can render them so. To show images of coy, bare-breasted women directed toward lascivious sexual interests in the pages of a national newspaper like *The Sun* is degrading.[26] But the degradation inheres not in the intrinsic immorality of such images themselves, though we might find them banal and sexually impoverished, but rather the display of such images in such a public forum. Indeed, the degradation is compounded not merely by the publicity of such pictures but by the fact that they are carried by a newspaper whose function is to report on issues of significance and public interest. To depict women as newsworthy solely by virtue of their sexual characteristics in this manner expresses an understanding of women that is demeaning and distortive.

MODERATE MORALISM

Given that the point of media representations is to cultivate our understanding, then in one sense media representations concerning sex and sexuality should seek to educate their audience. Thus, we might be inclined to think that "one clear ethical responsibility on the media—one they are a long way from fully accepting—is to fight bigotry and hypocrisy and to promote a new enlightened atmosphere about sex."[27]

The claim is that the function of the media, as a medium of education, is to wipe away the false prejudices and presumptions that we may have about sex and sexuality. But, unless we are dealing specifically with educational programs and films, we should not seek to bombard our audience with "the" ethically correct approach concerning sex. If all programs were of an educational "look and learn" form, then it is not clear that people would be interested in watching television or going to the movies for entertainment. Representations of sex that were forced to conform to a highly prescriptive understanding of sexuality would tend to be both tedious and facile since they would ring false to the phenomena concerned; for films and programs that are about or involve sex should reflect and engage with the real interests, attitudes, and emotions of the spectators.

Furthermore, it is not clear that it is a function of media representations to cultivate, prescribe, or promote *a* particular attitude about our personal manners and morals regarding sexuality. Rather, the point about representations generally is that they engage with our human interests and aim to deepen our understanding of such matters. Take a film such as Larry Clark's *Kids*, which portrays a host of ten- to twelve-year-olds indulging in sex and drugs in a rather aimless fashion. The film was considered so offensive that it was refused a general certificate in the United States. Although the violence and incessant, graphic sex may be rather hard to stomach, precisely because we would not wish to condone children behaving this way, the film itself portrays fairly convincingly the potentially wild, unsupervised, and promiscuous lifestyle into which urban children may be slipping. Thus not only is the portrayal relevant to our interests in the sense of understanding how things are or might be, but it is disingenuous to censure the film morally for the state of affairs that it seeks to represent. The film seeks to reveal to us an aspect of contemporary social behavior and attitudes among the very young regarding sex, violence, drugs, and the underlying nihilism that such behavior manifests. Hence the propagandist's and the fantasist's attitude toward representations of sexuality are flawed. For what is involved in both cases is a falsification or occlusion of human sexual reality in all its great variety, profusion, and intimacy.

The point is that proper representations aim to engage us imaginatively with the look, feel, and appropriate understanding of scenes, characters, narratives, and states of affairs. So the representation, using various artistic and media conventions, shapes our understanding of what the characters and world portrayed would be like. The purpose of doing this is to enlighten the audience, through their experience with the representation, about the multifarious ways in which we may understand ourselves, others, and the world. By contrast, fantastical representations play to our prurient interests and desires with no reference to how what is depicted might or could plausibly be. The primary focus of interest is in satisfying, usually through imitative and highly explicit images, the prurient desires of the audience. Hence such representations tend to be highly repetitive, superficial, and tedious since the engagement of our interest in understanding something about what is portrayed is besides the point. Rather, characters and narratives are important only insofar as they form a minimal backdrop against which the gratuitous representation of sexual features and activities can take place.

I am not denying that different levels of explicitness and certain concerns are appropriate for different levels of understanding. Hence the need for cinema certificates and television and advertising guidelines. Implicit in the role of the media in our society is the notion of a contract between the audience and the paper, magazine, or broadcaster. The customs of following certain genre constraints, scheduling concepts, and adequately labeling programs enables us to recognize the sexual content and nature of a program. Issues of offense and the immorality of media representations of sex and sexuality should focus not only on the fantastical nature of the images per se but also the inappropriate context within which they are often put. There are, for example, clearly appropriate expectations as to the acceptability of nudity or the depiction of sex in an adult drama, a situation comedy, and a children's program.[28] When Calvin Klein was forced to withdraw an advertising campaign featuring waiflike models advertising jeans and underwear, the complaint was that they looked like the opening scenes from a child porn movie. The images, deliberately shot in an amateurish style in black and white, included television commercials, bus posters, billboards, and magazine ads, with some being more overtly sexual than others. But we need to distinguish between the different media utilized on grounds of publicity. A billboard is necessarily in the public arena in a way in which television programs or magazines, which people choose to watch or read, are not.

The complaints arose because of the public nature of the advertisement campaign which was considered inappropriate for images of childlike characters clad in denim shorts revealing their underwear with legs splayed. For such an image plays on and fuels not just female anxieties but anxieties about the kind of sexual interest in children that the poster apparently invites us to take. There need not be anything immoral per se with sexual images or the explicit representation of sexual activities as long as their focus is not fantastical and they are believable in relation to the context, motivations, and lives of those portrayed and thus seek to deepen our understanding. Apart from the artistically tedious nature of fantastical representations, what they present is a moral affront insofar as they subjugate the true nature of what is represented for the sake of explicit sexual detail and innuendo.

Media representations of sex ought to be truly related to sexuality in our world, to give rise both to understanding and enjoyment. But it does not follow that sexually titillating images are necessarily degrading in the way often suggested. Of course, there is something wrong where explicitly sexually titillating images become commonplace in rather public contexts and where they come to predominate. This belies a certain kind of fascination with sexuality which comes to predominate popular media culture to the exclusion of much else and cultivates the misleading impression that bodice-ripping, passion-driven sex four or five nights a week is the norm. But the interest itself is not clearly immoral, and we learn about human sexuality by engaging with or looking at representations of characters and sexual situations both close to and far removed from our own. However, at some level, such representations had better touch on real desires and fears that we can recognize in relation to our world. If they do not, then at best the representation of sex is truly fatuous and, at worst, fantastical and pornographic, given the interest played to and the explicit focus on the sexual content involved for its own sake. In a media culture where the depiction of gratuitous sex, playing to fantastical desires, comes to predominate, there is clearly something very wrong.

NOTES

1. *The Independent on Sunday*, 4 October 1992, p. 20.

2. The genesis of this kind of thought is Immanuel Kant's *Groundwork of the Metaphysics of Morals*, trans. and ed. H. J. Paton, *The Moral Law* (London: Hutchinson, 1948), where one formulation of his categorical imperative is that we should "act in such a way that you always treat humanity . . . never simply as a means, but always at the same time as an end," p. 91.

3. For example, Susan Brownmiller, *Against Our Will: Men, Women and Rape* (New York: Simon and Schuster, 1975), pp. 389–396, assumes just such a link.

4. Catherine MacKinnon, *Only Words* (Cambridge, MA: Harvard University Press, 1993), pp. 95–97.

5. Andrea Dworkin, "Pornography and Grief," in her *Letters from a War Zone* (London: Secker and Warburg, 1988), p. 23. Similarly, Catherine MacKinnon has stated that "pornography works as a behavioral conditioner, reinforcer, and stimulus, not as idea or advocacy. It is

more like saying 'kill' to a trained dog—and also the training process itself." As quoted by Wendy Kaminer, "Feminists against the First Amendment," *Atlantic Monthly*, November 1992, pp. 111–118.

6. W. L. Marshall, "Pornography and Sex Offenders," in *Pornography: Research Advances and Policy Considerations*, ed. D. Zillman and J. Bryant (Hillsdale, NJ: Lawrence Erlbaum, 1989), pp. 185–214.

7. Nadine Strossen, *Defending Pornography: Free Speech, Sex and the Fight for Women's Rights* (London: Abacus, 1996), p. 127.

8. See Elizabeth M. Perse, "Uses of Erotica and Acceptance of Rape Myths," *Communication Research 21* (1994): 488–515.

9. In Aristotle's *Poetics*, trans. G. F. Else (Ann Arbor, MI: University of Michigan Press, 1970), the explanation of the psychological experience and effects of tragedy are articulated in terms of catharsis where, crudely, the expression draws out our emotions thus releasing what is bad while preserving what is good.

10. See Marcia Pally, *Sex and Sensibility: Reflections on Forbidden Mirrors and the Will to Censor* (Hopewell, NJ: Ecco Press, 1994), pp. 57–61.

11. See, for example, the classic study by S. E. Asch, "Opinions and Social Pressure," *Scientific American 193* (1955): 31–35.

12. Andrea Dworkin, "Against the Male Flood: Censorship, Pornography and Equality," in her *Letters From a War Zone* (London: Secker and Warburg, 1988), pp. 267–268.

13. See, for example, Mary Caputi, *Voluptuous Yearnings: A Feminist Theory of the Obscene* (Lanham, MD: Rowman and Littlefield, 1994); Feminists Against Censorship, *Pornography and Feminism,* ed. G. Rodgerson and E. Wilson (London: Lawrence and Wishart, 1993), pp. 67–75; and Ann Garry, "Pornography and Respect for Women," *Social Theory and Practice 4* (1978): 395–421.

14. Roger Scruton, "Fantasy, Imagination and the Screen," in his *The Aesthetic Understanding* (Manchester, U.K.: Carcanet, 1983), pp. 127–136.

15. Although this kind of distinction derives from Aristotle's *Nicomachean Ethics*, trans. J. A. K. Thomson (Harmondsworth, U.K.: Penguin, 1976), 1097b22–1098a20, pp. 75–76, it need not depend on debatable assumptions concerning metaphysical biology.

16. See Plato, *Gorgias*, trans. D. J. Zeyl (Indianapolis, IN: Hackett, 1987), 491e–497a, pp. 64–71, where Socrates shows that a life devoted to the fulfillment of all our appetites is self-defeating and thus what is pleasant is to be distinguished from what is truly good.

17. Scruton, "Fantasy, Imagination and the Screen," p. 128.

18. See, for example, R. J. McGuire, J. M. Carlisle, and B. G. Young, "Sexual Deviations as Conditioned Behaviour: A Hypothesis," *Behaviour Research and Therapy 2* (1965): 185–190.

19. Scruton, "Fantasy, Imagination and the Screen," p. 130.

20. Robert Nozick, *Anarchy, State and Utopia* (Oxford: Blackwells, 1974), pp. 42–45.

21. See V. F. Perkins, *Film as Film* (London: Penguin, 1990), p. 106.

22. See, for example, Gaylyn Studlar, "Masochism and the Perverse Pleasures of Cinema," in *Film Theory and Criticism,* ed. G. Mast, M. Cohen and L. Braudy, 4th edition (Oxford: Oxford University Press, 1992), p. 790, and Laura Mulvey, *Visual and Other Pleasures* (London: Macmillan, 1989), Chapter 3. See Berys Gaut, "On Cinema and Perversion," *Film and Philosophy, 1* (1), for a devastating critique of this line of thought.

23. Scruton, "Fantasy, Imagination and the Screen," p. 135.

24. See Roger Scruton, *Sexual Desire: A Philosophical Investigation* (London: Weidenfeld and Nicolson, 1986).

25. See Andrea Dworkin, *Woman Hating* (New York. E. P. Dutton, 1901), p. 101, where she states that sexual intercourse "means remaining the victim, forever annihilating all self-

respect. It means acting out the female role, incorporating the masochism, self-hatred, and passivity which are central to it."

26. See Piers Benn, "Pornography, Degradation and Rhetoric," *Cogito 7* (1993): 133.

27. Andrew Belsey, "Privacy, Publicity and Politics," in *Ethical Issues in Journalism and the Media,* ed. Andrew Belsey and Ruth Chadwick (New York: Routledge, 1992), p. 89.

28. See Andrea Millwood Hargrave, *Sex and Sexuality in Broadcasting* (London: John Libbey, 1992), pp. 53–59.

6 Violence in the Media

INTRODUCTION

Recently there has been a dramatic increase in popular disenchantment with violence in the media. Given that we think that media representations can cultivate insight into our world, it would be surprising if they did not, conversely, possess the potential to desensitize. But to see how this might be so we must start by unpicking the theoretical presumptions brought to bear in media analysis. The point of our engagement with media representations inheres in the constructive engagement of our imagination, in which our pleasure lies, and thus the promotion of understanding. Two key claims, I argue here, flow from this recognition. First, our evaluation of media representations necessarily includes our moral evaluation of the states of affairs as represented. Second, relative to the level of understanding brought to bear, representations of violence typically do cultivate violent behavior. Thus the usual liberal arguments against condemning violence in the media are inadequate. For we do have reason to believe that violence in the media may well lead to harm.

When Oliver Stone's *Natural Born Killers* was released in 1994, the film generated a huge controversy about the apparently ever-increasing levels of violence in films and television. The film itself portrays two serial killers, played by Woody Harrelson and Juliette Lewis, who career viciously through America littering their trail with innumerable corpses. The way the narrative is revealed to us utilizes rapid montage sequences and the stylized cinematic conventions from MTV popular culture in a way that both grabs our attention and highlights the heavy-handed satire on the way the media itself ends up glorifying the most vicious of crimes and nihilistic of criminals. But the film generated even more controversy after it came to be linked to at least six deaths in the United States and, in Paris, to a couple who killed four people. Indeed a fourteen-year-old from Dallas, Texas, who stood accused of killing a girl of thirteen, confessed that his motivation was the apparent desire to become "famous, like the natural born killers."[1] Only a year before in England, on 12 February 1993, a two-year-old child named Jamie Bulger had been taken by the hand in a large shopping mall, dragged two and a half miles to a railtrack, tortured, and then brutally murdered by two ten-year-old children. The murder of Jamie Bulger was explicitly linked by the trial judge, Justice Morland, to *Child's Play 3*, a film featuring Chucky, a possessed, sadistic toy character.[2] In *Child's Play 3*, we are presented with a doll who, possessed by a psychopath, proceeds to commit seven murders, shown in vivid detail ranging from throat-slitting to exploding bodies. At the climax of the film, Chucky, covered in blue paint, loses various limbs and is shredded in a wind machine. Indeed, a few days before Justice Morland's remarks, a defendant in another case, involving the torture and murder of the teenager Suzanne Capper, had allegedly referred to herself as "Chucky" throughout the ordeal.[3] Indeed such was the reaction in Britain that the release certificate for *Natural Born Killers* was delayed by four months, and Quentin Tarantino's *Reservoir Dogs* video release certificate was withheld for many months.

Despite increasing popular worries about such media representations of violence, the response by most media experts is dismissive. The usual variables, ranging from social deprivation to possible sexual abuse, are highlighted, but worries about violence in the media are typically labeled the worries of middle-class reactionaries, the puritanical, or the darkly political.[4] Indeed, worries about violence in the media are often treated as merely another episode in a long history of moral panics.[5] Yet the reason for such moral panics, we are told, is the sensationalism of the media. But then if the media can create a moral panic without foundation, this can only be because the media do deeply influence our attitudes, beliefs, perceptions, and intuitions regarding our world. This is precisely why many people fear stereotyping or the disparagement of particular ethnic, religious, or cultural groups by the media. Hence, I want to suggest, there is something deeply sound about the popular disenchantment with representations of, in particular, violence in the media. After all it seems intuitively obvious that there are links between the kinds of films we enjoy and the nature of civil society. Given that media representations can cultivate our understanding of the world, it would be surprising if they did not, conversely, also possess the potential to corrupt it. But to see this we must first unpick the theoretical presumptions typically brought to bear on media analysis. Only then can we understand how the depiction of violence may affect the way we understand and act within our world.

Despite being a strong focus of academic investigation, our understanding of the nature and influence of media representations is, at best, partial. This is largely because the dominant models applied to analyzing media representations are motivated by theories of meaning, which are thus held to render movies potentially equivalent in significance to any other sphere of discourse.[6] Concomitantly, critical and cultural studies have also been fixated by a concern with relationships of power. Thus, whether in terms of *Screen* theory or the renewed empirical focus deriving from David Morley's *The "Nationwide" Audience*, representations of violence, sexuality, and their censorship are examined in terms of dominant or subversive ideologies.[7] Hence John Fiske explicitly states that one should conceive of television "texts" in terms of ideology: "Texts are the site of conflict between their forces of production and modes of reception. . . . A text is the site of struggles for meaning that reproduce the conflicts of interest between the producers and consumers of the cultural commodity."[8]

Effectively, media representations are thought significant to the extent that they may be taken to constitute meaningful theories or ideologies about the world, whether implicitly or explicitly held. Hence representations of violence are considered to depend for their value on the ideology they condone, subvert, or confront. Thus, the presumption goes, disenchantment with media violence only arises from those who would illiberally seek to enforce a particular conception of the good society on us all or from those who wish to protect the dominant relations of power from subversion.

Now I would not want to deny that we may rightly be worried about the motivations of certain interest groups or particular individuals, such as Pat Buchanan or Adrian Rogers.[9] As Dewe Mathews suggests, it may be that "if censorship is to survive and retain its political sanction, it has to exploit demands for social intervention. Of course those demands have to be valid, but even more importantly, they have to enhance the power of the censor. In other words they have to ask for more censorship. . . . Above all it is the spurious use of legitimate concerns which underlines censorship's dependency on moral absolutes."[10]

Yet this is only a contingent concern. It does not follow that, as a matter of principle, there is nothing more fundamental to the popular complaint against violence in the media. As a historical or empirical thesis about the psychology of those who vociferously object to representations of violence, it may even be true that many of the complainants are politically motivated. Yet the truth of this thesis says little about whether or not there is something deeply problematic about the way that violence is represented. The complaint made with the purpose of furthering political ends may itself be sound, irrespective of whether the political ends are themselves justified. The fact that people may contingently use an issue or institution to further their own agenda does not, of itself, suggest that the actual complaint must be ill-founded.

The reason many media experts cannot make sense of popular worries, except in politically jaundiced terms, is precisely because media representations are reduced to matters of linguistic meaning or manifestations of power relations: promoting a given proposition or theory about the world. What this reveals is a complete neglect of the point, purpose, and inherent value of audience engagement with media representations in the first place. Indeed, on this basis, it remains manifestly unclear why representations of violence, or certain kinds of violence, could have any significant attraction or subsequent effect on viewers at all. After all, why watch *Unforgiven, Falling Down,* or *Reservoir Dogs* if they only afford an analysis that either confirms or subverts our supposed theory of the world? Why not just stay at home and read the papers or the cultural theorists?

A proper understanding of the distinctive value of media representations in our engagement with them must recognize the primary role and delight afforded by the imagination. Furthermore, only if we recognize the crucial role that imagination plays in our everyday lives, in terms of understanding both ourselves and others, can we begin to see just why we are rightly worried about representations of violence in the media. What will emerge is a picture of our engagement with representations of violence which shows how violent films could cultivate within us the delight taken in violence and a lack of compassion for those who are the subjects of violence. Such an argument in no way commits us to the claim that other variables, such as poverty or education, are irrelevant. But it is to claim that the socialization process that guides and shapes the character traits we develop and how they are manifested is affected by the images that the media places before us.

INTERPRETING FILMS

The problem is that a media representation is typically considered significant if and only if it concerns or manifests propositions or theories about the world. Yet why is this presumption held to be so obvious? One way, and I think the most fruitful, to make sense of this claim is to think of media representations as related to the human world in the way that scientific hypotheses are related to the natural world. That is, ultimately, they are speculations about how our world is, could be, or, perhaps, should be.

Now, science cannot hypothesize about the human world as it can about the natural world, because of the necessary intentionality of human action. Understanding ourselves, others, and the human world requires us to grasp the intuitions, feelings, and concepts under which people act. Hence science cannot wholly capture our subjective aspect: that is, our evaluation of reasons in the light of goals, interests, and plans of action that we may have. Thus various essential attributes of *my* self—ranging from why I love Amy, rather than Sophie or Karen, to why I am a philosopher, a Christian, or prefer Prague to Paris—cannot be wholly captured by scientific explanation.[11] Thus we may think that media representations may informatively analyze and investigate the distinctly human world in a way that science cannot.

Of course, the relations between the postulated possible or impossible worlds represented and our world may be complex. Nonetheless we might think of representations as throwing some significant light on the world within which we move. For example, looked at in this light, Martin Scorsese's adaptation of Edith Wharton's *Age of Innocence* may be taken as an analysis of how mere custom can only be inadequate to the realization of romantic love, individual freedom, and integrity. Now, as I will argue, there is truth in the idea that a representation *shows* us the possibilities inherent in a particular human world. However, this cannot be properly captured by a picture that conceives of media representations as, primarily, objects for critical analysis rather than representations that the audience engages with and imaginatively experiences.

The fundamental problem is that a representation's significance and value is reduced, falsely, to its status as a particular representation of a possible or impossible world. The politically motivated analysis of media representations implicitly misconceives them as scientific hypotheses about our human world. Hence we are left with an impoverished understanding of media representations, which are reduced to the status of philosophy examples or propaganda: mere illustrations. Thus their significance can only be trivial and their distinctive value pictured solely in terms of a distinctive form of entertainment. Yet, at least typically, we do not approach representations as objects for critical interpretation to test a hypothesis about our world.

In the first instance it is not even clear that a whole range of representations, including films such as *Jaws, IT*, the *Friday the 13th* series, and *Jurassic Park*, are of any particular ideological significance at all. At best such films might be roller-coaster rides through a gamut of emotions from fear and suspense to relief. At worst they might merely be shallow shock stories that fail to sustain any deep feelings of terror or even concern at the fate of their gullible and foolhardy characters. Conversely, such a picture cannot explain how representations that are heavily and explicitly ideological, such as Eisenstein's *Potemkin*, may nevertheless be enjoyed by many who do not share or would vehemently repudiate the ideology prescribed. After all, if a representation's value depends on the theory manifested, then its value must be coextensive with our evaluation of that theory as presented. Yet although one might evaluate the communism manifest in *Potemkin* as simplistic, one may still value Eisenstein's film highly.

It might be objected that we should distinguish significant media representations—ones that seek to influence the way that we categorize and act within our world—from those that serve merely to entertain. Thus we should only be concerned with the many representations that do manifest certain claims about the world, whether implicitly or self-consciously so. So though we might not be concerned with trivial amusement films such as *Jaws*, which are thus presumed harmless, we should nevertheless be concerned with "significant" ones such as *Henry: Portrait of a Serial Killer* or Siegal's original *Invasion of the Body Snatchers*. At the explicit level of analysis, Siegal's film concerns an invisible alien threat to personal identity and thus to humanity in general. Superficially, it might seem to do no more than any other entertaining horror movie. But even at the explicit level of analysis it raises significant questions about the nature of personal identity. Furthermore, whether intended or not, it is also implicitly expressive of a very great fear arising from a particular understanding of the world at a particular time: namely, that the free world was itself under threat from communists—people who externally seemed just like "us" but were "alien" and inexplicably contaminated by an evil ideology, which threatened to spread worldwide.

Now I would not want to deny that films may fundamentally be about our world or that some representations are more significant than others. Yet if this were all there were to films then some rather uncomfortable conclusions would follow. First, from this point of view, the propositions or theory suggested by a media representation must either be trivial or properly assessed by the relevant mode of enquiry. Thus, on this basis, and given the collapse of communism as a viable ideology, it would seem that *Invasion of the Bodysnatchers* is rendered redundant by history. Indeed, Kaufman's remake of the original movie must, on this basis, be considered conceptually stillborn: after all, in the conclusion to the remake, the aliens emerge victorious.

Similarly, it would be, properly speaking, a matter for psychology and philosophy, respectively, to formulate and adjudicate over any significant claims about human character and epistemology made in a particular film. Films certainly cannot test the coherence and soundness of any theses they may suggest about, say, self-deception, moral psychology, and knowledge claims. Thus even "significant" media representations cannot transcend the apparent dichotomy of entertainment and significance. The film may be considered enjoyable, but any significant claims made within it more properly belong within the domain of the relevant sphere of enquiry. Once again, on the basis presumed, it remains mysterious as to why we bother with films except as mere vehicles of distracting pleasure. Yet we commonly expect good media representations to be not merely entertaining but themselves to offer some significant insight into the world in a way that mere theory or academic investigation, as a matter of principle, cannot.

To consider a film significant to the extent that it manifests a theory or proposition is crudely to reduce it to the level and function of propaganda. Of course, once one swallows this assimilation, it may appear perfectly obvious that one of the prime functions of films is the repetition, extension, or repudiation of certain relationships of power or ways of categorizing our world. Thus, in terms of ideological equivalence, even the most banal media crudities may be treated as if they were equal to the most profound and insightful representations. But the reduction is a false one. The particular ideology or understanding that a representation articulates, expresses, or promotes is not necessarily identical with the value of the object *qua* media representation.

This point can be brought out if we consider Ed Wood Jr.'s infamous *Plan 9 from Outer Space*.[12] In terms of ideology it can be taken to express the same kinds of fears and understanding implicit in Siegal's *Invasion of the Body Snatchers*.

Yet because *Plan 9* is a truly awful film one cannot possibly get the same kind of enjoyment out of engaging with it as one does from *Invasion of the Body Snatchers*. *Plan 9* was basically built around a few minutes of footage shot before Bela Lugosi's death; sets fall apart, the script is disjointed and nonsensical in parts, actors change halfway through, and the aliens are truly laughable. Hence though two films may express the same ideology in similar ways, one may be awful and the other truly gripping. Thus the value inherent in our engagement with films—and with media representations generally—cannot be reducible to the theory or ideology of the world prescribed.

Lastly, merely conceiving of representations as objects that critically analyze our world cannot but fail to explain how it is that we may and do value representations whose "messages" are contradictory. According to this argument, our enjoyment and evaluation of any given film will be determined by how sound we think the representation is, in terms of the claims made about our world or the ideology promoted. Yet we clearly can and do enjoy films whose claims about our world are incompatible. For example one may enjoy and value a film such as *Nosferatu* where female sexuality is portrayed as the inherently passive, chaste, and vulnerable prey to the devious, lascivious nature of male sexuality. Nonetheless, and at the same time, one may enjoy and value films such as James Cameron's *Aliens* or David Cronenberg's *They Came From Within*, where female sexuality is represented as being intrinsically aggressive, predatory, and parasitic.

Indeed we may often value alternative and incompatible interpretations of the same representation. Thus, for example, the cinematic conventions utilized and the events represented within *Jacob's Ladder* are perfectly consistent with at least two incompatible interpretations, both of which we may value equally. On the one hand, spectators can imagine that Tim Robbins and his Vietnam platoon were the subjects of a devious, disastrous experiment by the U.S. military to enhance their fighting capacity. On the other hand, one can consistently imagine that what was represented was merely the hallucination of a man dying in a field hospital in Vietnam. The inherent ambiguity may be consistently and fruitfully disambiguated in a plurality of possible interpretations across the number of times that we imaginatively engage with it. Thus we may value incompatible interpretations of both the world represented and our world. Therefore the value of a representation cannot wholly inhere in how it postulates that our world might be.

INHERENT VALUE

Now, that we may value incompatible understandings in no way entails that we do not value the film's content.[13] Indeed we respond to the film's cognitive features in their own right and appreciate them as valuable to the work *qua* representation. Furthermore, truth is only one aspect of cognitive value. Hence, though a work may promote a flawed view of the world, and thus mar it in this regard, we may nevertheless value it in other respects. Thus, if a representation is original, interesting, and stretches our understanding of a medium, or subverts a genre, that also contributes to its cognitive value.

Nevertheless, in engaging with films, we do not just value what is represented, but how we are directed to imagine and thus understand it. A film prescribes what we or another would or should feel and think in a particular imaginative world. Only once we fully appreciate this can we adequately make sense of the way that we properly distinguish between good and bad media representations. That is, we value films in their own right where they engage and prescribe vivid imaginings.[14] Of course, we may value a media representation instrumentally: because it relays news or information to us. But if this is all we value it for, then quite how we get the information—whether by television, radio, or word of mouth— becomes irrelevant. But where we value a media representation as such, this is precisely because it prescribes and promotes our imaginings in peculiarly powerful ways. Hence we distinguish tabloid news or propaganda from imaginatively rich and valuable representations, such as Prévert and Carné's *Les Enfants du Paradis*, Kubrick's *The Shining,* or Ridley Scott's *Blade Runner.* Thus, as a constituent part of the kind of imaginings promoted, the distinct media, conventions, and genre of the representation in question are crucial with regard to its inherent value. What the traditional picture effectively occludes is the primary importance of a rich, vivid, imaginative experience—a matter that is irreducible to propositional and conceptual analysis.

But if representations merely prescribe vivid imaginings, and in so doing give rise to pleasure, how could they possibly threaten the well-being of certain individuals or the very fabric of our society? Many of us enjoy violent movies and do not proceed to maim, rape, and murder. Media representations, through prescribing and promoting our imaginings, can and do cultivate our understanding of ourselves, others, and the world. When we imagine, we do not merely conceive of and theoretically evaluate states of affairs; rather, imagining is constituted both by elements of thought and irreducible sensuous experience, typically conjoined with a sense of what something would feel like or what our emotional response to it would be. Now, imagining in this sense is fictionality-indifferent. That is, we can imaginatively engage with representations that concern facts about the world, and it may be an essential part of the imagining that this is so. But, whether fictional or not, the imaginative understanding promoted by a work, through what we imagine, may be fundamentally related to and thus possibly true or false of our world.[15]

One of the primary means by which our imaginative understanding is developed, both in imaginatively engaging with our world and media representations, is through character identification. Now, of course, things are highly complex. Nonetheless, character identification, through imagining what another thinks, feels, and senses in a particular situation, is fundamental to our ability to understand others. Hence it is important to clarify, briefly, what is involved in character identification and just why it is of crucial import. Someone might think that identification with an older brother or soap character involves merely drawing attention to an observed, or perhaps wished for, similarity—for example, that they are good at tennis, witty, glamorous, attractive, or hard done by. Of course, the similarity must be thought significant, otherwise there is little point in highlighting the supposed resemblance. However, noticing an apparent similarity is insufficient. Rather, we also think that we know what others think, feel, or perceive, through having imagined what it would be like for us to be in their shoes. This imaginative simulation is to be distinguished from the related imagining of what "I" would feel or do in another's position. That is merely to put myself into another's epistemic background. But in identifying with another I am imagining what it would be like to look out on the world with *his or her* eyes.[16] The whole point of identification lies in the fact that, despite epistemic and character differences, we imagine what another thinks and feels.

Imaginative simulation is crucial if we are to understand, and perhaps appropriately sympathize with, others.[17] It is a matter of how, given their character, they conceive of their situation and are predisposed to think, feel, and act. For example, we may meet someone and wish to develop what might otherwise remain an insignificant, fleeting relationship; what we need to know is how the other person would understand and respond to our attempts to do so. We do not then refer to some theory about interpersonal social interaction; rather, we try to imagine what he or she would feel if we tried to get to know that person better. Thus, if our imaginings are sensitive and sound, we should be in a better position to know whether or not to pursue what we desire. If we are attempting to understand deeply another individual or culture, we do not seek to apply a theory that they must tacitly possess to do what they do, whether it be religious worship, falling in love, following football, or watching movies. Rather, we need to grasp how they themselves subjectively feel and think in their pursuit of whatever their project or goal is.

Given the general importance of what we imagine in cultivating our understanding, we can now see that, through our powerful and vivid imaginative experience, a representation may enable a form of knowledge by acquaintance. Thus the understanding promoted by a media representation, through our imaginative acquaintance, may directly or indirectly affect the way we come to look on and thus act within the world. The significance of what we imagine arises from the imaginative experience afforded by the representation and how we think that it relates to our actual experience and situation. That is, what we engage with in our imaginative lives may deepen or alter our understanding, cultivating the multifarious ways we may look upon our human world. For example, in Ridley Scott's *Blade Runner* the construction of androids' memories suggests that social engineering controls and determines who and what we are. Even at the end it still seems possible that Deckard's predictability is symptomatic of his being manipu lated or controlled. The complexities of the imaginings prescribed are rich and complex, producing an unremittingly bleak indictment of man's degeneration into nihilism. Yet the ideal of human love, ironically enough only manifested by nonhuman persons, is reaffirmed as a humanly sound motivating vision. For though memories may be manipulated, and perhaps innocence, in time, destroyed, there remains the chance to start again.

In *Blade Runner*, through prescribing our identification with Deckard, our imaginative sympathies are engaged and a particular understanding promoted. This stands in direct contrast to the understanding that could so easily have been prescribed: an easy identification with humanity and thus a categorization of the rebellious androids as a dangerous threat to humankind. Such a superficial understanding would have proscribed our sympathies for the androids, thus negating the need for compassion, love, and "human" concern. Through our imaginative engagement with *Blade Runner*, at least as it is in the director's cut, we are forced to question our general understanding of the nature of deviants. Where we might previously have presumed that outgroups—for example, racial or sexual minorities—were not worthy of moral inclusion, *Blade Runner* suggests otherwise. Hence it may lead us to reflect, among other things, about the nature of personal identity, moral concern, and love. Thus it is that media representations, even entirely fictional ones, can deepen our imaginative sense of the world—why one does or should feel and act in relation to others.

VICIOUS DELIGHT AND CAUSAL INFLUENCES

However, the flip side of the coin is that representations such as Pedro Almadovar's *Tie Me Up, Tie Me Down* can promote and cultivate a flawed or superficial imaginative understanding of reality: the characters are superficial, their motivations and feelings caricatured, and the development from pornographic obsession to love is facile. It fails to vivify the central characters as driven by imaginatively understandable and complex human desires. Hence one may imaginatively understand a work but reject it on the grounds that the prescribed imaginings and understanding are fantastical or inadequate to possible human life. Thus, for example, Dilys Powell is deeply critical of *Last Tango in Paris* because ultimately she takes it to be "about manufactured characters, about a false situation, about a piece of fake brilliantly executed, indeed, but still a piece of fake."[18]

It is important to realize that this line of thought does not involve the wholesale condemnation of representations of violence per se. For example, the violence in Clint Eastwood's *Unforgiven* is a necessary feature of the imaginative understanding, of both the West and humanity, that is promoted—namely, that the asocial individual outside the moral community of the family can only degenerate into brutal nihilism. Of course, we might criticize the simplistic picture of man's casual, inherent violence. Nevertheless, the film serves to subvert the typical imaginative understanding of the Western, where the autonomous individual is seen as necessarily heroic in his rejection of authority and social morality. Thus we might recognize that though partially inadequate, the violence in and understanding promoted by *Unforgiven* may deepen our own imaginative understanding in a way most Westerns do not.

We are now in a position to see why violent films such as *Good Fellas* or *Pulp Fiction* are both valued and flawed. *Good Fellas* engages our imaginings so that we can appreciate and delight in highly stylized, extended, and random Mafia violence. It promotes an imaginative understanding of the Mafia as generally an admirable, familial community impelled by a distinctive vision of the world involving close blood attachments, protection, and self-sacrifice. We can recognize Martin Scorsese's artistic techniques, mastery of the medium in the film's prescription of our imaginings, and the pleasure afforded by the mere violence of the imaginings prescribed. Indeed, it is important that we do recognize the appeal of violent, horrific, or scary representations: the force of this point should not be neglected. Normally negative evaluative thoughts and feelings, which are individuated according to their typically unpleasant formal objects, may nevertheless be experienced as pleasant under atypical conditions. The enjoyment afforded by horror movies or violent programs is not, *pace* Noël Carroll, merely a cognitive matter.[19] It is a mistake to think that the pleasures afforded by horror movies arise solely from their violation of our categorial schemas. The repulsion and fear are not necessarily just unfortunate by-products that we must experience to derive enjoyment from the intellectual and psychological curiosity provoked and subsequently sated. After all, we may, and often do, just enjoy being scared, repulsed, or relieved. Hence some people enjoy violent films, roller-coaster rides, racing-car driving, or mountaineering merely because of the thrill of fear and danger that they afford.[20]

Nonetheless the imaginative understanding manifest in *Good Fellas*—that casual violence directed at those outside the Mafia is of little concern—is itself radically flawed. Hence, though the violence in *Good Fellas* may afford pleasure, our recognition of the film's value and enjoyment of it at the meta-level should be marred, because the violence is inappropriately represented as part of an admirable response to the world and others. Indeed even where our moral sense may mar our endorsement of the film, it still does not wholly dissolve the pleasure that may be derived from the representations of violence. Significantly, though, the imaginative understanding promoted by *Good Fellas* is not just inappropriate, in the sense in which *Unforgiven* presents only a partial understanding; rather, it is fundamentally at odds with the most morally significant aspects of Mafia life. It constitutes a fundamental and radical misunderstanding of what it represents. Hence it cannot promote true insight but only a radically unsound imaginative understanding of a vicious ethos.

Similarly, the stylized, jokey violence of Quentin Tarantino's *Pulp Fiction* ultimately mars the film because its only underlying rationale inheres in the appeal to the visceral delight it may afford. But this is precisely to promote a delight in, and radical misunderstanding of, the nature of human violence. Despite its stylization, orchestration of talent, and at times exceptional tone, *Pulp Fiction* can only remain fundamentally flawed. Where we are prescribed to enjoy the infliction of pain and suffering for its own sake, and where the suggested relationship of violence to our world is inappropriate, a representation's value is marred and its consequent effects may well prove positively harmful.

It might be objected that we do not know that media representations affect how we understand, imaginatively or otherwise, our world. Understanding the world and media representations may involve the same faculty—the imagination—but they are necessarily two distinct activities distinguished by, respectively, belief and fantasy. What we fantasize about cannot bear any significant relation to what we actually believe.[21] Furthermore, the empirical evidence concerning the effects of violence in the media is, perhaps, rather inconclusive.[22] After all, someone may watch the most gratuitously violent film, which promotes a complete disregard for and pleasure taken in the horrific infliction of pain and suffering on others, and yet remain a perfectly well-balanced moral individual. Indeed even if one were to assume that there is a causal relationship of some sort, it is not clear which way the causal arrow would run: whether violent films corrupt or whether the corrupted watch violent films.

It would be false to claim that representations that promote a gratuitously violent understanding of the world are *necessarily* corruptive. However, given the nature of our engagement with media representations, we have reason to believe that repeated exposure to gratuitously violent understandings of the world and others will tend to corrupt.[23] The relationship is not a necessary one, because although the cultivation of our understanding disposes us to act in certain ways, it cannot wholly determine it.[24] Hence we can *try*, and thus may succeed or fail, to suppress or cultivate certain habits and dispositions. Nevertheless, as advertisers rightly assume, media representations can appeal to and cultivate a general attitude that disposes us to act in certain ways. How else could one explain the imitative actions of people in response to particular representations, ranging from advertisements to popular songs and films?[25]

Through prescribing imaginings and identification with certain characters, an audience may increasingly be encouraged to draw pleasure out of the infliction of violence on others who, for whatever reason, are defined as an outgroup and therefore as worthless. Thus our appetites for violent pleasures may not only be condoned and indulged but enlarged. Hence the baser pleasures may increasingly come to dominate our imaginative understanding of the world in general.[26] Typically concomitant with this is the proscription of our imaginative sympathies for those who are the subjects of the violence. That is, to indulge and cultivate the pleasure derived from the infliction of violence, our imaginative sympathies and understanding of those subjected to it are precluded.

At a very simplistic level although our sensitivities to the infliction of violence are cultivated in one aspect—to derive pleasure from it—our sensitivity for those suffering is precluded. Of course, we may experience a much more complex reaction to violence than this. First, the genre within which violence is depicted will obviously shape our response. For example, showing the violence and horrors of war may play an important part in reporting on the nature of aid-relief efforts in Somalia or genocide in Rwanda. Showing the nature of massacres and injuries inflicted may play a crucial role in providing evidence for the reality of what may be happening. Yet the same photographic image in a wholly different context—say, a magazine devoted to cultivating a delight in death and the horrors of war—may be wholly unacceptable. Even within the realm of the fictional our reaction to a violent act portrayed in a cartoon may sharply diverge from our reaction to the same act depicted in a snuff movie. Nonetheless, even allowing for such complexities, at least certain kinds of violent representations may, minimally, reinforce and deepen a corrupt imaginative understanding of our world. Representations of violence may tend to deaden our moral response to the infliction of violence on those with whom we do not or would not wish to identify. Even in the case of news, the more explicit the depictions of violence and its horrific results, the greater the likelihood that we may become desensitized to the vicious realities involved. But the point applies particularly to cases where difference is depicted as a sufficient criterion for moral disregard or qualifying someone as deserving violent treatment on the basis of, for example, sexual orientation, nationality, class, race, religion, or politics.

Representations of violence are particularly worrying when we consider the increasingly free and easy access that children have to such films,[27] because children, unlike adults, may well have no other experiences of the kinds of events and feelings supposedly represented. Thus they may come to assume that the distortive nature of love, sex, and violence portrayed do, in fact, manifest normal and morally appropriate behavior. The influence of such representations may also be exacerbated not only where the child has no other experiential base with which to compare and evaluate the depictions, but where he is emotionally neglected and thus has no general understanding of related emotions, attitudes, and behavior. Children learn their social and moral behavior primarily by example. If a child's primary example for some of the most fundamental human behaviors consists of representations of violence, then there is something tragically wrong. More generally, the predominant production of films cultivating this kind of pleasure may express fundamental aspects of our social understanding of the nature of sex, love, and violence. Thus the increasing production and enjoyment of such films may be symptomatic of a degenerating culture which positively values the infliction of and fetishization of violence.

A LIBERAL DILEMMA

One consequence of this line of thought is that only those with a sense of the significance and place of others in our world can properly appreciate and judge media representations of violence, whether it be *Unforgiven, Good Fellas,* or

Pulp Fiction. Indeed, even those who possess an adequate moral understanding are not themselves immune to the corruptive aspects of violent representations. After all, though our moral sense may mar the pleasure derived from a representation of violence, it does not wholly dissolve it. Nonetheless, the pleasure should be marred because, at the meta-level, we should recognize that the violent attitudes and behavior represented are undesirable. Thus, given moral understanding, a gratuitously violent representation can only be unconditionally enjoyed as a fantasy—that is, at the cost of severing any putative relation between the prescribed imaginative understanding of the film and one's own understanding of the world. The problem is that, psychologically, we may be unable to sever the suggested relationship and thus be unable to enjoy the representation at all. Alternatively, those whose moral understanding is inadequate may misinterpret how a violent film actually relates to our world. For example, though Eastwood's *Unforgiven* essentially involves violence, it does not prescribe a violent disregard for others as appropriate. Yet spectators whose understanding is dictated by the pleasures that the represented violence affords may misconstrue the imaginative understanding prescribed. Indeed we might explain such a misinterpretation in terms of the perverse desire to wallow in the violence as represented. Thus when we are confronted with a tragic, brutal, and final confirmation of Eastwood's sad descent into nihilism, some spectators might laugh sadistically at the last brutal murder of a helpless, wounded man. The inability of some spectators to distinguish between the understanding promoted by *Unforgiven* and the casual pyrotechnics of violence manifest in films like the *Lethal Weapon* series betrays a worrying inability to perceive what is going on beyond the basic narrative sequence and pleasures afforded by the violent events.

Perhaps the problem is best exemplified by *A Clockwork Orange.* The infliction of extreme, intense, and highly stylized violence portrayed in Stanley Kubrick's film can be enjoyed in its own right and is enhanced by our prescribed identification with Alex and his droogs. Indeed, the power of the film in this regard is, at least in Britain, legendary. Kubrick withdrew the rights for it to be shown in the United Kingdom following a spate of crimes and copycat rapes, mimicking characters and scenes from the film.[28] The problem inheres not just in the representation itself, but also the moral understanding a spectator may bring to bear in his or her engagement with and evaluation of it. The imaginative delights and appeal to baser pleasures in representations of violence is dangerous. The danger lies in both the possible corruption of a preexistent moral understanding and the cultivation of a radically mistaken, immoral understanding of the world and others. This serves to explain precisely why it is that we should be suspicious of violent movies. The problem is not merely one of offense but concerns the age-old Platonic paradox: art's power inheres in its capacity both to enlighten and to corrupt. In a culture increasingly tolerant of the appetite for violence, violent films may not only reflect but cultivate the delight taken in it. What is peculiar about films that indulge and revel in the gratuitous infliction of violence, and sadism generally, is the celebration of this delight.

Where we can rely on an adequate moral understanding, then typically we trust ourselves to enjoy and recognize the pleasures afforded by violent representations for what they are, without allowing our imaginative understanding and actions to be affected. However, where someone's moral understanding is inadequate, then representations of violence may only confirm a tendency to disregard the suffering and well-being of others. Yet just as anorexics cannot recognize the fact that they are dangerously thin, so those devoid of moral sense may not see the necessity for a proper imaginative understanding of and concern for others. Thus, given that some people have a far more developed moral understanding than others, it seems obvious that only those with a sufficiently developed moral understanding should have access to gratuitously violent films, especially those as appealing and subtle as *A Clockwork Orange*.

It might be objected that the conclusions drawn are viciously elitist. Who is to say who possesses an adequate moral understanding or what constitutes gratuitous violence? Of course, when we get down to matters of policy, these are crucial questions. Indeed, it is primarily at this level that considerations of power relations are significant. Yet this shows only that the strongest arguments for minimal censorship lie not in the usual liberal complaint that violent films are harmless, but that legitimizing censorship may often enable the censorship of certain things, in the interests of a particular group, detrimental to justice and democracy.[29]

But such pragmatic considerations do not, in principle, hold against the arguments put forward above. It is rather obvious, especially when we consider children, that there are different levels of understanding. To recognize that this is so is not to be elitist in a vicious sense. After all, when a child steals we do not tell him or her what we actually think about stealing: that stealing is only a *prima facie* wrong and may be justified under certain conditions—for example, to fulfill a stronger *prima facie* duty such as protecting one's family from starvation. Instead, we say that stealing is wrong, that Jesus, Ghandi, or Grandma would not do it, or, even better, tell them a story to show why stealing is wrong. This is not because we are hypocrites. Rather it is because certain explanations are appropriate for different levels of understanding, whether one is dealing with children or with adults.

At a different level, we recognize that some people possess a more highly developed moral understanding than others. Hence we might go to someone for advice, not just because their perspective is different from ours, but because we think they have a wisdom we lack. The problem is that, especially at the lower levels, our moral understanding remains vulnerable to corruption or degeneration—because representations of violence simply cultivate the baser pleasures and because the imaginative understanding prescribed may be radically flawed or too subtle.

Of course, our moral senses are typically in a continual process of development, extending and deepening our moral understanding. Moreover, one of the primary ways of deepening our understanding is through engaging with the multifarious representations of possible and impossible worlds available to us. Hence we must encourage and cultivate the imaginative, critical appreciation of art, film, television, and other media that enable us to interpret our world and understand others. But it also follows that we should protect the most vulnerable, especially children, from exacerbating the baser appetites that representations of violence provoke and satiate. If we fail in this regard, then the corruption of moral understanding and the dissolution of a fully human regard for others is to be laid at civil society's doorstep.

Ideally we should seek to censor violent representations according to the level of understanding the relevant audience is likely to bring to bear in their engagement with it.[30] The freedom of media expression must be qualified by our obligation not to harm both particular individuals and society at large. It follows that filmmakers, program producers, and writers should be concerned to exercise their judgment more in acts of self-censorship. Moreover, the families and groups that constitute civil society should also look to exercise their own discretion. Hence, in the United States, for example, cable television's self-administered voices-against-violence initiative adopted in 1993 should be clearly welcomed.[31] Among the measures developed there was a clear commitment to inform viewers more clearly about the levels of violence in a given program by developing a violence-rating system, as well as an explicit aim to avoid the gratuitous depiction of violence. Such initiatives obviously dovetail nicely with the instalment of a V chip in every television to enable parents to control what their children can and cannot see on television. It is quite reasonable to expect the amount of screen violence to be reduced, for the social benefit of all. But in a culture increasingly accepting of vicious representations of violence, where parents increasingly fail to care for or censor their children's viewing habits and general behavior, and where industry cooperation fails, the state must have a *prima facie* obligation to exercise its powers of censorship. Indeed, we can now make sense of the complaint that the liberal state's failure to censor fails not just the victims of violent crimes, and not just those who perpetrate these crimes, but their families and society at large. Previously the presumed understanding of media representations tended to dismiss such worries altogether. What I have suggested is an account of our imaginative engagement with representations which renders plausible the popular disenchantment with violence in the media, especially where the violence represented promotes a radical misunderstanding of others and the world. It is an insight that strikes at the very heart of the liberal presumption against censorship.

The liberal may, for laudable motives, shy away from such an uncomfortable state of affairs. But it looks a though a failure to censor, at least under certain conditions, may constitute an abrogation of the point and purpose of the state in the first place. It is to allow the very preconditions of a liberal state—security, stability, and tolerance—to be uprooted. Typically the liberal consensus has tended to dismiss popular worries about violence in the media. Hence liberals tend to shrink away from considering any positive obligations there may be to censor the media. Unfortunately the way that we actually engage with and understand media representations suggests otherwise. Rather than perpetuate the rhetorical condemnation of all censorship, this constitutes a dilemma that any mature liberal must confront. It is to this very task that the next chapter is dedicated.

NOTES

1. Mike Ellison, "The Power and the Gory," *The Guardian*, Tuesday, 25 October 1994, Arts Section, p. 5.

2. Judge Morland even went so far as to remark, in his summing-up, "It is not for me to pass judgement on their upbringing, but I suspect that exposure to violent video films may in part be an explanation."

3. There is some doubt as to whether the boys actually saw "Chucky 3," as Martin Barker points out in *The Times Higher*, 3 June 1994, p. 12. Nevertheless, as David James Smith, *The Sleep of Reason* (London: Century, 1994), makes clear, it is at least distinctly possible that both children saw it, given that *Child's Play 3* was the last video rented by the father of one of the boys and that they had free and easy access to the videos that he rented.

4. See, for example, Kenneth R. Clark, "Yes, TV Violence Is Awful, but What's the Cure?" in *Impact of Mass Media*, ed. Ray Eldon Hiebert, 3rd edition (New York: Longman, 1995), pp. 241–244, and Nick Cohen's feature article "The Fear, the Shame, the Guilt," *The Independent*, 21 February 1993, p. 21.

5. See, for example, David Gauntlett, *Moving Experiences: Understanding Television's Influences and Effects* (London: John Libbey, 1995), and Geoffrey Pearson, "Falling Standards: A Short, Sharp History of Moral Decline," in *The Video Nasties*, ed. Martin Barker (London: Pluto, 1984).

6. A classic example is Robert Hodge and David Tripp's *Children and Television* (Oxford: Polity, 1986), which conceives of the construction and interpretation of meaning in semiotic terms. Hodge and Tripp essentially dispute the fixity of signs, arguing that meaning must, in part, be determined by the background codes that children themselves bring to bear. But this is still to remain prey to the notion that all one is engaged in is "reading off" signs from images to get a fix on the world. See Matthew Kieran, "The Impoverishment of Art," *British Journal of Aesthetics 35* (1995): 14–25, for an argument that outlines the inadequacies and corruptive effects that this kind of approach has had in relation to artistic practice.

7. A classic example of *Screen* theory is Jean-Luc Comolli and Jean Narboni's "Cinema/Ideology/Criticism," in *Film Theory and Criticism*, ed. G. Mast, M. Cohen, and L. Braudy (New York: Oxford University Press, 1992), pp. 682–689. David Morley, *The "Nationwide" Audience* (London: British Film Institute, 1980), though foregrounding the engagement of actual viewers and challenging the "textual determinism" of *Screen* theory nevertheless presumes the all pervasive significance of ideology.

8. John Fiske, *Television Culture* (London: Routledge, 1988), p.14.

9. Dr. Adrian Rogers is a founder member and official consultant to the Conservative Family Campaign and is well known in Britain as an aggressive campaigner for family values.

10. Tom Dewe Mathews, *Censored: The Story of Film Censorship in Britain* (London: Chatto and Windus, 1994), p. 289. Martin Barker, "Sex, Violence and Videotape," *Sight and Sound 3 (1993): 10–12*, mistakenly presumes that because demands for censorship have been or are politically motivated it follows that therefore all such complaints must be

11. The idea that intentionality is what distinguishes a mental from a physical state originated with Franz Brentano's *Psychology from an Empirical Standpoint*, vol. 1, ed. O. Kraus, trans. Antos C. Rancurello, D. B. Terrell, and Linda L. McAlister (London: Routledge, Kegan and Paul, 1976). The importance of the subjective aspect of the human world has most recently been foregrounded by Thomas Nagel, *The View From Nowhere* (Oxford: Oxford University Press, 1986).

12. I owe this example to Berys Gaut.

13. Monroe Beardsley, *Aesthetics* (New York: Harcourt, 1958), pp. 426–429, claims falsely, in relation to artworks, that the fact that we value incompatible representations of the world shows that a work's content cannot be significantly related to its intrinsic value.

13. Kendall Walton, *Mimesis as Make-Believe* (Cambridge, MA: Harvard, 1990), argues for the centrality of playing games of make-believe when we engage with representations of any kind. Psychological research that would support such a conception in relation to television includes Jerome L. Singer and Dorothy G. Singer, *Television, Imagination and Aggression* (Hillsdale, NJ: Lawrence Erlbaum, 1981).

15. See Michael D. Slater, "Processing Social Information in Messages: Social Group Familiarity, Fiction versus Nonfiction, and Subsequent Beliefs," *Communication Research 17* (1990): 327–343.

16. Noël Carroll, *The Philosophy of Horror* (New York: Routledge, 1990), pp. 88–96, wrongly marginalizes the importance of character identification on the basis that the criteria for such identification are too strong. But character identification cannot be, *pace* Carroll, the exact simulation of every thought, feeling, and sensation in every respect. Apart from anything else, the intentional gaze of the identifier is obviously other-directed, while that of the person being identified with is self-regarding. Identification with another, through imaginative simulation, can hardly require the simulation of another's states in *every* respect.

17. See *Natural Theories of Mind*, ed. Andrew Whiten (Oxford: Blackwell, 1991), for recent developments in contemporary psychological research that suggest the primary importance of mental simulation in attempting to understand others.

18. Dilys Powell, ed. C. Cook, *The Dilys Powell Film Reader* (Oxford: Oxford University Press, 1991), p. 221.

19. See Carroll, *The Philosophy of Horror*, pp. 159–194.

20. M. J. Apter, *Reversal Theory: Motivation, Emotion and Personality* (London: Routledge, 1989), reviews recent psychological research that underwrites the fact that, under certain circumstances, we can and do enjoy what is otherwise typically unpleasant. See also Berys Gaut, "The Paradox of Horror," *British Journal of Aesthetics, 33* (1993): 339–344.

21. Roger Scruton, *Art and Imagination* (London: Routledge, 1981), pp. 89–98, argues for something like this kind of distinction on the basis that imagining necessarily goes beyond belief.

22. See, for example, David Buckingham, *Children and Television: An Overview of the Research* (London: British Film Institute, 1987), and Martin Barker, *The "Video Violence" Debate: Media Researchers Respond* (April 1994), School of Cultural Studies, University of the West of England. It is important to recognize that even those researchers who argue that there is some kind of link between video violence and behavior admit that the experimental evidence remains inconclusive. See, for example, Elizabeth Newsome's report, *Video Violence and the Protection of Children* (March 1994), Child Development Research Unit, University of Nottingham.

23. See Haejung Paik and George Comstock, "The Effects of Television Violence on Antisocial Behavior: A Meta-Analysis," *Communication Research 21* (1994): 516–546.

24. The presumption that our understanding and evaluations wholly determine our actions must be false given the phenomena of temptation and weakness of will. As Plato recognized,

because of our nonrational appetites, *pace* Socrates, we may be tempted to act in ways despite what we know or understand to be the case. See Plato, *The Republic*, trans. D. Lee (Harmondsworth: Penguin, 1974), Book IV, Section 2, 439a–439d, pp. 209–217.

25. An infamous advertising case in the United Kingdom concerns a Tango ad that had to be taken off the air precisely because children were imitating it. The ad portrayed a large orange man slamming his hands against the ears of a child in the playground. Unfortunately this became a playground craze, resulting in severe deafness in some cases. Such cases are hardly new or particular to film or television—after all, Goethe's morbidly sentimental *Werther* reportedly induced widespread melancholia and a rash of suicides.

26. The base pleasures are so called because they remain independent of our evaluation of them. The exacerbation and dominance of the life of appetites over reason resembles the Calliclean conception of the good life as articulated in Plato's *Gorgias*, trans. D. J. Zeyl (Indianapolis, IN: Hackett, 1987), 491e–1.492c, pp. 64–65.

27. The case of cinema censorship is, practically speaking, more straightforward than that of video censorship in one crucial regard. Namely, film viewing can be controlled by age restrictions and admissions policies. Video and television pose a particularly acute problem precisely because so many children have free and easy access to highly "adult" videos and cable networks.

28. See Mathews, *Censored*, pp. 208–210, for a typical account, which labels those who would attempt to link such actions with the film as indulging in "the easy excuse rather than the complex explanation."

29. Classic examples of such censorship range from Eisenstein's classic *Battleship Potemkin,* banned for obvious political reasons all over the Western world and in the United Kingdom from 1926 to 1954, to the prolific use made of the libel laws by Robert Maxwell to cover up his fraudulent business practices.

30. See Judith Van Evra, *Television and Child Development* (London: Lawrence Erlbaum, 1990), pp. 3–28, and Catherine N. Doubleday and Kristin L. Droege, "Cognitive Developmental Influences on Children's Understanding of Television," in *Children and Television*, ed. G. L. Berry and J. K. Asamen (Newbury Park, CA: Sage, 1993), pp. 23–37, for arguments based on psychological research to suggest that a child's level of development is a strong determinant of how he or she interprets and responds to television.

31. The initiative was constituted by "a comprehensive set of initiatives to deglamorize violence on television; to allow parents to better know and control what their children may be watching; and generally to reduce the level of violence seen on television." See *Voices Against Violence: A Cable Television Initiative*, p. 1, produced by the National Cable Television Association, Washington, DC.

7 *Harm, Offense,
and Media Censorship*

INTRODUCTION

The foundation of any liberal conception of the law is the presumption that the mere immorality of a particular act, whatever it is, cannot justify any legal proscription against it,[1] for the point and purpose of the liberal state is to maintain the rights and just conditions required for individuals to lead their lives as they freely choose. This includes the right to act immorally as long as such acts do not harm or infringe the rights of others. So the main justification for outlawing certain kinds of activities concerns the condition of harm to others.[2] Hence murder or torture is illegal because it involves taking the life of another or inflicting pain on a person without his or her consent. We should also note, however, that the harm condition is not a sufficient condition to outlaw an activity. For example, protecting people's right to travel by car leads to harm: if we allow cars on the road, a certain number of people will be maimed or killed on the road each year.[3] Of course, a liberal state may, through traffic regulations and prohibitions against drunken driving, do all it can to minimize the number of people harmed in this way. Nonetheless, the state protects the fundamental right of the individual to choose how to lead his or her life and thus how to travel, even in the knowledge that harm may result.

We have seen that we have some reason to believe that certain kinds of news reports, programs, pornography, and violent films may harm people. This gives us some reason to consider whether they should be censored or not. But even if harm is involved, further argument is required to justify censorship. Furthermore, the question of offense is often thought to legitimate censorship. Hence films that are sexually indecent or explicit or obscenely violent may perhaps be censored even where no harm is involved. Essentially there are two distinct grounds for holding to this claim. The first involves construing certain kinds of offense as a form of harm; if certain programs or publications are both public and offensive, then their offensiveness may count as a kind of harm. The second variant holds that to take account of the harm condition is itself overly restrictive—it must be supplemented by the principle that the offensiveness of an activity can constitute grounds for prohibiting it.

THE CASE AGAINST CENSORSHIP

Before proceeding to consider the arguments against censorship, we need to make a basic distinction. We are concerned with state censorship, which involves coercion by the state to prevent or withhold the publication or broadcasting of particular opinions, images, or films. This is to be distinguished from instances of self-censorship, where a paper or network organization decides to censor or withhold a news report or film for reasons that may range from the purely commercial to judgments concerning taste and decency. This is an important distinction. There may be cases where broadcasting a certain report or film is morally unjustifiable, and hence it would be morally correct for an editor or corporation to remove it from the schedules. Nonetheless, if the program is not pulled, the state may still not be justified in exercising its powers of censorship; as we shall see, there are good grounds for holding that the evil of state censorship may be greater than the evil that would result from allowing unethical reporting or broadcasting.

Given the liberal presumption that a just state is one that protects and enables its citizens to lead their lives as they choose, the arguments against censorship are very strong indeed. Perhaps the best articulation of these arguments, both negative and positive, are to be found in John Stuart Mill's *On Liberty*.[4] Censorship constitutes an attack on the autonomy of the state's citizens, undercutting the rationale that justifies the state's rule and authority, because it involves measures whose very aim is to prevent opposing opinions from being heard and, as such, these measures are objectionable. This holds irrespective of the truth, falsity, or implausibility of opinions proffered and no matter how offensive they may be.

To start with, newspaper reports, billboard advertisements, television programs, and films should not be censured, because even if they proffer false views, censoring them would prevent us from understanding why what is true is in fact the case.[5] Consider, for example, the case of the Holocaust, or the recent controversy over intelligence and race.[6] Many people are inclined to think that reports, books, and programs that claim that the Holocaust never happened or that Blacks are naturally less intelligent than Caucasians ought to be censored; in both cases, what is being claimed is an explicit denial—in some cases motivated by racial hatred   of what we all take to be obviously true. The mere articulation of such falsehoods, it is often thought, viciously perpetuates such pernicious views.

But if the articulation of such views were banned, then we would not be motivated to think about the evidential and rational basis for claiming that, for example, the Holocaust did occur, and we thus would be less likely to understand it. It would merely be held as a dead dogma or prejudice, among many others, rather than a belief that we understand and can rationally justify. Claims should be subjected to the light of evidence and reason and not merely understood as the assertion of conflicting prejudices, where mere weight of numbers determines what should be believed. Moreover, even if we do know the evidence and rational grounds for a particular belief, we should always remain open to the possibility that there are grounds for holding different beliefs. If we fail to remain open to this possibility, grounds given for holding to our own would be far weaker. Hence we should be able to see why someone is tempted to think, on the basis of IQ studies, that Blacks are naturally less intelligent than Caucasians. We should then be able to point both to better grounds for holding our own view and to an explanation as to why the evidence offered against us does not really count as such or is minimal in weight. Thus our own understanding of what is true is thereby deepened, and we can give better reasons to others to persuade them rationally to agree with us.

This naturally leads us onto the second argument that Mill gives against censorship: many prejudices and dogmas that we presume to be true often turn out, due to human fallibility, to be entirely false. If views are censored on the presumption that they are false, then we would never find out which views are in fact true, only partially true, or completely false. Thus not only would our knowledge about the world not increase, but, significantly, many things that we ought to know would never be found out.[7] If Galileo had been successfuly censored by the Catholic Church, our understanding of the universe would have been poorer for hundreds of years to come. Similarly, if journalists had been prevented from publishing evidence that showed that many people tried by McCarthy's commission in the 1950s were not communists, then perhaps the injustices perpetrated would never have come to light. Thus the dubious nature of McCarthy's commission would not have been exposed, and people would have been more likely to believe, falsely, that Hollywood itself was a haven for communists whose sole aim was to subvert the American way of life.[8] In an uncritical culture, where the freedom of expression is constrained by the state, political corruption, vicious elitism, and the perpetuation of false myths and prejudices are far more likely to flourish.

Of course, it is more usually the case that most newspaper reports or television programs contain partial accounts of what is the case, rather than either the complete truth or utter falsehoods. But by silencing those who dissent from received or majority opinion on a matter, we sacrifice the possibility of getting at a more complete version of the truth. Had the news reports issuing from West nam from 1962 onward, which certainly contained elements of truth, been effectively censored, as both the military and the White House increasingly wished they were, then the progress toward a more complete account of the true state of affairs in Vietnam and the nature of U.S. involvement would not have become clear.[10]

The third argument Mill gives is that the censorship of certain views by the state tends to be self-defeating.[11] The point of censorship is, presumably, to prevent pernicious views being aired and thus gaining credence. This is very often quite difficult to do, as can be seen from the British government's censorship of IRA and Sinn Fein spokesmen in the 1980s. For the media still interviewed IRA and Sinn Fein figures but broadcast their views using actors' voices instead. But even if such censorship could be effective, the main problem remains, for where governments censor a particular view, then the public are not free to assess whether or not the view has any substance. Hence, quite naturally, we are inclined to think that there may well be something to what is being said and that the censorship is, really, a form of unjustified persecution. If there really were no credence in the view expressed, then surely the government would not be afraid of it being broadcast for us to assess and reject. Naturally, then, the censorship of a view tends to lend it, falsely, a certain possible weight and credence. Better to have a false and pernicious view out in the open where it can be assessed on its own merits by the public than allow it to gain unwarranted credence through the act of censorship. It is self-defeating to use the purported truth of a government's position as the basis for silencing contradictory ones; by silencing opposing opinions, governments destroy the credibility of their own.

It is important to recognize, in the three considerations raised above, that Mill is not endorsing a crude form of relativism that holds that all opinions are equally good. The force of these considerations arises precisely because some opinions are better than others—they are more coherent, consistent, informative, and faithful to the empirical facts of the case than others. Rather, the point is that only in a free society are we ever likely to arrive at better, more complete, and truer opinions. Only through testing our opinions against those of others and being called to justify them, where we are free from coercion, can we expect to progress toward understanding the truth of the matter.[12] Hence the media have certain rights and privileges, which arise from their duties as the fourth estate, to provide the public with the information, opinions, and debate required to enable members of the public to judge for themselves as individuals and citizens what it is they want and why.

Another important argument Mill gives is the beneficial side-effect to society as a whole of allowing everyone, including vociferously opposed minorities, to have their say without fear of being silenced by the state.[13] Imagine a society where a small minority thought that the prevalent social structures were deeply iniquitous. If a government suppresses the expression of that view through censorship, then the resentment of that minority will be much stronger than if they had freely been allowed to air their grievances and had open to them the possibility of persuading others of their point of view. Since they are effectively denied a voice in the political and civil culture of their society, the implication is that they are not worthy of equal concerns as fellow citizens. In such circumstances the minority group will obviously feel marginalized and alienated from society as a whole. Hence they are more likely to detach themselves from society and possibly attempt to subvert the existing social structures in harmful, violent ways. By contrast, if those in a minority group are free to speak and thus have the opportunity to put their views forward, they are far more likely to continue to identify themselves with society as a whole, because they are able to participate in and contribute to a debate about the justice and good of that society and their place within it. Both the minority group's and society's self-development and integrity are thus maintained.

The last argument Mill raises against censorship is, in effect, a negative one, but no less powerful for all that.[14] Even where we consider censorship to be justified in a particular case, say to protect national welfare, the legitimization of it in one specific instance may lead to censorship in illegitimate areas, which would be very damaging indeed. We may recognize that a state within which there is no censorship is far from ideal. After all, the commitment to freedom of expression, in the name of the public interest, is often used by the media as a cynical camouflage to justify the coverage of stories that bear no relation to the public interest whatsoever and may harm the lives of those whom the story concerns. Revealing that a one-time celebrity such as Arthur Ashe suffers from AIDS or giving the name of a rape victim may lead to great suffering and harm for the individuals concerned. Similarly, a report that reveals secret U.S. foreign policy goals may result in harm to the national interest. Nonetheless, a law designed to legitimate state censorship in such cases could be far more harmful to everyone. For such a law to be workable, it would have to be a very blunt, crude instrument. Thus it would end up legitimating censorship in all sorts of areas that could never be justified and would result in very great harm indeed. The public interest may then be used, illegitimately, to justify the censorship of cases of injustice, whether at the individual or state level, that we should know about. For example, had the U.S. government been permitted to censor investigative programs on the grounds of public interest, it is possible that the events surrounding the Iran–Contra affair would never have come to light.

However, despite the strength of Mill's arguments against censorship, we do tend to think that, in certain cases at least, censorship is clearly justifiable. With regard to state or public security it does seem that the state can legitimately withhold or prevent the publication of certain information. For example, imagine that the press corps in the Gulf War acquired the plans detailing the Allies' projected attack against Saddam Hussein's forces. Clearly, if the information were published before the battle, the Allies would face countermeasures from Saddam Hussein and possibly defeat. Assuming that the war itself was just and that the lives of many Allied troops were at stake, if a paper attempted to publish the Allies' battle plans, the government would be justified in censoring the report concerned because, for the germane period up to and including the attack, this information should be withheld from the public arena. By parity of reasoning, the same point applies to intra-state security operations; we tend to think that were a television program about to broadcast details of a projected FBI swoop on a group of terrorists, the government, in the name of the public interest, would be justified in censoring it.

Furthermore, we tend to think that censorship is justifiable not only in cases where the public interest or lives are at stake. Certain individuals are, under particular circumstances, justified in demanding state protection that may involve media censorship. Imagine the case of a woman who has been raped, has reported it to the police, but has clearly expressed the wish for her identity to be protected. By chance or police error, a reporter manages to work out the exact identity and address of the victim and writes a report giving her details. If the story were to be published, not only would the woman's wishes clearly not have been respected, but her life may well be harmed in a number of ways. Her family, friends, neighbors—even strangers in her hometown and elsewhere—will find out that she was the victim. Thus they may pass judgment on her and treat her in all sorts of distressing and possibly damaging ways (which they would not otherwise have done), without even knowing more than the details outlined in the report. Furthermore, her life itself may become the object of media attention and harassment in any manner of unpleasant and unnecessary ways. It seems clear, in such a case, that we would think it legitimate for the government to step in and prevent her personal details from being published.

The third kind of area where we often think state censorship is justified concerns instances of vitriolic racist reports, programming, and films. This is not to deny Mill's general point that, as a matter of principle, all views should be allowed expression in a liberal state. Nonetheless where the expression of certain views, in this case violently racist ones, will probably lead to harm to others, they should be censored, for the fundamental justification of the liberal state is to protect—including protection from harm—the conditions required for all to live their lives freely. As Mill himself recognized, where the context and expression of a certain view is such that it has a serious chance of leading to harm, then the state is justified in censoring that view: "Even opinions lose their immunity when the circumstances in which they are expressed are such as to constitute their expression a positive instigation to some mischievous act."[15]

For example, if a particular Ku Klux Klan rally in the deep south is likely to lead to violence against local Blacks then, in the name of protecting the latter from harm, the state may justifiably step in and prevent the rally from going ahead. Opinions that, through their expression in a particular way or due to circumstance, are likely to cause harm to others may freely be censored by the state.

Although a lot more needs to be said about these considerations, what they do point us toward is a legitimate basis for claiming that, in certain prescribed instances, state censorship may not only be permissible but obligatory. True, even where there is no long-term benefit from broadcasting a particular view, and even where there may be possible social costs, the initial position is that the program should be permitted since the expression of political, social, or moral views can only further rather than hinder the development of a free society. Nonetheless, state censorship is only a *prima facie* wrong. Where a news report or the broadcasting of a certain kind of program is likely to result in serious harm to others, the state may justifiably exercise its powers of censorship to protect the freedom of all to lead their lives as they wish, free from harm. Where there is no probable threat of serious harm, views, programs, or films should not be censored, because this would constitute an assault on our freedom of speech and thus on the kind of free society required for us to live our lives as we so choose.

THE HARM CONDITION

However, the argument sketched out in favor of justifiable censorship, on the grounds of harm, needs to be more carefully filled in. The first issue that needs to be addressed is just what constitutes the notion of "harm." Intuitively, it seems like a fairly clear notion, because we can all cite actions such as murder, torture, and injury which involve the unwanted annihilation of life or infliction of pain. But if we examine the notion further, it seems slightly vague. Consider, to use Anthony Ellis's argument, the case of rape.[16] Typically, rape involves the infliction of obvious harm through vicious physical violence. But violence is a contingent feature of rape and not intrinsic to it. It is not just the violence that may be involved that makes rape objectionable (though where the rape is violent, the wrong of the action is compounded). Of course, rape may traumatize victims in such a way that their capacity to form meaningful sexual relations in the future is deeply marred. But this is far from necessarily the case.

Where no violence or traumatization is involved, and even though the victim feels abused and unhappy, this does not clearly fall within our intuitive notion of harm at all. Nonetheless, we do consider rape to be deeply harmful. Hence we have laws against it and punishments that reflect the serious nature of the wrong done. What this tells us is that harm is not reducible to the amount of violence or gratuitous pain inflicted, but that we can be harmed in far deeper, more subtle ways. Hence our understanding of just what constitutes harm should be broadened out.

One possible way of extending our intuitive notion of harm is to consider something to be harmful if and only if it mars, constrains, or abuses someone's interests. Hence *The Williams Report* suggests that, "Laws against public sex would generally be thought to be consistent with the harm condition, in the sense that if members of the public are upset, distressed, disgusted, outraged, or put out by witnessing some class of acts, then that constitutes a respect in which the public performance of those acts harms their interests."[17]

But how, exactly, are our interests harmed if we are disgusted, outraged, or "put out" by something? What we should focus on here is the intrinsic link between where our interests lie and our desires.[18] Our interests are harmed not just where our capacities are marred, as in the case of physical injury or the sexual traumatization that may result from rape; they may also be harmed where something frustrates certain fundamental desires that we may have. In the case of a rape that does not involve injury or traumatization, our interests are still harmed because our desire not to have sex with a person is ignored. Similarly, if we are forced against our wishes to look at pornographic, violent, or obscene images, then perhaps our interests have been harmed. Thus, consistent with the harm condition, we may have a justifiable reason for wanting such images legally prohibited.

But this is far too quick. Normally we think that only in certain kinds of cases does the frustration of a desire count as a harm. In the case of rape, the desire frustrated and abused is one that is intimately bound up with our identity and autonomy as a person. Conversely, the display of a pornographic billboard advertisement or the broadcast of a gratuitously violent movie is not tied to our fundamental identity or autonomy as a person at all. We may desire that other people should not see or watch such things, but we are ourselves free to look away or turn the television set off.

This distinction is far from arbitrary since the point of the harm condition, and thus of legislation with respect to it, is to protect and sustain the conditions required for meaningful choice. For individuals to function and develop in society, we require a level of public order, stability, tolerance, and protection from physical coercion and theft. So we should construe "harm" in terms of what is required to sustain these things. Something that is destructive of these conditions, whether public or private, constitutes a harm. Hence rape—irrespective of the degree of violence or traumatization caused—really does constitute a harm, whereas airing views or images that are offensive to some does not. In the latter case we are free to ignore whatever is proffered us. In the case of rape, the victim has no choice. Thus only those activities that directly constrain the lives of others should be prohibited. This certainly gets us some way toward, and makes sense of, the underlying justification for traffic regulations, parking restrictions, or nuisance laws, since prohibited activities such as these have the effect of undermining the choices open to others.

In relation to the media, we can thus make sense of the importance of libel laws prohibiting and compensating for character defamation. After all, our material prosperity, our capacity to function in our jobs, our social and self-image which depends on our personal reputation, and our ability to live our lives as we would choose are intimately bound up with such considerations. If a newspaper wrongly slanders a doctor's character and ability, he may be sacked; through the resultant consequences including unemployment, a lack of trust in him by his future patients, and a wary attitude towards him by his friends and colleagues, his own self-image may suffer in innumerable and undeserved ways.

Nonetheless, the sphere of legislation appropriate under the harm condition remains relatively narrow, for something can only be a harm where it is motivated by or constitutes an attack on or constriction of an individual's autonomy. Hence the frustration of many desires that we have will not count as a harm at all. The prohibition of media and programs that offend against social customs or majority moral or religious views is clearly ruled out. Such a prohibition would not protect the prerequisites of individual autonomy but, rather, constitutes an attack on it.

This is not to deny that certain groups definitely wish, on moral grounds, that obscene images, pornographic or violent movies, and blasphemous programs should not be shown. That such images are displayed or programs shown does actually frustrate their preference. But this cannot constitute a harm. The immorality, obscenity, or blasphemous nature of an image, and the frustration of moral preferences, cannot count against its legality. It is perfectly understandable why certain people regard pornographic films, gratuitously violent dramatic reconstructions, or Salman Rushdie's *The Satanic Verses* as blasphemous or obscene. Indeed, we might even agree with them. But such frustration cannot count as a harm, because the liberal state should not prohibit or censor on moralistic grounds. After all, most people usually prefer others not to do what they themselves consider to be immoral. Puritans would, for moral and religious reasons, undoubtably prefer that people did not go out dancing or shopping on Sundays. But the frustration of what they wish that other people would do is not a harm. Prohibition would be to constrain rather than protect the preconditions required for individual choice.

OFFENSE AS HARM

However, in emphasizing the significance of distress and disgust, *The Williams Report* may be pointing toward the idea that the very suffering of deeply unpleasant feelings that are characteristic in the case of offense perhaps itself constitutes a harm. But we need to be clear about the notion of offense underlying the claim.[19]

In one sense, to offend someone is merely to annoy them. If I swear at someone or spit in the street, people may be annoyed by what I have done and resentful that I should treat them or the public walkway in such a manner. Similarly, I may be annoyed that the youth of today should go around looking so untidy and slovenly. But since offense in this sense merely concerns my annoyance, there are no grounds for considering it a form of harm. I may be annoyed and disgusted for all sorts of reasons, many of which may reflect my own peculiarities rather than anything essentially harmful about what has been done

There must be something more to the notion of offense involved if this line of thought is to be worth considering. Of course, if the annoyance itself were to create the serious risk of imminent disorder then the liberal state may have to step in. For example, the state may ban a Ku Klux Klan march through a Black area because of the likelihood of riots and resultant loss of life. But this is motivated not by the condition of annoyance provoked but by the requirement to protect people's lives.

A more substantial notion of offense is that of moral disgust or outrage, which is what obscenity gives rise to. Offense in this sense is not reducible to whether actual feelings of disgust or repulsion are felt; rather, something is deemed to be offensive in this sense because there is something fundamentally morally offensive or repugnant about the image or program concerned. So we can claim that something is obscene without ourselves actually experiencing any feeling of disgust, repulsion, or loathing. For example, we may claim that the display of nude women in newspapers, as in the case of *The Sun*, the gratuitous violence of Oliver Stone's *Natural Born Killers*, or the portrayal of sexuality in Nagisa Oshima's *In the Realm of the Senses* are degrading because they exploit women, or demean human life, or demean human sexuality, respectively, but we may do this without necessarily feeling any disgust ourselves. Essentially this is to express a moral judgment about the nature of the image or the program and the way we are prescribed to understand what is being depicted. Prohibition on these grounds, then, would clearly be motivated by the claim of offending against a particular moral view or principle and is thus inconsistent with the harm condition.

But there is a further sense of "offense" that captures the kinds of experiences that we may suffer when repelled by something—namely, deeply unpleasant emotions of abhorrence, loathing, anger, or repulsion. So the thought might be that people have a right, in line with the harm condition, to be protected from the constitutively unpleasant feelings of outrage and disgust rather than merely seeking to enforce particular moral judgments on others. After all, we think we have a right to be protected from being made to feel fearful or anxious by physical intimidation or stalking.

Yet, first, not everyone finds the feelings of fear, repulsion, and disgust unpleasant. After all, if this really were the case then the activities of mountain-climbing, car-racing, going to horror movies, or, indeed, watching very violent films would be unintelligible. For the most part such activities are not enjoyed merely because of the pay-offs involved—from looking out on beautiful scenery, competitively testing one's driving skills against others, to learning about what we find most frightening about the human condition. They are also enjoyed because of the elements of fear and loathing intrinsic to such activities.[20] Mountain climbers and racing-car drivers talk of the thrill of fear, which depends on the possibility of death, and moviegoers often complain that a film just was not horrific or violent enough. So an image or program that gives rise to feelings of disgust may actually delight and be enjoyed by some or indeed many people. Hence, as long as we have a choice of whether or not to see the images and programs that disgust some people but delight others, there can be no law prohibiting them consistent with the harm condition.

Second, and more fundamentally, even if an image actually does disgust nearly everybody, this cannot constitute a good reason for prohibiting it. The question to be asked is this: just why do the unpleasant feelings of disgust arise in the first place? Presumably such feelings are thought to result from a moral or aesthetic judgment about the heinous, obscene nature of the image concerned. For example, the feeling or horror we might feel at Bennetton's exploitation of the image of a man dying of AIDS for one of their advertising campaigns is the proper expression of one's firm judgment that such an image is or embodies a commercial trivialization of the plight of the individual concerned and the fate of those suffering from AIDS generally. In other words, we judge the image to be morally pernicious. But, as has already been argued above, the frustration of desires concerning what others ought to see and do cannot constitute a harm. Feelings, no matter how unpleasant, cannot count as harmful if they are, in essence, the expression of a moral view.

Still, we could make a possible reply by making a further distinction between mere offense and indecency. What *The Williams Report* seemed to be getting at was the essentially public character of something that gives rise to moral feelings of disgust and outrage. Many things that we would consider indecent and offensive if they were they uttered or proclaimed publicly are not considered offensive in private at all. As Hart puts it: "Homosexual intercourse between consenting adults in private is immoral according to conventional morality, though not an affront to public decency, though it would be both if it took place in public. But the fact that the same act, if done in public, could be regarded both as immoral and as an affront to public decency must not blind us to the difference between these two aspects of conduct."[21]

Thus perhaps it is the public indecency of an image, independently of whether it causes offense to some or many, that constitutes grounds for prohibiting it. I take it that indecency is committed when an image or act that should essentially be considered private is displayed in public where others cannot but help see it.

However, views as to which acts or images are only appropriate for private indulgence is itself a moral stance. For example, sex is typically held to be an essentially private matter and not something that should be displayed for public spectacle and consumption. Hence the public display of sexually explicit images, from billboards to magazines, is typically regarded as indecent and, at least in some, arouses feelings that they would rather not have. But this stance depends on a particular, moral understanding of the proper aim of human sexual relations and activities, because if sex is to be properly understood as an essentially private communion between two souls, then the public display of it is indecent. But then the public indecency depends on a moral judgment concerning the appropriate sphere for certain kinds of images and activities. Offense caused by public indecency provides, for the liberal, no good grounds for prohibition, because the offense arises from a moral understanding and evaluation of the object concerned.

THE PRINCIPLE OF OFFENSE

The second kind of argument for censorship does not claim that certain kinds of offense constitute a harm. Rather, it suggests that we ought to supplement the harm condition with the principle of offense. The offensiveness of an opinion, image, or film may provide grounds for censoring it. So we should always ask whether expressing a view on television, placing a particular billboard advertisement, or broadcasting a certain film offends those who have not sought it out and, moreover, whether they could reasonably have avoided it.[22] If an image is both offensive and cannot reasonably be avoided, then this provides grounds for censoring it.

It is crucial to recognize that the importance of offense here is not supposed to derive from its expression of a moral judgment. Rather, censorship on such grounds aims to protect the public from opinions, images, and programs that can justifiably be regarded as an unreasonable nuisance. Dropping litter, spitting in the street, obscene billboard advertisements, offensive talk-shows, or the predominance of sexually lewd or violent movies on television ought to be constrained because, for many exposed to them at least, they constitute a nuisance.

Now is it reasonable to consider such things a nuisance and thus prohibit them. In the case of a man who compulsively swears and spits, we are either objecting because of the threat to public hygiene or because his manners are appalling. If such behavior really does constitute a threat to public hygiene, then under the harm condition we have good grounds for prohibiting such behavior. But if it merely constitutes an affront to social manners, then the grounds for prohibition are weak, indeed weaker than if the offense were based on a moral judgment: manners are merely a social convention, whereas morals concern what is good in a way significantly independent of particular social conventions.

A more important kind of offense involves the gratuitous display of contempt for and insult to others' deeply held values. For example, if I walk around with the insignia of the Ku Klux Klan, this will give deep offense to many because of its associations with the barbarity toward and vicious murders of many Blacks in the Deep South. Moreover, this may be compounded where my wearing of the insignia is not a matter of naive ignorance but motivated by the deliberate intention to insult Blacks. My aim is to flaunt the attitude that Blacks are worthy of little human consideration and thereby to rile as many Blacks as I come into contact with. But it is not yet clear that this gives sufficient grounds for the prohibition of such behavior, unless it is likely to lead to a serious breach of the peace, which falls under the harm condition. The offense, as such, is based on moral outrage and thus cannot constitute grounds for prohibition. Consider, by analogy, posters advertising Gay Pride with two men kissing, or a gay talk-show deliberately setting out to offend and provoke orthodox Christians. Although in the latter the deliberate intent to cause offense is morally heinous, nonetheless the offense caused and the nuisance felt by orthodox Christians springs from a moral judgment concerning the blasphemous and immoral nature of the stance being advocated. The mere fact that an opinion, image, or program offends a particular moral or religious sensibility cannot constitute grounds for restriction or censorship.

Lastly, there is the idea that certain kinds of offense are indecent and lead to unpleasant feelings of embarrassment, shame, and repulsion. Of course, for the argument to work, the notion of indecency here had better be distinct from the one canvassed above—namely, that something is indecent because it is the (morally) inappropriate display of something that should remain private. But an interesting account of indecency has been suggested by Joel Feinberg. Immorality may exacerbate the indecent nature of what is expressed, but indecency is the public display of something that is inherently unpleasant to observe, hear, or come across. Public nudity, for example, is embarrassing since it draws the eye and provokes thoughts that are normally repressed. "The conflict between these attracting and repressing forces is exciting, upsetting, and anxiety producing . . . the result is not mere 'offense,' but a kind of psychic jolt that in many people can be a painful wound. Even those of us who are better able to control our feelings might well resent the nuisance of having to do so."[23] We may, Feinberg claims, justifiably demand protection from this kind of unpleasantness.

Now the inherent unpleasantness of an image, say, had better not amount to the claim that it is an affront to accepted social or moral norms, because there may be nothing inherently unpleasant about confronting certain norms. For example, Neil Jordan's *The Crying Game* certainly tests many people's normal evaluative assumptions about transsexuals and the nature of romantic love but is not, itself, an unpleasant film. What may be identified as unpleasant or uncomfortable is the positive evaluation of a complex relationship which challenges most people's normative assumptions about sexual love. But then this is to move back to offense arising from moral judgments. So the unpleasantness of an image, program, or film cannot lie in its abrogation of standard social or moral norms.

Indecency arises from the intrinsically unpleasant nature of the image, program, or film concerned. A particularly grotesque image of a corpse or a sexually explicit program may provoke us to attend to and contemplate certain conflicting emotions and thoughts that we find deeply distressing and painful to cope with. Why this stressful conflict arises in different people may vary, from the thought that contemplation of such an image is itself immoral to the frustration at having certain desires provoked without the possibility of acting on them. Whatever the reason for such conflict, it is the inner conflict and stress caused by the image or program concerned that makes it unpleasant. We have a right to be protected from such unpleasant turmoil where it is caused or determined by others rather than ourselves.

Yet, first, as Ellis points out, it is not clear that we actually desire, let alone need, such protection. A sexually alluring image may not just give rise to conflicting emotions but may afford great delight. Human life would be all the more impoverished if we were to attempt, unrealistically, to do away with all spontaneous thoughts and emotions caused by the expression of certain views, the display of certain images, or the broadcasting of certain films. Second, inner conflict and stress arise from all sorts of things over which we have no control ourselves, and which we would not consider ought to be prohibited. Certain people become very vexed at the intrinsically unpleasant nature of certain youth cultures, from punk to grunge, but it would be ridiculous to prohibit them (not to mention well-nigh unenforceable). Similarly, watching cringingly dreadful films may cause deep embarrassment and vexation, but it would be ridiculous to prohibit them. Lastly, the display of certain images or programs, from nude bodies to boxing promotions, may give rise to vexed and conflicting thoughts and desires. If we thought them immoral, we obviously would wish that people did not delight in such images or activities. But the cost of enacting and enforcing a law to prohibit either of them, for the reasons Mill gives, would be so high as to far outweigh any particular inconvenience or conflict that we might feel.

As Ellis argues, the reason the offense caused in such cases is significant is because our attitude to indecency has a moral aspect to it. Yet, according to liberalism, moral judgments have no business influencing what, legally speaking, is or is not permissible. The law is there to protect our capacity to lead our lives as we so choose—and that includes, unless harm to others is involved, the possibility of choosing to do, watch, or express that which is immoral.

OFFENSE AND INDIRECT HARM

However, Ellis's conclusion rests on the failure to see the force of a crucial distinction. The claim is that views, images, and programs that lead to, or are likely to result in, direct harm to particular individuals may justifiably be censored. Hence, for example, we can justifiably ban a Ku Klux Klan march through, images in, or programming directed at a Black area if riots are likely to break out and the march is likely to lead to the direct harming of particular individuals. But significant harm need not be direct in this sense at all, for we can be harmed—quite significantly—in ways that are much more insidious and indirect.

Consider, at the individual level, the nature of gossip and slander. If someone gossips behind my back, this may not lead to any direct harm at all. Nonetheless, it may significantly affect how my friends, colleagues, and clients come to treat me in the future. They may be less likely to trust my professional abilities; hence my ability to develop myself in my job is clearly harmed, promotion is less likely to come my way, and my position in the office may be challenged at every step so that eventually I feel unable to function at all and am forced to leave. Similarly, my friends may suddenly become less trusting, the kinds of confidences and activities that we had enjoyed up until recently are suddenly cut short, and I become excluded from the friendships that I had previously enjoyed. Both at a professional and personal level, gossip can clearly harm me, even where I am not aware of it. Moreover it is important to see that such gossip can be harmful even where it is not clearly slanderous and thus based on falsehoods. The malicious gossip may not make any false claims about my actions or things I have or have not said. A clever gossip would be unlikely to be so obvious, since he or she is more likely to be challenged and less likely to be believed; rather, a Machiavellian gossip will point to my actual views and actions but seek to insinuate ulterior motives underlying them. Thus good relations toward my boss are interpreted as slimy and pernicious operating; similarly, altruistic acts toward my friends are, it is suggested, to be interpreted in terms of my self-interest rather than any true concern for my friends. Hence a truly effective gossip will cultivate an attitude of cynicism toward all my actions.

The very same kind of harm can be extended from the consideration of individual people to, for example, the slander of particular groups. Hence the rationale underlying laws against viciously racist literature, broadcasting, and reporting is exactly the same. Namely, the capacity for Blacks to pursue their lives as they would choose is clearly constricted if, for example, newspaper reports and television programs represent Blacks as necessarily lazy, filthy, subhuman, and so on, for their capacity to realize gainful employment, get housing, be treated with respect, and be taken seriously is constricted by the promulgation of viciously racist literature and programming. Such images and programs are akin to an assault on certain people's identity as autonomous individuals rather than the mere frustration of a particular choice or preference that they may have.

Racism is not damaging merely because, in particular contexts, the expression of racist views is likely to lead directly to harm to particular individuals in a resultant riot. Rather, racism's pernicious nature lies in the harm that results more generally and indirectly, for it cultivates a pernicious general attitude toward people from certain ethnic groups, Blacks or Jews, say, which harms their fundamental interests as autonomous human beings. Clever racist literature points to indisputable facts—for example, that Jews have historically been very good at business and money-lending and successful in many societies, while significantly remaining apart from them—but the interpretation of these facts is given in terms of corruption, the perversion of honesty, and a parasitical culture whose aim is to devour and take over its host society. The cultivation of such attitudes, where successful, clearly leads to harm, albeit indirectly, because people who come to believe these views, and thus adopt an anti Semitic attitude, will obviously treat Jews in ways that they otherwise would not have done. They are less likely to employ a Jewish person if they assume Jews are endemically dishonest, or to listen to the opinions and arguments of someone who is Jewish, since the presumption is that Jews are motivated solely by their pernicious, money-grabbing aims. It also becomes harder for Jews to achieve certain personal and social goods. People are more likely to object to synagogues being put up in their community and less likely to entertain the possibility of befriending a Jew. So anti-Semitic literature can lead to significant indirect harm, where it succeeds in influencing public attitudes, since at the political, social, and personal level the ability of Jews to pursue fundamental aspects of their lives is constricted in a vicious manner. The frustration of fundamental political, social, and personal interests, which are tied up with our identity and autonomy, constitutes a significant harm that the state should prevent.

It is important to note, however, that the scope of the argument from indirect harm is much wider than the particular instance of racist reporting and programming. The general criterion concerns whether significant harm results regarding any group. Thus, for example, certain religious groups may legitimately demand protection from certain kinds of offense. Christians and Moslems may find their lives harmed in similar ways where a hostile secular culture is predominated by programs and films that are derisive and mocking and deliberately set out to blaspheme against their religious beliefs and way of life. The perpetuation of programs that cultivate the attitude that religious belief is no more than superstitious nonsense, fail to take religious claims seriously and mock it merely as something akin to a sad and naive faith in Santa Claus clearly makes it more difficult to live a religious life freely. At the political level, the claim that certain policies, ranging from abortion to lack of welfare provision for the poor, go against certain religious commitments and are therefore wrong will not be taken seriously at all. At the social level, the ability to bring one's child up within a religious tradition becomes much harder where it is publicly mocked.

Another kind of case might be where only a few people constituting a small minority in society wish to pursue their personal lives outside the sphere of marriage. In a culture where media reporting and programming is based on the assumption that homosexual couples, couples living together outside wedlock, or single parents should be consistently derided and mocked for their fecklessness, immorality, and parasitic free-riding off the welfare of others, it is obviously much harder to live freely the life that one would choose. Where an attitude like this prevails, at a personal level, such couples may be openly mocked or chased out of their homes and their children cruelly bullied in school and made to feel that their parents are monstrous by virtue of such behavior. At a political level, their voice as citizens may well typically be discounted and their problems ignored because of a general attitude that such people are not really worth thinking about or are not of equal worth as members of that society.

Thus offense, where we have good grounds to believe that it will constitute a significant indirect harm, can and does provide grounds for censorship. However, it is crucial to recognize that this judgment does not depend just on the nature of a particular report, program, or film. A film that directly offends against the sensibilities of, for example, heterosexual married couples and represents an attitude of scorn for such a lifestyle should not be censored in a society where this is the presumed norm; for the free pursuit of such a life will not be indirectly harmed by such a film where the predominant attitude is one that this is a perfectly acceptable and legitimate lifestyle. By contrast, a film that is offensive to Jews, Blacks, or single parents, where the cultural position of such people in society is precarious, is a candidate for censorship. It is not the offense per se that legitimates censorship; rather, it is whether the offense cultivates and perpetuates an attitude that is likely to contribute to or reinforce the harmful discounting or disdain for people in these groups, which is a judgment that can only be made in relation to the culture as a whole.

It is important to recognize that, although many gratuitously offensive images and programs that may fall under this heading do not have to be seen by those who are offended, the claim still holds, for those who are offended and indirectly harmed by the contents of racist programs or blasphemous films will, as in the case of gossip, be indirectly harmed by the consumption of these things by other people. The problem lies not with any offense given but with the consumption of what is gratuitously offensive in circumstances where this will contribute to the significant indirect harm of particular groups in society.

However, we should go on to add a significant qualification. Consider a news documentary that reveals new statistics and insights showing that a significant number of single mothers do go out of their way to have babies in order to gain greater welfare support. Let us assume that this news documentary offends the sensibilities of a precarious group in society—single mothers—and does reinforce the generally harmful attitude that single parents are feckless parasites. But this is not yet sufficient to legitimate censorship, for the program may give good, coherent reasons and evidence to believe the claims they are making to be true. So although indirect harm may result, the fact that we have good reason to believe that the claims are justified means that the program should be broadcast. It is clearly in the public interest to know such facts, which are important for public policy matters, and the offense given is not a result of the nature of the program as such but merely the sensibilities of those in the group concerned and their reaction to the program. Similarly, it may be true that most inner-city crime is committed by Blacks. A program that develops this claim, giving good reasons and evidence, may be offensive to many Blacks and reinforce harmful stereotypes. Nonetheless, it is clearly legitimate and, where this relates to significant public policy matters, the media have a clear obligation to broadcast such a program despite the offense caused.

Where the criterion of indirect harm kicks in is where programs or reports are both gratuitously offensive, by their very nature, and lead to indirect harm. A program that lambasts single parents or Blacks as feckless, criminal, and parasitic, without any kind of reasoned, coherent, informative argumentation or consideration of the actual evidence, is gratuitously offensive and not really concerned with arriving at a true understanding of the plight or state of the groups concerned. Similarly, religious programming or films that seek solely to scoff and scorn religious belief per se are inherently offensive where no effort is made to understand the basis of religious belief and no argument is given.

The considerations raised above give us good grounds for allowing that censorship of news reporting, programming, and films is justified, though only on tightly circumscribed grounds. Where a report, program, or film is likely to lead to serious, direct harm of others or where the gratuitous offense inherent in them is likely indirectly to harm a particular, precarious group in society, then censorship is legitimate. The argument also gives grounds for holding that the liberal state has certain positive obligations regarding those whose position in society is rather precarious. For example, where a particular culture or subgroup finds that its views, opinions, and perhaps even cultural goods, such as its language, are in danger of withering away in the public arena, then the state has an obligation to make sure that the members have channels of public access both to express their culture and communicate their views.[24]

The only relevant consideration that we have failed to entertain concerns the question of artistic merit, for it may be true that a film that is gratuitously offensive to a particular, precarious group in society, and thus may indirectly harm them, may possess much artistic merit. But, on the argument above, such films could legitimately be censored. Yet we find it harder to swallow the claim that valuable artistic works that are offensive in this way should be banned than we do where programs or films that possess little or no such artistic merit are involved. It is clear that, for example, Ezra Pound's *Cantos*, Martin Scorsese's *Last Temptation of Christ*, or Oshima's *In the Realm of the Senses* may be both offensive and, under certain circumstances, indirectly harmful. Yet their artistic merit, though of varying quality, nonetheless inclines us to think that our culture would be worse off were the broadcasting of them to be censored.

To see why this should be so we need to have some kind of understanding of why art, as such, is important and valuable. The value of an artwork cannot lie in its being merely beautiful or aesthetically pleasing. After all, if that is where art's primary value lies then it would not be clear why we think that attending to artworks is more significant than the pleasures afforded by beautiful, natural landscapes or by activities ranging from ten-pin bowling to playing cards. Rather, we typically value artworks, at least representational ones, because of their cognitive value, for the point of depicting a particular character—whether it be Captain Ahab or Jesus Christ—in a certain way is to prescribe in the viewer a particular imaginative understanding of the character's emotions, motives, ideals, character, and dilemmas that they confront or are caught up within.[25]

Of course, many television programs, dramas, and films are fictional, genre-specific, and only indirectly related to our own world.[26] But, for us to be entertained by them and value them as art, they must be related significantly to how we conceive of and understand our own world. For example, it is a staple convention of science-fiction films to portray an alien threat that seeks, in some form, to infect and thus destroy us. In the 1950s such a device was often used as a blatant cold-war allegory, as, for example, in Siegal's *Invasion of the Bodysnatchers*. Such films, though apparently at the furthest remove from our everyday worlds, actually concern and engage with the most fundamental concerns, drives, and desires manifested in ordinary life. This is, after all, why films and dramas may be profound in a way that transcends genre, time, and culture.

Yet, it might be thought, why give art special status? Even the profoundest of programs and films cannot touch our own world, for a work's putative insights about the world are only properly assessable within the appropriate intellectual discipline. We do not watch Kenneth Branagh's *Frankenstein* and then presume that experimentation with life itself is profoundly immoral. Rather, we enjoy the film but consider the issues raised, say in relation to genetic engineering, quite separately. Furthermore, the fact that we can and typically do value films containing seemingly contradictory "insights" seems to back this picture up. The pleasures afforded by Tarantino's *Pulp Fiction* depend on, in part, backgrounding a natural presumption in favor of the significance of human life. Conversely, Oliver Stone's *Natural Born Killers* depends on foregrounding such a presumption, in order to function as a critique of contemporary popular culture. Thus, in order to enjoy both films, we must call upon apparently incompatible attitudes toward human life. Therefore, given that films cannot provide "insights" about the human world, they should not be afforded special status when weighing up the matter of censorship.

But that our appreciation of different works requires apparently incompatible attitudes does not show that we do not expect a film to illuminate our world. After all, we rightly criticize films for failing to provoke an appropriate response to the events depicted. Hence, it would be a significant criticism of Branagh's *Frankenstein* were we to find the psychological motivations of Victor, perhaps arising from the gruesome loss of his mother in childbirth, wholly unconvincing. Similarly, we may legitimately criticize Francis Ford Coppola's *Dracula* because it fails to scare us—for, given the nature of Dracula, we ought to feel afraid. Moreover, insights about our world are not the only things we value in a film. We value a film if it is original and interesting, deepens our understanding of the medium, or prescribes us to imagine something in a particularly vivid way. Hence we value films both for their content and the way that we are prescribed to imagine what is represented. Thus we may enjoy a film because of the way it prescribes particular imaginings, even though we may think that the putative insights about, say, human psychology or the state of affairs that it depicts are false. So Leni Riefenstahl's triumphalist Nazi film of the 1936 Nuremberg rallies, *Triumph of the Will*, is flawed because it misrepresents the nature of Nazism. All its aesthetic power and imagery is devoted to representing Hitler and

Nazism as the glorious savior of the human race. It glorifies and celebrates what is, in essence, a vicious and immoral creed. Nonetheless, in terms of its imagery, originality, and appreciation of the aesthetically attractive nature of Nazism, it is a valuable work.[27]

As we have seen from the arguments considered, such works may indirectly threaten the very fabric of a liberal society, for even fictional films—through engaging our imaginings—promote particular self-understandings. We imagine what it would be like to be a particular person or in a certain state of affairs. Such imaginative simulation is crucial in our ordinary lives if we are properly to understand others, whether at an individual or cultural level. Ordinarily, we do not refer to abstracted hypotheses that explain another's behavior. Rather, we seek to imagine how, given their nature, other people conceive of their situation and are prone to feel and act.

Given that our imaginings enable us to grasp our own world and that of others, it should seem obvious that films may affect, directly or otherwise, the way that we conceive of and thus act within the world. Films, through engaging our imagination, promote particular self-understandings. Hence what we watch, through showing us various ways in which we may look upon our world, may deepen or distort our understanding. This serves to explain precisely why it is that we should rightly be suspicious of violent or racist movies. The problem is not one of mere offense, it is the age-old Platonic paradox: art may both enlighten and corrupt.[28]

For example, in a culture increasingly tolerant of the appetite for violence, violent films may not only reflect but cultivate the delight taken in it. Perhaps this is the reason why Quentin Tarantino's films have enjoyed such a rich vein of success. They touch upon an element of sadism flowering within our culture: the delightful stylization, enjoyment of, and reveling in the infliction of violence. What is peculiar about Tarantino's films, and sadism generally, is the celebration of this delight. Such a positive evaluation of violence and the concomitant indifference to others may, in a society threatened by increasing levels of violence, dissolve the ties that bind us within the larger liberal society. Similarly, deeply racist or blasphemous films may cultivate an indifference or hostility toward the groups concerned and thereby indirectly harm the ability of particular citizens within our society to lead their lives as they would choose.

Yet where films or dramas possess intrinsic artistic merit, even though they may lead to indirect harm in the sense discussed, they should not be censored except in the most extreme of instances; because the cost of indirect harm is worth paying in order to enable people to watch programs, dramas, or films of artistic merit. Similarly, the indirect harm of allowing cars on the road—the deaths of a few individuals each year—is considered worth paying because of the social benefits that car travel brings with it. This is perfectly consistent with the claim that those films or programs that are gratuitously offensive and indirectly harmful, and lack artistic merit, should be censored. D. W. Griffiths' *Birth of a*

Nation should be available to the general public and the media free to broadcast it. But gratuitously racist films of little or no artistic merit, in a society where racism constitutes a grave social ill, should not be broadcast at all.

CONCLUSION

No doubt for some, the position for which I have argued will seem deeply unsatisfactory because it is neither a clear-cut defence of an absolute right to freedom of expression nor an argument that applies cleanly to all programs or films that may be considered offensive. Moreover, such a view will no doubt attract charges of elitism. Who should say whether someone can adequately understand a particular film? Who is to say what constitutes gratuitous violence? When and where may a gratuitously offensive film constitute an indirect harm? Moreover, will the legitimation of censorship in very particular cases not lead to its illegitimate use in many other areas?

Of course, such questions are crucial and a question of judgment. But it is unmistakably true that judgment is required. True, we may be mistaken in our judgment of particular cases and circumstances; all human judgment is fallible. But, at best, such considerations show that it may be difficult to judge when and where certain kinds of gratuitously offensive programs and films may constitute an indirect harm. Furthermore, the regulatory authority that judges such matters had better be at a great distance from the political government of the day, for the justifiable case for censorship may, illegitimately, be used by political governements to protect their own interests in ways that are detrimental to justice and democracy. Thus the regulatory bodies whose job it is to make such judgments and enforce censorship where required had better be made up of a body of politically disinterested people whose powers do not depend on or are subject to undue influence from the particular government of the day. Furthermore, the regulatory framework need not be so imprecise as to permit censorship in illegitimate areas. The grounds for censorship can and must be clearly circumscribed. For example, a liberal state could pass a law, as is the case in Britain, that the identity of a rape victim should remain anonymous in the period up to and including the trial. Similarly, any move by the regulatory body to cut or ban the broadcast of a program or film must be based on a strong case that suggests that the gratuitously offensive nature of the film, in the present circumstances, constitutes or is likely to lead to direct or indirect harm.

The point here is that such worries do not hold, in principle, against the case for media censorship per se. Freedom of expression is qualified by the obligation not to harm, whether in relation to a particular individual or civil society as a whole. Hence we require a much greater emphasis on the need for self-censorship by film makers, ranging from the commissioning to the editorial process, and by the families or groups that constitute civil society. However, where society itself is riven with harmful attitudes that may be cultivated or reinforced by gratuitously offensive films, which thus constitute an indirect harm, the liberal state can legitimately allow for a politically neutral regulatory body to exercise fairly strong powers of censorship where the media community fails to do so.

Furthermore, to my mind, the complexity of the position that I have argued for and its recognition of the need to exercise judgment is precisely where its virtue lies—for the point of a right to freedom of expression is underwritten by the general liberal commitment to protect the conditions of stability, tolerance, and freedom from harm which enable people to lead their lives as they freely choose. So where protection of the right to freedom of expression threatens those very conditions, then it must give way. This is compatible with the liberal separation of legal constraints and morality, for mere indecency or gratuitous offense do not themselves constitute grounds for legitimating censorship.

Recognizing the importance of context and circumstance in determining whether a film constitutes an indirect harm is crucial; the same film may be gratuitously offensive and indirectly harmful in one culture but not so in another. In a secular society, no one may take offense at antireligious programming. In a society where religious traditions are not under threat, an antireligious program may be found to be gratuitously offensive but not constitute an indirect harm. But in a society where racism is a deep problem or religious ways of life are deeply threatened, programs that are gratuitously offensive may constitute an indirect harm and thus may legitimately be banned or censored. The very same gratuitously racist film may in one context be legitimately censored—in Germany after World War Two such material threatened to destabilize the fragile shoots of a liberal society—and yet in another should not be; in a strong liberal society where racism is not endemic and does not threaten the preconditions of the liberal state, such films are not harmful. Furthermore, the position argued for recognizes the general importance we place on programs and films that attain a certain artistic merit and recognizes that even where they do constitute an indirect harm, this may be a cost worth paying.

The complexity and context-sensitivity of such a position is a virtue and not a fault, for the evolution and maintenance of a liberal society is a great historical achievement and one that we must be careful to sustain. What is required to maintain the conditions of a liberal society will vary over particular times and cultures. This is precisely why sophisticated liberalism is more adequate to the dilemmas posed by imagery, programs, and films that harm and offend people than an ahistorical liberalism that blindly and damagingly holds to an absolute right to the freedom of expression. Typically illiberal measures are sometimes required to maintain the conditions of meaningful choice that the liberal state must protect and sustain.

NOTES

1. See, for example, Jeremy Waldron, "Legislation and Moral Neutrality," in his *Liberal Rights* (New York: Cambridge University Press, 1993), pp. 143–167, and Gordon Graham, *Contemporary Social Philosophy* (Oxford: Blackwells, 1988), pp. 121–137.

2. Graham Gordon, "Sex and Violence in Fact and Fiction," in ed. M. Kieran, *Media Ethics* (London: Routledge, forthcoming), makes this point.

3. John Stuart Mill, *On Liberty* (Harmondsworth: Penguin, 1982), especially pp. 59–74, 141–162.

4. Ibid., pp. 75–118.

5. Ibid., pp. 96–108.

6. David Irving's *Hitler's War* (London: Hodder and Stoughton, 1977) argues that the Holocaust did not happen strictly speaking and that what genocide did take place was clearly not the result of Hitler's intentions or the ideology of Nazism. The controversy over race and IQ has recently been sparked off again by Richard J. Herrnstein and Charles A. Murray's *The Bell Curve: Intelligence and Class Structure in American Life* (New York: Free Press, 1994), and in Britain in April 1996 the psychologist Christopher Brand's *The G Factor* was withdrawn by its publishers, John Wiley and Sons, the day before its publication, on the grounds that his conclusions were racist, as reported by Aisling Irwin and Olga Wojtas, "Racist I.Q. Book Withdrawn," *The Times Higher*, 19 April 1996, p. 1.

7. Mill, *On Liberty*, pp. 77–96.

8. See Richard M. Fried, *Nightmare in Red: The McCarthy Era in Perspective* (New York: Oxford University Press, 1990), and Edwin R. Bayley, *Joe McCarthy and the Press* (Madison, WI: University of Wisconsin Press, 1981).

9. Mill, *On Liberty*, pp. 108–115.

10. See Phillip Knightley, *The First Casualty. From the Crimea to Vietnam: The War Correspondent as Hero, Propagandist, and Myth Maker* (New York: Harvourt, Brace, Jovanovich, 1975), pp. 374–400.

11. Mill, *On Liberty*, pp. 91–94, 150.

12. Ibid., pp. 107–116.

13. Ibid., p. 115.

14. Ibid., pp. 151–162.

15. Ibid., p. 119.

16. Anthony Ellis, "Offense and the Liberal Conception of the Law," *Philosophy and Public Affairs 13* (1984): 3–23, from which this and the next section of the chapter closely draw.

17. *The Williams Report; Report of the Committee on Obscenity and Film Censorship*, ed. Bernard Williams (London: Cmnd. 7772, 1979), p. 99.

18. See David Lewis, "Dispositional Theories of Value," *Aristotelian Society Supplementary Volume*, Vol. LXIII, 1989, pp. 113–137.

19. See Ellis, "Offense and the Liberal Conception of the Law," pp. 12–19, for a more detailed discussion of the nature of offense.

20. M. J. Apter, *Reversal Theory: Motivation, Emotion and Personality* (London: Routledge, 1989), reviews recent psychological research that underwrites the fact that, under certain circumstances, we can and do enjoy what is otherwise typically unpleasant.

21. H. L. A. Hart, *Law, Liberty and Morality* (Oxford: Oxford University Press, 1963), p. 45.

22. Joel Feinberg, *Social Philosophy* (Englewood Cliffs, NJ: Prentice-Hall, 1973), pp. 36–54.

23. Ibid., p. 44.

24. See Onora O'Neill, "Practices of Toleration," in *Democracy and the Mass Media*, ed. J. Lichtenberg (New York: Cambridge University Press, 1990), pp. 155–185.

25. See Matthew Kieran, "Art, Imagination and the Cultivation of Morals," *Journal of Aesthetics and Art Criticism 54* (1996): 337–351, for a development of this position.

26. The following draws from Matthew Kieran, "Violent Films: Natural Born Killers?" *Philosophy Now 12* (1995): 15–18.

27. I would like to thank Berys Gaut for suggesting this example.

28. Plato, trans. D. Lee, *The Republic* (Harmondsworth: Penguin, 1974), Book X, 602c–608b, pp. 432–439.

Bibliography

Abramson, Jeffrey B. "Four Criticisms of Press Ethics." In *Democracy and the Mass Media*, edited by Judith Lichtenberg, pp. 229–268. New York: Cambridge University Press, 1990.

Aibel, Robert. "Ethics and Professionalism in Documentary Film-making." In *Image Ethics*, edited by Larry Gross, John Stuart Katz, and Jay Ruby, pp. 108–118. New York: Oxford University Press, 1988.

Anselm. *De Veritate*. In *Truth, Freedom and Evil, Three Philosophical Dialogues*, edited by Jasper Hopkins and Herbert Richardson. New York: Harper & Row, 1967.

Apter, M. J. *Reversal Theory: Motivation, Emotion and Personality*. London: Routledge, 1989.

Aristotle. *Nicomachean Ethics*. Harmondsworth: Penguin, 1953.

Aristotle. *Poetics*. Ann Arbor, MI: University of Michigan Press, 1970.

Asch, S. E. "Opinions and Social Pressure." *Scientific American 193* (1955): 31–35.

Ballard, J. G. "The Secret History of World War 3." In *Best Short Stories 1989*, edited by Giles Gordon and David Hughes, pp. 1–12. London: Heinemann, 1989.

Barker, Martin. "Sex, Violence and Videotape." *Sight and Sound 3* (1993): 10–12.

Barker, Martin. *The "Video Violence" Debate: Media Researchers Respond*. School of Cultural Studies, University of the West of England, April 1994.

Barth, Karl. *Church Dogmatics*. Edinburgh: T. & T. Clark, 1961.

Baudrillard, Jean. "The Gulf War Has Not Taken Place," *Libération*, 29 March 1991.

Baudrillard, Jean. "The Reality Gulf." *The Guardian*, 11 January 1991.

Bayley, Edwin R. *Joe McCarthy and the Press*. Madison, WI: University of Wisconsin Press, 1981.

Beardsley, Monroe. *Aesthetics*. New York: Harcourt, 1958.

Beauchamp, Tom L., and James F. Childress. *Principles of Biomedical Ethics*, 3d edition. New York: Oxford University Press, 1989.

Bell, Martin. *In Harm's Way*. London: Hamish Hamilton, 1995.

Belsey, Andrew. "Privacy, Publicity and Politics." In *Ethical Issues in Journalism and the Media*, edited by Andrew Belsey and Ruth Chadwick, pp. 77–92. New York: Routledge, 1992.

Belsey, Andrew, and Ruth Chadwick. "Ethics as a Vehicle for Media Quality." *European Journal of Communication* 10 (1995): 461–473.

Benn, Piers. "Pornography, Degradation and Rhetoric."*Cogito* 7 (1993): 127–134.

Bernstein, Carl, and Bob Woodward. *All The President's Men*. New York: Secker and Warburg, 1974.

Berry, C. "Learning from Television News: A Critique of the Research." *Journal of Broadcasting 27* (1983): 359–370.

Bok, Sissela. *Secrets*. New York: Pantheon, 1982.

Boynton, R. M. *Human Color Vision*. New York: Holt, Rinehart & Winston, 1979.

Bradlee, Ben. *Conversations with Kennedy*. New York: Norton, 1975.

Brentano, Franz. *Psychology from an Empirical Standpoint*. London: Routledge, Kegan and Paul, 1976.

Brownmiller, Susan. *Against Our Will: Men, Women and Rape*. New York: Simon & Schuster, 1975.

Buckingham, David. *Children and Television: An Overview of the Research*. London: British Film Institute, 1987.

Capa, Robert. *Slightly Out of Focus*. New York: Henry Holt, 1947.

Caputi, Mary. *Voluptuous Yearnings: A Feminist Theory of the Obscene*. Lanham, MD: Rowman and Littlefield, 1994.

Carroll, Lewis. *Sylvie and Bruno Concluded*. London: Macmillan, 1893.

Carroll, Noël. *The Philosophy of Horror*. New York: Routledge, 1990.

Catalano, Kevin. "On the Wire: How Six News Services Are Exceeding Readability Standards." *Journalism Quarterly 67* (1990): 97–103.

Chomsky, Noam. *Necessary Illusions*. Toronto, Ontario: CBC Enterprises, 1989.

Christians, Clifford G., Mark Fackler, and Kim B. Rotzoll. *Media Ethics: Cases and Moral Reasoning*, 4th edition. New York: Longman, 1995.

Christians, Clifford, John Ferré, and Mark Fackler. *Good News: A Social Ethics of the Press*. New York: Oxford University Press, 1993.

Churchill, Winston. "Speech." *Hansard*, 11 November 1947, col. 206.

Clark, Kenneth R. "Yes, TV Violence Is Awful, but What's the Cure?" In *Impact of Mass Media*, edited by Ray Eldon Hiebert, 3d edition, pp. 241–244. New York: Longmans, 1995.

Clark, Stephen R. L. "Abstract Morality, Concrete Cases." In *Moral Philosophy and Contemporary Problems*, edited by J. D. G. Evans. Cambridge: Cambridge University Press, 1978.

Clarke, P., and E. Fredin. "Newspapers, Television and Political Reasoning." *Public Opinion Quarterly 42* (1978): 143–160.

Cohen, Elliot D., ed. *Philosophical Issues in Journalism*. New York: Oxford University Press, 1992.

Cohen, Nick. "The Fear, the Shame, the Guilt." In *The Independent*, 21 February 1993, p. 21.

Coleman, Milton. "18 Words, Seven Weeks Later." In *The Washington Post*, 8 April 1984, C8.

Comolli, Jean-Luc, and Jean Narboni. "Cinema/Ideology/Criticism." In *Film Theory and Criticism*, edited by G. Mast, M. Cohen, and L. Braudy, pp. 682–689. New York: Oxford University Press, 1992.

Cooke, Alistair. *The Americans: Fifty Talks on Our Life and Times*. New York: Alfred A. Knopf, 1979.

Dahlgren, Peter, and Colin Sparks, eds. *Communication and Citizenship*. London: Routledge, 1991.

Daniel, Stephen H. "Some Conflicting Assumptions of Journalistic Ethics." In *Philosophical Issues in Journalism*, edited by Elliot D. Cohen, pp. 50–58. New York: Oxford University Press, 1992.

Day, Louis A. *Ethics in Media Communication: Cases and Controversies*. Belmont, CA: Wadsworth, 1991.

Denton, Robert E., Jr., ed. *Ethical Dimensions of Political Communication*. New York: Praeger, 1991.

Deppa, Joan. *The Media and Disasters: Pan Am 103*. London: David Fulton, 1993.

Doubleday, Catherine N., and Kristin L. Droege. "Cognitive Developmental Influences on Children's Understanding of Television." In *Children and Television*, edited by G. L. Berry and J. K. Asamen, pp. 23–37. Newbury Park, CA: Sage, 1993.

Dworkin, Andrea. *Letters from a War Zone*. London: Secker and Warburg, 1988.

Dworkin, Andrea. *Woman Hating*. New York: E. P. Dutton, 1984.

Ellis, Anthony. "Offense and the Liberal Conception of the Law." *Philosophy and Public Affairs 13* (1984): 3–23.

Ellison, Mike. "The Power and the Gory." In *The Guardian*, Tuesday, 25 October 1994, Arts Section, p. 5.

Evans, J. D. G., ed. *Moral Philosophy and Contemporary Problems*. Cambridge: Cambridge University Press, 1987.

Feinberg, Joel. *Social Philosophy*. Englewood Cliffs, NJ: Prentice-Hall, 1973.

Fink, Conrad. *Media Ethics*. New York: McGraw-Hill, 1988.

Fiske, John. *Media Matters: Everyday Culture and Political Change*. Minneapolis, MN: University of Minnesota Press, 1994.

Fiske, John. *Television Culture*. New York: Routledge, 1988.

Fried, Richard M. *Nightmare in Red: The McCarthy Era in Perspective*. New York: Oxford University Press, 1990.

Fulton, Marianne. "Changing Focus." In *Eyes of Time: Photojournalism in America*, edited by Marianne Fulton, pp. 208–220. New York: New York Graphic Society, 1988.

Garry, Ann. "Pornography and Respect for Women." *Social Theory and Practice 4* (1978): 395–421.

Gauntlett, David. *Moving Experiences: Understanding Television's Influences and Effects*. London: John Libbey, 1995.

Gilmore, Gene, and Robert Root. "Ethics for Newsmen." In *Ethics and the Press*, edited by John C. Merill and Ralph D. Barney. New York: Hastings House, 1975.

Gitlin, Todd. *The Whole World Is Watching*. Berkeley, CA: University of California Press, 1980.

Goldstein, Tom. *The News at Any Cost*. New York: Simon & Schuster, 1985.

Goodwin, H. Eugene, and Ron F. Smith. *Groping for Ethics in Journalism*, 3d edition. Ames, IA: Iowa State University Press, 1994.

Gordon, Graham, "Sex and Violence in Fact and Fiction." In *Media Ethics,* edited by M. Kieran. London: Routledge, forthcoming.

Graber, Doris. *Processing the News*. New York: Longman, 1984.

Graham, Gordon. *Contemporary Social Philosophy*. Oxford: Blackwells, 1988.

Green, Bill. "Janet's World." In *The Washington Post*, 19 April 1981, pp. A1, A12–A15.

Gross, Larry, John Stuart Katz, and Jay Ruby, eds. *Image Ethics*. New York: Oxford University Press, 1988.

Hardin, C. L. *Color for Philosophers: Unweaving the Rainbow*. Indianapolis, IN: Hackett, 1988.

Hargrave, Andrea Millwood. *Sex and Sexuality in Broadcasting*. London: John Libbey, 1992.

Hart, H. L. A. *Law, Liberty and Morality*. Oxford: Oxford University Press, 1963.

Hartley, John. *Understanding News*. London: Methuen, 1982.

Hausman, Carl. *Crisis of Conscience: Perspectives on Journalism Ethics*. New York: Harper Collins, 1992.

Herrnstein, Richard J., and Charles A. Murray. *The Bell Curve: Intelligence and Class Structure in American Life*. New York: Free Press, 1994.

Hewstone, Miles, and Charles Antaki. "Attribution Theory and Social Explanations." In *Introduction to Social Psychology*, edited by Miles Hewstone, Wolfgang Stroebe, Jean-Paul Codol, and Geoffrey M. Stephenson, pp. 111–141. Oxford: Basil Blackwell, 1988.

Hiebert, Ray Eldon, ed. *Impact of Mass Media*, 3d edition. New York: Longman, 1995.

Hodge, Robert, and David Tripp. *Children and Television*. Oxford: Polity, 1986.

Irving, David. *Hitler's War*. London: Hodder and Stoughton, 1977.

Irwin, Aisling, and Olga Wojtas. "Racist I.Q. Book Withdrawn." In *The Times Higher*, 19 April 1996, p. 1.

Iyenger, S., and D. R. Kinder. *News That Matters: Television and American Opinion*. Chicago, IL: Chicago University Press, 1987.

Jacobs, Ronald N. "Producing the News, Producing the Crisis: Narrativity, Television and News Work." *Media, Culture and Society 18* (1996): 373–397.

Kaminer, Wendy. "Feminists against the First Amendment." *Atlantic Monthly*, November 1992, pp. 111–118.

Kant, Immanuel. *Groundwork of the Metaphysics of Morals*. In *The Moral Law*, translated and edited by H. J. Paton. London: Hutchinson, 1948.

Kant, Immanuel, *The Philosophy of Immanuel Kant*. Chicago, IL: University of Chicago Press, 1949.

Karnow, Stanley. *Vietnam: A History*. New York: Viking Press, 1983.

Katz, Ian. "Juiciest of Tales." In *The Guardian*, Monday, 23 January 1995, Tabloid Section, pp. 2–3.

Kautsky, K. *The Dictatorship of the Proletariat*. Ann Arbor, MI: University of Michigan Press, 1964.

Kellner, Douglas. *The Persian Gulf TV War*. Boulder, CO: Westview Press, 1992.

Kieran, Matthew. "Art, Imagination and the Cultivation of Morals." *Journal of Aesthetics and Art Criticism 54* (1996): 337–351.

Kieran, Matthew. "The Impoverishment of Art." *British Journal of Aesthetics 35* (1995): 14–25.

Kieran, Matthew. "Violent Films: Natural Born Killers?" *Philosophy Now 12* (1995): 15–18.

Kieran, Matthew, ed. *Media Ethics*. London: Routledge, forthcoming.

Kieran, Matthew, David Morrison, and Michael Svennevig, *Regulating for Changing Values: A Report for the Broadcasting Standards Commission*. London: BSC, 1997.

Klaidman, Stephen, and Tom L. Beauchamp. *The Virtuous Journalist*. New York: Oxford University Press, 1987.

Knightley, Phillip. *The First Casualty. From the Crimea to Vietnam: The War Correspondent as Hero, Propagandist, and Myth Maker*. New York: Harcourt, Brace, Jovanovich, 1975.

Koch, Tom. *The News as Myth*. New York: Greenwood, 1990.

Kurtz, Howard. *Media Circus*. New York: Random House, 1994.

Lambeth, Edmund B. *Committed Journalism*, 2d edition. Bloomington, IN: Indiana University Press, 1992.

Lemert, J. B. *Criticizing the Media*. Newbury Park, CA: Sage, 1989.

Lepore, Ernest, ed. *Truth and Interpretation*. Oxford: Blackwell, 1984.

Lester, Paul. *Photojournalism: An Ethical Approach*. Hillsdale, NJ: Lawrence Erlbaum, 1991.

Lewis, David. "Dispositional Theories of Value." *Aristotelian Society Suplementary Volume*, LXIII (1989): 113–137.

Limburg, Val E. *Electronic Media Ethics*. Boston, MA: Focal Press, 1994.

Locke, John. *A Letter Concerning Toleration*. New York: The Library of Liberal Arts, 1955.

Locke, John. *Two Treatises of Government*. New York: Cambridge University Press, 1963.

Machiavelli, Niccolò. *The Prince*. New York: Dover, 1992.

MacKinnon, Catherine. *Only Words*. Cambridge, MA: Harvard University Press, 1993.

Maclean, Anne. *The Elimination of Morality*. London: Routledge, 1993.

Marshall, W. L. "Pornography and Sex Offenders." In *Pornography: Research Advances and Policy Considerations*, edited by D. Zillman and J. Bryant, pp. 185–214. Hillsdale, NJ: Lawrence Erlbaum, 1989.

Mathews, Tom Dewe. *Censored: The Story of Film Censorship in Britain*. London: Chatto and Windus, 1994.

McChesney, Robert W. "The Battle for the U.S. Airwaves, 1928–1935." *Journal of Communication 40* (1990): 29–57.

McGuire, R., J. M. Carlisle, and B. Young. "Sexual Deviations as Conditioned Behaviour: A Hypothesis." *Behaviour Research and Therapy 2* (1965): 185– 190.

McNair, Brian. *Glasnost, Perestroika and the Soviet Media*. London: Routledge, 1991.

McQuail, Denis. *Media Performance: Mass Communication and the Public Interest*. Newbury Park, CA: Sage, 1992.

Merill, John C., and Ralph D. Barney, eds. *Ethics and the Press*. New York: Hastings House, 1975.

Meyer, Philip. *Ethical Journalism*. New York: Longman, 1987.

Midgley, Mary. *Heart and Mind*. London: Routledge, 1981.

Midgley, Mary. "Trying Out One's New Sword." In *Vice and Virtue in Everyday Life*, edited by Christina Sommers and Fred Sommers, 5th edition, pp. 174–180. Fort Worth, TX: Harcourt Brace, 1993.

Milgram, Stanley. *Obedience to Authority: An Experimental View*. New York: Harper & Row, 1974.

Mill, John Stuart. *On Liberty*. Harmondsworth: Penguin, 1982.

Moore, Roy L. *Mass Communication Law and Ethics*. Hillsdale, NJ: Lawrence Erlbaum, 1994.

Morley, David. *The "Nationwide" Audience*. London: British Film Institute, 1980.

Mulvey, Laura. *Visual and Other Pleasures*. London: Macmillan, 1989.

Nagel, Thomas. *The View From Nowhere*. Oxford: Oxford University Press, 1986.

National Cable Television Association.*Voices Against Violence: A Cable Television Initiative*. Washington, DC: National Cable Television Association, 1994.

Newsome, Elizabeth. *Video Violence and the Protection of Children*. Report, Child Development Research Unit, University of Nottingham, March 1994.

Nisbett, R. E., and L. Ross. *Human Inference: Strategies and Shortcomings in Social Judgment*. Englewood Cliffs, NJ: Prentice-Hall, 1980.

Nozick, Robert. *Anarchy, State and Utopia*. Oxford: Blackwells, 1974.

Oakeshott, Michael. *Experience and Its Modes*. Cambridge: Cambridge University Press, 1933.

O'Neill, Onora. "Practices of Toleration." In *Democracy and the Mass Media*, edited by J. Lichtenberg, pp. 155–185. New York: Cambridge University Press, 1990.

Orwell, George. *1984*. London: Secker and Warburg, 1974.

Paik, Haejung, and George Comstock. "The Effects of Television Violence on Antisocial Behavior: A Meta-Analysis." *Communication Research 21* (1994): 516–546.

Pally, Marcia. *Sex and Sensibility: Reflections on Forbidden Mirrors and the Will to Censor*. Hopewell, NJ: Ecco Press, 1994.

Parent, W. A. "Privacy, Morality, and the Law." In *Philosophical Issues in Journalism*, edited by Elliot D. Cohen, pp. 92–109. New York: Oxford University Press, 1992.

Patterson, Philip and Lee Wilkins, eds. *Media Ethics: Issues and Cases,* 2d edition. Dubuque, IA: Wm. C. Brown, 1994.

Pearson, Geoffrey. "Falling Standards: A Short, Sharp History of Moral Decline." In *The Video Nasties*, edited by Martin Barker. London: Pluto, 1984.

Pedelty, Mark. *War Stories*. New York: Routledge, 1995.

Perkins, V. F. *Film as Film*. London: Penguin, 1990.

Perse, Elizabeth M. "Uses of Erotica and Acceptance of Rape Myths." *Communication Research 21* (1994): 488–515.

Philo, Greg. *Seeing and Believing*. London: Routledge, 1990.

Plato. *Protagoras and Meno*. Harmondsworth: Penguin, 1956.

Plato. *The Republic*. Harmondsworth: Penguin, 1974.

Plato. *Gorgias.* Indianapolis, IN: Hackett, 1987.

Powell, Dilys. *The Dilys Powell Film Reader.* Oxford: Oxford University Press, 1991.

Powell, Jody. "No Consequences." In *Impact of Mass Media,* edited by Ray Eldon Hiebert, 3d edition, pp. 119–122. New York: Longman, 1995.

Powes, Jr., Lucas A. *The Fourth Estate and Constitution: Freedom of the Press in America.* Berkeley and Los Angeles, CA: University of California Press, 1991.

Price, V., and J. Zaller. "Who Gets the News? Alternative Measures of News Reception and Its Implications for Research." *Public Opinion Quarterly 57* (1993): 133–164.

Rabinow, Paul, ed. *Foucault Reader.* New York: Random House, 1984

Rachels, James. "Why Privacy Is Important." In *Philosophical Dimensions of Privacy,* edited by Ferdinand D. Schoeman, pp. 290–299. New York: Cambridge University Press, 1984.

Rachlin, Allan. *News as Hegemonic Reality.* New York: Praeger, 1988.

Rodgerson, G., and E. Wilson, eds. *Pornography and Feminism.* London: Lawrence and Wishart, 1993.

Rosenblum, Mort. *Who Stole The News?* New York: John Wiley, 1993.

Scruton, Roger. *Art and Imagination.* London: Routledge, 1981.

Scruton, Roger. *The Aesthetic Understanding.* Manchester: Carcanet, 1983.

Scruton, Roger. *Sexual Desire: A Philosophical Investigation.* London: Weidenfeld and Nicolson, 1986.

Seib, Philip. *Campaigns and Conscience: The Ethics of Political Journalism.* Vancouver: University of British Columbia Press, 1994.

Singer, Jerome L., and Dorothy G. Singer. *Television, Imagination and Aggression.* Hillsdale, NJ: Lawrence Erlbaum, 1981.

Slater, Michael D. "Processing Social Information in Messages: Social Group Familiarity, Fiction Versus Nonfiction, and Subsequent Beliefs." *Communication Research 17* (1990): 327–343.

Smith, Anthony. *The Newspaper: An International History.* London: Thames and Hudson, 1979.

Smith, Anthony, ed. *Television: An International History.* Oxford: Oxford University Press, 1995.

Smith, David James. *The Sleep of Reason.* London: Century, 1994.

Snoddy, Raymond. *The Good, The Bad and The Unacceptable.* London: Faber, 1993.

Sommers, Christina, and Fred Sommers, eds. *Vice and Virtue in Everyday Life,* 5th edition. Fort Worth, TX: Harcourt Brace, 1993.

Stocking, S. Holly, and Nancy LaMarca, "How Journalists Describe Their Stories: Hypotheses and Assumptions in Newsmaking." *Journalism Quarterly 67* (1990): 295–301.

Strossen, Nadine. *Defending Pornography: Free Speech, Sex and the Fight for Women's Rights.* London: Abacus, 1996.

Studlar, Gaylyn. "Masochism and the Perverse Pleasures of Cinema." In *Film Theory and Criticism,* edited by G. Mast, M. Cohen and L. Braudy, 4th edition. Oxford: Oxford University Press, 1992.

Tester, Keith. *Media, Culture and Morality,* London: Routledge, 1994.

Tuchman, Gaye. *Making News.* New York: Free Press, 1988.

Van Avermaet, Eddy. "Social Influence in Small Groups." In *Social Psychology*, edited by Miles Hewstone, Wolfgang Stroebe, Jean-Paul Codol, and Geoffrey M. Stephenson, pp. 372–380. Oxford: Basil Blackwell, 1988.

Van Dijk, T. A. *News Analysis*. Hillsdale, NJ: Lawrence Erlbaum, 1988.

Van Evra, Judith. *Television and Child Development*. London: Erlbaum, 1990.

Vaux, Kenneth L. *Ethics and the Gulf War: Religion, Rhetoric and Righteousness*. Boulder, CO: Westview, 1992.

Waldron, Jeremy. *Liberal Rights*. New York: Cambridge University Press, 1993.

Walton, Kendall. *Mimesis as Make-Believe*. Cambridge, MA: Harvard, 1990.

Warren, Samuel, and Louis Brandeis. "The Right to Privacy." In *The Journalist's Moral Compass*, edited by Steven R. Knowlton and Patrick R. Parsons, pp. 84–87. Westport, CT: Praeger, 1995.

Weaver, Paul. *News and the Culture of Lying*. New York: Free Press, 1994.

Whiten, Andrew, ed. *Natural Theories of Mind*. Oxford: Blackwell, 1991.

Williams, Bernard, ed. *The Williams Report; Report of the Committee on Obscenity and Film Censorship*. London: HMSO, Cmnd. 7772, 1979.

Williams, Juan. *Eyes on the Prize*. New York: Viking Press, 1987.

Williams, Kevin. "Something More Important than Truth: Ethical Issues in War Reporting." In *Ethical Issues in Journalism and the Media*, edited by Andrew Belsey and Ruth Chadwick, pp. 154–170. Routledge: New York, 1992.

Winston, Brian. "Tradition of the Victim." In *Image Ethics*, edited by Larry Gross, John Stuart Katz, and Jay Ruby, pp. 34–57. New York: Oxford: 1988.

Wisnia, Saul E. "Private Grief, Public Exposure." In *Impact of Mass Media*, edited by Ray Eldon Hiebert, 3d edition, pp. 113–118. New York: Longman, 1995.

Index

About the Author

MATTHEW KIERAN is Lecturer in Philosophy at the University of Leeds, England. He also teaches media ethics and researches for the Broadcasting Standards Commission in the United Kingdom. His articles on aesthetics, ethics, and social philosophy have appeared in such journals as the *Journal of Aesthetics and Art Criticism* and the *Journal of Communication*.

ISBN 0-275-95634-2

90000>

EAN

9 780275 956349

HARDCOVER BAR CODE